Picture Windows

LONG ISLAND

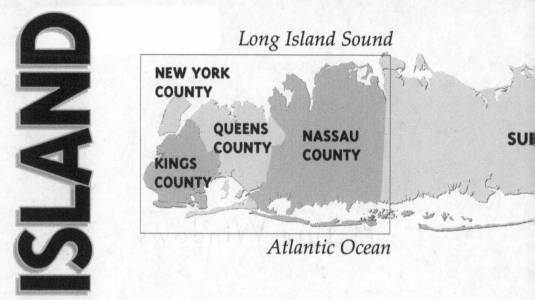

Cartography by Stephan Van Dam

Long Island Sound

NEW YORK COUNTY

QUEENS COUNTY

KINGS COUNTY

NASSAU COUNTY

SU

Atlantic Ocean

MANHATTAN
(NEW YORK COUNTY)

Long Island Sound

LaGuardia Airport

Hudson River

③ Queensboro Bridge

Long Island Expwy

Brooklyn Bridge **①** **②**

Manhattan Bridge

QUEENS

New York Harbor

BROOKLYN
(KINGS COUNTY)

JFK Airport

Jamaica Bay

Atlantic Ocean

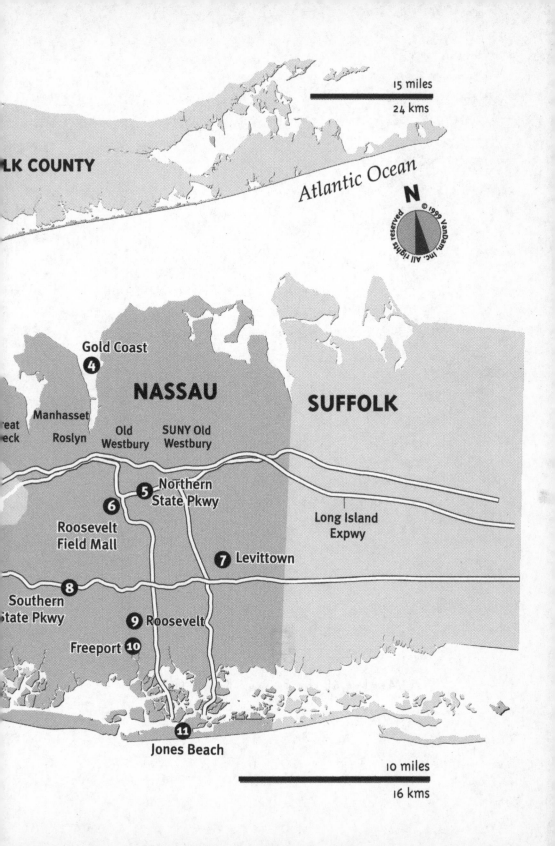

A Member of the Perseus Books Group

Picture Windows

How the Suburbs Happened

Rosalyn Baxandall and Elizabeth Ewen

Excerpt from "Day-Dreams," copyright 1926, renewed 1954 by Dorothy Parker, from DOROTHY PARKER: COMPLETE POEMS by Dorothy Parker. Used by permission of Penguin, a division of Penguin Putnam Inc.

PHOTO CREDITS:
Rural town life. Photographer unknown. New York Public Library Picture Collection.
Gold coast invasion; Otto Kahn. Nassau County Museum Srs. Collection.
Long Island Studies Institute at Hofstra University. Reformatted by Patricia Ryan.
Long Island. Found by Andrew Mattson. Retouched by Patricia Ryan.
Freeport 1926; Klan march. Nassau County Museum Srs. Collection.
Long Island Studies Institute at Hofstra University. Photographer unknown.
New York Public Library Picture Collection.
Good house are. Catherine Bauer, *Modern Housing.*
Sunnyside, Queens; Chatham Village; Pedestrian underpass.
Clarence Stein, *Toward New Towns for America.*
Which Playground? Mary Lou Williamson, *Greenbelt: History of a New Town.*
Courtesy of the Library of Congress.
Greenbelt, Md. Clarence Stein, *Toward New Towns for America.*
Irish Channel; Nathan Straus, *The Seven Myths of Housing.*
Citizens of Lubbock. Nathan Straus, *Two-Thirds of a Nation.*
Assembly-line homes; Architectural Forum, 1949.
First again. New York Times.
Roosevelt Field. Photographer unknown. New York Public Library
Picture Collection, 1960.
Pioneer Generation/Levittown. Photographs by Lucille and
Morton Gold. Levittown, 1954–1957.

A CIP catalog record for this book is available from the Library of Congress.

ISBN 0-465-07013-2

Book design by Victoria Kuskowski

To those visionaries of the past who dared to imagine a new America, and to those of the future—our students at SUNY/ Old Westbury.

The terms "neighborhood" and "community" are often used interchangeably. . . .
But neighborhoods have to do with natural topographic transitions highlighted by
administrative boundaries and even transportation lines. Community refers to the
delicate lattice of human networks and social institutions. Community also represents the shared meaning of residents, a moral order and ideals, memory and expectations; it satisfies emotional needs for understanding and control over the
structures of power and forces that govern us—needs that are upheld, if only in the
breach, in streets and homes, businesses and public institutions. More than the benefits of specific rights and entitlements, communities provide citizens with a sense of
control and empowerment.

—HILLEL LEVINE AND LAWRENCE HARMON,
The Death of an American Jewish Community

Contents

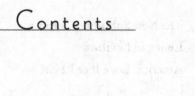

Acknowledgments

Many people along the way have helped us to explore suburban history. In particular we would like to thank Roger Wunderlich, historian and editor of the *Long Island Historical Journal*, for sharing his extensive knowledge of Long Island history. Robert Keeler, reporter for *Newsday* and author of *Newsday: A Candid History of the Respectable Tabloid*, generously shared his extensive files with us. Marquita James, professor and former Freeport high school teacher, enriched our understanding of the influence of the civil rights movement on suburban racism. Andrew Wiese shared his Ph.D. thesis on racism in suburbia and subsequent articles. Filmmaker Tami Gold showed us home videos of her family's voyage to Levittown in 1947 and gave us photographs. Allen Hunter provoked our thoughts by providing articles with different points of view. Stephan Van Dam stimulated our sense of context with geographical ideas and visual eloquence. Patricia Ryan provided us with ideas and artwork. Robin Drew was extremely helpful in transcribing our interviews. Andrew Mattson shared his enthusiasm and collection of suburban artifacts. Julie Tate, while working as an editor of *Grand Street*, opened our eyes to the New Deal's Greenbelts. Mark Seader, a student of architecture, made us aware of Radburn. Architect Simon Breines shared his recollections of living in Sunnyside and working with Catherine Bauer, Lewis Mumford, and Clarence Stein.

The Levittown and Freeport libraries were particularly helpful. The Old Westbury Foundation helped provide us with funds for transportation and transcription. Local residents amplified our files. Ruth Grefe shared her huge diary with us, and Dan Mandel and Jomer Rand gave us their clippings and scrapbooks.

We would like to thank the following students for opening up suburban doors: Margaret Schrage, Gloria Kunen, Irene Weinberger, and La-Keisha Dandy. Most helpful were longtime residents Norman Appleton, Nancy Arroyo, Dorothy Bass, Mae Brandon, Millie Cantor, Rose Cimino, Roberta Coward, Ramona Crooks, Hazel Dukes, Donna Gagliano, Clara Gillens, Ruth Grefe, Doris Hood, Rabbi John Juliano, Isa Abdul Kareem, Reuben Katz, Michael Kirwin, Dan Mandel, Meta and Charles Mereday, Ilda Northern, Lila Page, Barbara Patton, Julie Pearse, Harriet Popkin, Jomer Rand, John Rice, Jr., Vera Rivers, Karen Robers, Betty Scott, Harve Sinklar-Herring, Yvonne Simmons, Louise Simpson, Chris Sprowal, Roberta Stim, Dorothy Storm, Robert Sweeney, Pat Sullivan, Reverend Reginald Tuggle, Vicki Truxson, Barbara Ware, Helena White, Lotte Wolf, Jean Wyatte and Frances Wunderlich.

Eric Jorgenson, our research assistant, found many invaluable treasures. Carol Hanisch was a great help in editing. Early on Steve Fraser encouraged us to examine the suburbs by exploring the historical overview. Libby Garland's comments on the penultimate draft were extremely insightful. Our editor, Tim Bartlett, did yeoman service in fine-tuning the book. We want to thank him for his expertise, patience, and time. Vanessa Mobley provided wise counsel on many parts of the book and was particularly helpful in shaping the photo insert.

Phineas Baxandall, Sheila Rowbotham, and Ira Jacobson read chapters and made many helpful suggestions as well as giving emotional sustenance. Paul and Sam Ewen were enthusiastically supportive—if critical that we were writing a book on "the burbs." Stuart Ewen helped at every stage with the conception and execution of this long project. His insight and patience were intellectually and emotionally sustaining.

Most of all we would like to thank our students at the State University of New York at Old Westbury, who confronted our suburban stereotypes and let us witness the suburban experience through their eyes.

Introduction

It is 1999 and we are standing in the living room of a ranch house on a street called Whisper Lane in what is probably the nation's most famous suburb: Levittown. The house has been transformed since it was built in 1949: new upstairs bedrooms, the carport replaced by a garage, the exterior enhanced by deep green shutters and light olive trim, the kitchen expanded, and the backyard framed by a flagstone patio. Peering out the picture window, we talk about the suburbs.

People take the history of suburban migration for granted, as if the suburbs had sprouted overnight as a result of the post–World War II economic boom and newly built highways. The human aspect is largely absent from conventional suburban history. Yet suburbs didn't just happen; their history has been submerged behind a mythic facade. Suburban history, we come to realize, is as many-layered as the house in which we stand.

It was our own journey into suburbia, as Manhattan professors, commuting to the State University of New York at Old Westbury near Levittown, that brought us to this project. Initially we didn't understand that suburbia even had a history, we imagined it as an anesthetized state of mind, a no place dominated by a culture of conformity and consumption. We maintained a vision of the suburbs defined by endless malls, tidy streets with manicured lawns, and houses with little character. This image was not ours alone. Both critics and celebrants imagine suburbia as fixed and timeless, existing without conflict or change.

Our students in Old Westbury made us realize how little our clichés had to do with their experience. Unlike the characters in "Leave it to Beaver" or "Father Knows Best," these students—Long Island housewives returning to college after many years, young African-American, Hispanic, and immigrant women and men juggling jobs, school and family—led lives as intricate as any urban dweller. Curious to discover whether their experiences were anomalous, we ven-

tured into the epicenter of mythic suburban conformity—Levittown—to interview some of its residents. Our goal was to understand how the "boring burbs"
had changed into the diverse communities our students described. Residents
there recounted a complicated place, long shaped by conflict and community activism. It is this story of suburbia's complex past, as well as its multilayered present, that we want to tell.

Long Island is the ideal laboratory for such research. Its proximity to New
York City makes it appealing for successive waves of suburban settlers. Long Island acted like a magnet, first for wealthy industrialists in the late nineteenth
century, who turned Long Island's North Shore into a glittering Gold Coast,
complete with baronial palaces and private golf courses and beaches. In the
1920s Long Island attracted upper-middle-class urbanites, who longed to escape
city congestion and live in smaller but deluxe houses imitative of the Gold Coast
generation. After World War II the South Shore drew urban working and middle-class white families, who came seeking a prosperity and a home of their own.
In the 1960s and 1970s African Americans joined the trek, seeking integrated,
peaceful, suburban communities. Most recently a host of new immigrant groups
has bypassed the city entirely, moving directly to Long Island.

In spite of its proximity to New York City, Long Island remained bucolic until the turn of the century. Undeveloped, it was perfect for suburban development—a place to experiment with modern industrial and technological
innovations. Where else could Robert Moses build parkways and bridges linking city and suburb, opening up beaches and parks for the less affluent? What
other place would allow William Levitt to construct affordable assembly-line
houses, and William Zeckendorf to build the first mall, Roosevelt Field? All of
this transformed the rural island into the bedroom of New York City. Eventually
in the 1970s the bedroom disappeared and Long Island suburbs became self-
sufficient—a place where people not only lived but worked and played. Over
time, Long Island has reflected as well as contributed to America's changing social and historical contours.

While much scholarship and popular fiction on suburbia focuses on upper-
middle-class suburbs like Scarsdale, New York, Greenwich, Connecticut, and

Grosse Pointe, Michigan, we chose to study working- and middle-class Long Island suburbs, the kind that most Americans inhabit. Levittown was a natural, but it was also predominately white, it does have similar income levels to two neighboring communities: Roosevelt, mainly African American and Freeport, an integrated town.

To find residents other than our students to interview, we composed a leaflet explaining our project and put it in local newspapers, libraries, community centers, clinics and gave one to everyone came across. Nervous at first that no one would reply, we were surprised when the response snowballed. People busily arranged meetings for us. Women in particular were so excited to talk that they invited us into their homes, called their friends, gave us coffee and cake, and with great relish described their initial adventures as suburban "pioneers."

Not yet seasoned, often we started with the wrong questions. Not able to determine over the phone the ethnicity of those requesting interviews, we frequently were taken aback by our own tendencies to stereotype. We would drive up to a split-level house on a cul-de-sac expecting to talk with a group of white women, and instead found a group of African-American women or an interracial group.

During these early interviews, we began to understand that underneath the media's depiction of suburban serenity is a rich and stormy history. We uncovered signposts dim to us: community activism and political battles in Levittown, women changing their lives due to the liberation movement, struggles over integration in schools and housing, and even suburban race riots.

To learn about this largely unrecorded history, we went to the back issues of the local press. Its coverage of conflict and upheaval was skimpy and incomplete. To fill in the blanks, we interviewed town officials, real estate agents, policemen, parents, teachers, principals, lawyers, architects, activists, clergy, reporters, and residents. All in all we interviewed more than 230 people, some more than once and others for hours in multiple sessions. Along the way, people generously provided their diaries, scrapbooks, clipping files, and other memorabilia.

Hearing these dramatic tales of suburban clashes led us to question our own antisuburban snobbery, having been schooled in a tradition that celebrated urban American over all others. This intellectual disdain for the humdrum typical Main Street middle-class life had its roots in the twenties, the first decade of suburban expansion. The city—especially New York—was considered cosmopolitan, and the countryside was seen as a slice of nature's paradise, but suburbia was suspended somewhere in the blah middle. In 1921 Lewis Mumford one of modern America's most important social critics, warned that the suburbs were becoming a new wasteland:

> The 19th century American town, with none of the cultural resources that cities like Oxford and Paris had inherited from the middle ages and the renaissance, was the negation of the city—and suburbia was the negation of that negation. The result was not a new synthesis, but a further deterioration.[1]

Some of Mumford's contemporaries echoed his critique of suburbia. Popular writer and historian Frederick Lewis Allen derisively commented on what he called the "suburban nightmare":

> The groves where we now look for anemones in spring will be sliced through with orderly little streets down which orderly little commuters will hurry to catch the seven-forty-dash eight train for town while their wives look into each others back windows and tell each other that you never would believe, my dear, what's going on at Mrs. So and So's right in plain sight of everybody."[2]

Christine Frederick, a well-known proponent of scientific management and the standardization of home life, believed that what people looked for in suburbs—modern conveniences, the automobile, privacy, access to the country, and a healthy life—was in fact best found in the city. In her words, "I have enjoyed myself like Thoreau in the privacy of his forest retreat while living in a New York apartment, but in the suburb I have never felt like anything but a worm trying to crawl over a much be-travelled roadway." Suburbia, she believed, was socially and aesthetically empty. Frederick was particularly dismayed by what she viewed as the connection between architectural and behavioral conformity:

These suburban houses for instance, I suppose architects get pleasure out of the neat little toy houses on their neat little patches of lawn and their neat colonial lives, to say nothing of the neat little housewife and their neat little children—all set in neat rows—for all the world like children's blocks . . . the very aspect of it offends me deeply. It is so sugary and commonplace and pathetic in its pretense of an individualism which doesn't exist.[3]

Why did city folk display such malice and venom in their depictions of suburban dwellers? Why did modernists like Frederick, Allen, and Mumford, proponents of mass production and garden cities, stick their noses up at the suburban exodus? Why was such a profound socially conscious critic like Mumford so culturally condescending? Why was the suburb and suburbanite seen as the epitome of crass commercial culture and the death of sophisticated, highbrow civilized living?

Suburbs do reflect certain aspects of a conformist culture, such as homogeneity of stage of life, commonality of class, and keeping up with the Joneses. Suburbs have neither the beauty and wildness of the country nor the urbanity and vibrant clashes of the city. Yet there are different kinds of suburbs. In the 1920s such critical attacks were launched at upper-middle-class suburbs. By the 1950s, working- and middle-class suburbs became the focus of the antisuburb barrage.

Suburbia—especially the Levittowns—rarely have generated an active intellectual life. Most intellectuals born in suburbs and small towns flee, only to spend their lives in a vain attempt to rid themselves of their backgrounds. Suburban phobia remains an intellectual cliché, the mantra of the urban refugee against the commercial culture of H. L. Mencken's "booboisie." In the mass exodus of the late 1940s and 1950s this theme gathered steam, even though the class composition of those moving changed. Urban intellectuals such as Mumford, academics such as David Reisman and William Whyte, novelists such as John Keats, Vance Packard, and John Cheever, and feminists such as Betty Friedan all blamed the suburbs for the cultural ills of society: 1950s conformity, the highest levels of mass consumption in history, "low-brow" new media like television, and the problem that had no name, the so-called boredom of the over-educated housewife.

Everything about suburbia, exteriors and interiors alike, was magnified and dissected. Even though homes and apartments everywhere contained a mixture of labor-saving devices and ordinary household objects, the accumulation of these things in the suburbs took on a sinister air. John Seeley, Alexander Sim, and E. W. Loosley in their book *Crestwood Heights* claimed that the suburban house had become nothing more than an odd and chilling repository of an exceedingly wide range of artifacts, from freezers and furnaces to mousetraps and mix masters.[4] John Keats in his novel *Crack in the Picture Window* chimed in, claiming that the suburbs resembled George Orwell's *1984*. Combining sexism and anticommunism, Keats created a suburb, Rolling Knolls, where people lived, "in vast communistic, female barracks. This communism . . . began with the obliteration of the individualistic house and self-sufficient neighborhood, and from there on, the creation of mass-produced human beings as the night follows the day."[5] Keats's depictions of suburban life were so exaggerated that he even proclaimed that new suburban houses were "doll houses which out slum the slummiest of our prewar slums."[6]

These virulent denouncements were based on class and ethnicity as well as sex. The 1950s critics attacked not only the suburbs but the new residents themselves.[7] The opening of home ownership to a new class of people represented a changing relationship between the propertied and the propertyless. While this new class believed that it finally was being allowed a piece of the dream, urban tastemakers feared this dream would turn into its opposite, a suburban ghetto. At issue here was whether the new suburbs would bring to fruition a world in which workers would work less, would be better educated, and live in standardized but well-built homes. Or would suburbia turn into a cultural wasteland of conformity as Mumford and others feared?

Even though the suburbs have grown more vital and the majority of Americans choose to live there, the snobbery continues unabated, articulated by a variety of intellectuals. To James Howard Kunstler, author of *The Geography of Nowhere*, and Marc Auge, author of *Non Places*, the suburbs have become synonymous with an empty, anticivic, spiritually dead, dysfunctional society that is slowly enveloping the world. Even cities are becoming suburbanized. As Kunstler puts it, suburbia is "deleterious, insalubrious; it is damaging to our culture, to our aspirations, to our humanity. . . . It may get so bad that suburbia will collapse before people are ready or willing to reinvent civic life."[8] This theme is echoed by "neotraditionalist" architects and planners, such as Andres Duany and Elizabeth Plater-Zyberk. For them "The suburb is the last word in privatization and spells the end of authentic civil life."[9]

There is even a zinelike book from the hiphop generation entitled *Bomb the Suburbs* by William Upski Wimsatt. Upski (as he prefers to be called) argues, "It's the American state of mind, founded on fear, conformity, shallowness of character, and dullness of imagination." He feels the suburbs are bad for America "Socially, they intensify segregation and mistrust. Culturally, they erode the sense of history, narrow the outlook. . . . [Suburbanites] run around in a comfort warp, taking everything for granted and misusing what they have."[10]

None of these books reflects the voices of our students and the myriad Americans—white, black, immigrant, gay, straight, old, young, married, divorced, and single—who have selected to live in suburbia and have inscribed their signatures on its landscape. Moreover, none of these books has bothered to uncover the changing contours of suburban history.

Once we rejected antisuburban snobbery and began compiling oral histories and examining archival records, we found a suburban history that spanned the twentieth century. Indeed, the history of suburbia is at the heart of twentieth-century American history; over the years many believe that the fate of the nation is inextricably bound to the fate of suburbia. At every critical juncture the history of suburbia collides with that of housing and its pivotal role in the evolution of American society. The idea of suburbia was central to visionaries, planners, and socially conscious architects who began to imagine a new America. In their vision suburbia meant a place where ordinary people, not just the elite, would have access to affordable, attractive modern housing in communities with parks, gardens, recreation, stores, and cooperative town meeting places. These ideas were not just pipe dreams.

Towns like these were built in the 1920s and 1930s, first by nonprofit organizations and later by the federal government. The idea that every citizen deserved decent housing captured the public imagination. After the second world war the demand for public affordable housing was so strong that Senator Joseph Mc-Carthy had to hold open hearings for five months to move public sentiment away from the idea of government-sponsored housing and in favor of private real estate interests building mass housing.

Our interviews and research revealed that suburban life has both shaped and been shaped by some of the most important issues of the past century. We focus on three crucial themes. The first is the ongoing struggle between ideas about private versus public responsibility for instance, the belief that government should take care of Americans versus faith in private enterprise. The second is the relationship of ideas and images to real buildings and places: how battles between aesthetic ideas and differing cultural, political, and economic forces forged suburban developments. The third is the continuing attempt to claim the dream of inclusive democracy and prosperity, and create the kind of American community where people's ideas can be heard, fought over, and realized.

The suburban migration—like the settlement of the West, mass immigration to America, and the black migration from the rural South to northern cities—changed the face of America. Our book examines the intellectual, economic, and political forces behind the opening of the suburbs to middle- and working-class families. In order to capture the interaction between social and political forces and the dense diversity of experience, we juxtapose many voices: intellectuals, planners, politicians, master builders, and most significantly, those who live in suburbia and are the custodians of suburban history.

Part One

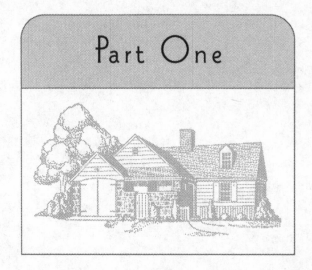

The Beginnings

Chapter One

The Gold Coast

The name Long Island evokes images of a new suburban life that many Americans first experienced during the prosperous years after the second world war. These images are partly accurate, yet the history of this 118-mile long, fish-shaped strip of land stretching east from New York City reaches back to America's beginnings.[1] Until postwar suburban development established Long Island as a laboratory for America's future, Long Island was a place firmly rooted in America's past.

Like many other rural and small-town areas in the United States, nineteenth-century Long Island was made up of small village communities, many of which dated back to the seventeenth or eighteenth centuries. In 1900, 60 percent of all Americans still lived in rural areas.[2] On Long Island, where there was little industry, the percentage was even higher. Its economy was provincial and preindustrial: a network of merchants, shopkeepers, artisans, farmers, and fishermen. Long Islanders generally lived on small plots of land, relying on nature's bountiful resources for subsistence. Rural folk pieced together a living from a variety of undertakings: vegetable and fruit farming; dairying; raising pigs, cows, and chickens; fishing the oceans, streams, and lakes; building houses and barns; and transporting lumber and crops. Though there was a cash economy, barter was still predominant. To some extent this way of life endured on Long Island into the early years of the twentieth century.

The unpublished writings of Ruth Grefe (who still lives in Roosevelt, a small village on Long Island's south shore) testifies to the persistence of a traditional life style. Her family's Long Island history dates back to 1644, when Alfred

Denton from Halifax, England, established the first Presbyterian Church in Hempstead. In Grefe's diary, written for her grandchildren, she described every-day life in the early 1900s in Roosevelt, a town she calls a "Land of Plenty."

Dad, a carpenter always had access to used lumber when a house was being torn down or re-molded. When a truckload of lumber was dumped in the driveway, Maddie [her younger sister] and I were always recruited to take nails out of it and stack it neatly . . . We used the wood for kindling. The woodbox in the kitchen had to be filled. Every Saturday we had to spend at least four hours at the stump pile splitting and sawing enough wood to feed our pipeless furnace for the week.

Roosevelt, in the old days, had an abundance of nuts, berries and nature's bounties Wild cherries abounded and in early or mid-summer we would pick them for jelly or for Mom and Dad to make wine from. At the bottom of Straw-berry Hill were wild grape which Mom made jelly from.

There were many apple trees around town and no one seemed to mind if you picked up the apples from the ground for applesauce—all you had to do was ask. Mom always gave away the excess pears and apples from our trees along with veg-etables from the garden and berries.

Mother and Dad got a cow a year or two after they were married. We had a cow barn in the back yard where she was kept. We had all the milk we could drink, plenty of whipped cream and pot cheese which Mom made when the milk soured. What we couldn't use we shared with neighbors.[3]

Yet America was changing. Between 1900 and the end of World War I, Long Island's North Shore saw unprecedented development.[4] What had been a rural outpost of farmers and fishermen was transformed into a palatial country retreat for a new class of men made wealthy by huge industrial and financial enterprises that were reshaping America's economic landscape. It began as a trickle in the 1860s after the Civil War and gathered steam throughout the 1890s.

During this era America's sixty richest men erected estates on Long Is-land's North Shore: J. P. Morgan, William Randolph Hearst, Russell Sage, Vincent Astor, W. R. Grace, Marshall Field, Henry Clay Frick, Jay Gould, Henry Ford, Thomas Edison, Pierre DuPont, William Whitney, Charles

Pratt, and William K. Vanderbilt, to name a few. In 1902 the *New York Herald* reported that "Long Island is rapidly being divided up into estates of immense acreage . . . beyond all precedence of American country life. Nowhere else certainly in America, possibly in the world, are to be found so many landed estates in any similar area."[5]

What made Long Island so appealing to the new ruling class, those who made fortunes from steel, oil, mining, railroads, and banks, was its proximity to the world's new commercial and financial center, New York City. Although they also built bungalows in Newport and Bar Harbor, Maine, for use in the summer, their Long Island estates were ideal for the spring and fall season and many winter weekends. The new rich were particularly attracted to the rolling and wooded North Shore. Here the varied landscape insured a uniqueness to each estate. They rejected the South Shore because it was "flat as a pancake," and seemed lacking in character.[6] The diverse North Shore terrain also was ideal for sporting activities, golf courses, polo grounds, boating, and bridle paths.

"They wanted to live like the nobility of Europe with huge estates secluded behind gates," says writer Suzanna Lessard, great-granddaughter of North Shore architect Stanford White. Lessard also observed that ironically, the estates of the robber barons set the precedent for Long Island's suburban sprawl.[7] Instead of generating clustered villages, Long Island grew rambling, isolated estates surrounded by vast tracts of private property.

Although the new capitalists built imitations of old-world baronial manors and hunted and fished in emulation of European aristocracy, their Long Island homes revealed a uniquely American twist: they used the newest industrial techniques and technologies in the construction of their fiefdoms. As the Prince of Wales observed while visiting the North Shore in 1924, "The paintings, tapestries, Old China and armor would have been common enough in a British country house; what was surprising was to find on the same property a squash court, a gymnasium, an indoor swimming pool and a Turkish bath."[8]

Building these new recreational edifices was a complex process requiring both Old European artisan master crafts and state-of-the-art technology, available only to the captains of industry. The sheer magnitude of construction required dozens of professionals and master craftsmen, some in totally new fields:

surveyors, architects, landscapers, interior decorators, masons, a variety of sewage, structural, and electrical engineers, well drillers, and elevator installers. Together these teams built long driveways that shielded the estates from public view, walls and gates (deemed necessary for security), the master house, gatehouse, stable, garage, pumping stations, water towers, power plants, greenhouses, casinos, indoor sports facilities, pool, bowling alley, racquet courts, boathouses, docks, guest houses, servant cottages, kennels, riding rings, golf courses, servant quarters, and repair facilities.

A large labor force was needed to keep the estates humming. A superintendent coordinated the efforts of specialized workers, including butlers, chauffeurs, gardeners, horse trainers, dog trainers, and cooks, as well as a host of laborers who worked as house servants, wood haulers, planters, and fireplace tenders. Each job had its place in a strict hierarchy organized along ethnic lines. Owners preferred their superintendents and butlers to be English; their gardeners, Scottish; their servants, Irish; and their common laborers, Polish or Italian. It was unusual for African Americans to be hired for estate work. The more specialized workers lived in servant quarters on the estate, were prohibited from owning automobiles, and were expected to be on call. Curfews were common. The laborers lived in nearby towns, and trucks from the estates picked them up each morning.[9]

By 1920 most of Long Island's North Shore was divided into nearly 600 large and small estates, home to the largest concentration of wealth and power in the United States. The elites were determined that no industrial development would mar their beaches, forests, hunting preserves, yachting, and country clubs. Class conflict might be an unavoidable by-product of the industries these men owned, but life on the North Shore would bear no evidence of the industrial turmoil that financed it. The North Shore let the industrial elites live out the fantasy of a leisured, preindustrial existence—albeit with all the modern conveniences money could buy.

Indeed, the architecture of the estates was calculated to mask all signs of physical labor: with servant entrances and narrow servant passages, masters would never bump into their servants on the staircase. In addition, small back service roads were designed for deliveries, work vehicles, and gardening equipment. On the Gold Coast, rooms were cleaned and gardens tended as if by magic.

The North Shore certainly earned its reputation as America's Gold Coast.[10] More than any other stretch of the nation, the Gold Coast glittered with private mansions, private country clubs, polo fields, and marinas. Estate owners outdid each other in displays of opulence. The F. W. Woolworth Mansion in Glen Cove had sixty-two rooms and included solid gold bathroom fixtures and a dining room ceiling gilded with 1,500 square feet of fourteen-carat gold. William Whitney's Old Westbury estate had an 800-foot-long racing stable, a mile-long track containing eighty-three box stalls, and a second story with a dining room, modern kitchen, gymnasium, dormitory, and library. The Marshall Field estate in Lloyd's Neck provided its guests with tennis, badminton, and squash courts, indoor and outdoor swimming pools, sailboats, motorboats, skeet ranges, and, lest their thirst for sport go unquenched, a thousand-acre hunting preserve. Investment banker Otto Khan wanted an open view on a hillside in Cold Spring Harbor, but he discovered that the hills around him were taken. He decided to build a small mountain of his own. Hauling the dirt and stone for the mountain required a railroad, so he built his own railroad line.[11]

On the estates, entertainment on a grand scale emerged as a way of life. Owners threw lavish parties for engagements, weddings, and debuts. Hosts hired famous performers and musicians and gave away expensive jewelry. At a debutante party for his daughter, Otto Kahn paid Enrico Caruso $10,000 to sing two songs. Other celebrations were less family-oriented. Elaborate estate parties were held in honor of the Prince of Wales's visit and the triumphant return of Charles Lindbergh. The magnates threw parties of a kind that few Americans had ever seen, outdoing each other with, among other things, swimming pools bearing thousands of orchids, diamond tiaras for lady guests, cigarettes wrapped and designed to be smoked in hundred-dollar bills.

Despite estate owners' wealth, their access to the North Shore of Long Island was difficult. In 1890 getting to the island from lower Manhattan meant taking a ferry to Brooklyn, where the nearest railroad station with access to Long Island was located. It was customary for Gold Coast millionaires to hire their own coaches, in which they could endure the rickety tracks in greater comfort and en-

joy each other's company in private. In 1910 a tunnel was dug under the East
River that allowed the railroad to proceed directly into Manhattan, making access easier. The tunnel was designed to serve the needs of the elite, yet the development of a direct route between Manhattan and Long Island laid the
infrastructure for later suburban development. Historians see the completion of
the tunnel as the moment when Long Island ceased being rural and started to become suburban.[12]

As one scholar noted, "Along with the railroad, the automobile played the
greatest part in changing the face and pace of Long Island."[13] At the turn of the
century the automobile was the new toy for the wealthy. Before the Model T, cars
were extremely expensive, one car costing several years of an average worker's
salary. In 1900 there were approximately 8,000 "horseless carriages" in the
United States.[14] But cars were common enough on Long Island's North Shore
that Gold Coast residents remade the landscape to accommodate them.

On the Gold Coast cars were de rigueur; the elite loved racing them, especially
the younger scions. William K. Vanderbilt II, an avid motorist and racing afi-
cionado, was instrumental in the construction of the first parkway in the United
States, the Vanderbilt Motor Highway Parkway, which extended from the
Queens border to Suffolk County, cutting through more than half of Long Island
and its Gold Coast. It was planned as a racing road, although toll-paying mo-
torists were allowed to travel on it. The automobile, along with its attendant infrastructure, was an important new element in the playground of the rich, one
that would create opportunities for the less wealthy. As Thomas Edison observed in 1904, "In time, the automobile will become the poor man's wagon . . .
he'll use it to haul his wood, convey his farm freight, get to and from the post office, and take the family to church."[15]

Even as they began to build roads that eventually would open Long Island to
the larger public, the robber barons in the meantime carefully constructed a political strategy to protect their enclave on the North Shore. Before 1898 Nassau
County was still part of Brooklyn, where politics was dominated by the Democratic party. When the historic charter of 1898 amalgamated the five boroughs of
New York and created the modern metropolis, however, Nassau County was deliberately carved out as a separate entity from the city. Influential Gold Coasters

used their power to make Nassau County into a Republican stronghold free from city-based Democratic politics. So durable was this Republican machine that it dominates Long Island politics to this day.

The elites now had unrestricted access to state government and the new Republican clout was soon felt in Albany. Gold Coast estate owners set about bending the laws to suit themselves. The legal incorporation of a village usually enabled communities to become self-governing bodies able to levy taxes and fund local improvements. This capacity to construct roads, develop water supplies, build parks, and apply zoning regulations often encouraged people to move to incorporated villages.

Gold Coast property holders, hostile both to taxation and the increase of the population in their dominions, recognized that the mechanism of incorporation could be quite useful—if only the rules were different.[16] State law called for a village to have at least 250 residents to become incorporated. Obligingly, Republican politicians working for the estate owners devised a new law passed in Albany that changed the minimum residency to fifty. With large extended families and staffs of loyal servants, this number could now be achieved by a single estate.

One of the most influential Republicans to help establish the new legislation was R. Eldridge, who occupied a huge estate in Saddle Rock, the first property to become an incorporated estate village in 1911. New residents had been moving to the area, and Eldridge worried that he soon would have to pay a large share of the public improvements that the unincorporated town was planning to build. It would be much less costly for him, he reasoned, to incorporate his estate, "to set up his own government and provide for his own needs," while ignoring the needs of nearby townspeople. On his estate he had fifty people, including servants, the exact number necessary for incorporation under the law he helped to enact. It is not surprising that Eldridge was "elected" the first mayor of Saddle Rock village, or that his wife was the second person to hold that office.[17] Laws enacted by estate villages prohibited parking on all village roads and forbade swimming in local lakes in order to "end once and for all the disturbing Sunday and holiday excursion crowds."[18]

The robber barons' determination to protect their opulent way of life was not without consequences for less well-to-do Long Islanders. The new titans of in-

dustry had a well-earned reputation for ruthless dealings with smaller competi-
tors, buying out those who would sell and pricing others out of the market. Just
as they devoured local small businesses to build their vast national corporations,
so too they gulped up small farm properties and undeveloped land to build their
giant estates. They bought as much North Shore land as possible, private and
public, to create a totally enclosed world of their own with no noisesome public
to bother them. In order to build the Payne Whitney estate, five family farms
dating back to the late seventeenth century were purchased, dispersing farmers
and their progeny. The utility magnate John Aldred and W. D. Guthrie purchased sixty homes from small-home owners in the Lattington sea town and demolished all sixty to improve their ocean views. Others bought and tore down
large resort hotels. Popular picnicking areas went the same way.[19]

Farm and fishing communities were deeply affected by the estate owners'
land-buying frenzy. Private estates created a contiguous barrier along the North
Shore and severely limited fishermen's access to the Long Island Sound. Once
publicly accessible forests and fields now became the posted province of the rich.
Farmers who long had relied on the bounty of lands were now summarily dispos-
sessed.

While some traditional Long Islanders welcomed the millionaires and ea-
gerly sold off their property, others deeply resented the intrusion. Reactions
ranged from bewilderment to anger to protest. In 1895 the farmers of Oceanside
signed a petition stating, "We the undersigned farmers . . . do hereby notify and
forbid the so-called Rockaway Hunting Club from crossing our land with horses
and dogs . . . We are determined to put a stop to this nuisance which has been going on for the past 8 years." Others felt their economic viability threatened and
took action to protect their livelihoods. In Oyster Bay in 1910 the baymen, feeling the effects of estate encroachment, reasserted their right to access the clamming beaches by circling the beaches with a wagon that cut through all the new
estate docks that blocked the baymen's way.[20]

In 1900 in Cold Spring Harbor, the only public road with open access to the
shore was closed by the new landowners, making it inaccessible to local people
who claimed bathing, clamming, and fishing rights. Several townspeople
protested, arguing that the dispute should be settled by reference to official maps

of the area. But the maps had disappeared mysteriously, and without them it was impossible to prove the existence of the public road. The villagers appealed to the local officials, but as one surviving member of the group stated, "The politicians always backed the estate people."[21]

Antagonisms between local workers and the elite came to a head in 1902, when William K. Vanderbilt II secretly (under the alias Mr. Smith) purchased 600 acres surrounding Lake Success, the largest freshwater lake in Nassau County, to build his own estate, Deepdale. He then tried to purchase the entire lake and the last remaining public access road from the town of North Hempstead. Boaters and fishermen, together with men who earned their living harvesting ice in the winter, made up the opposition. In this case the locals convinced municipal authorities not to sell and defeated the estate owner.[22]

Unruffled, Vanderbilt quickly became involved in a new dispute—this time over his proposal to take over Long Island's unpaved roads and spread 90,000 gallons of oil on them for the Vanderbilt Cup, a 300-mile race through Nassau County. The oil was needed to bank down the dirt, making it easier for racers to speed. He argued that the race would focus international attention on Long Island by attracting tens of thousands of visitors and the press. Politicians, auto clubs, and local businessmen were enthusiastic. In 1904 the American Automobile Association announced the race and its prize: a 481-ounce silver cup donated by Vanderbilt. Nassau County supervisors voted to approve the race.

Many Long Islanders saw the vote as a victory for arrogant, irresponsible plutocrats. They formed the Peoples' Protective Association, quickly gathering 300 signatures to prevent the race from occurring on public roads. Farmers protested that oil and grease would pollute their produce and harm their horses. The New York World noted that "War, grim war of the bucolic variety, looms up in Nassau because of the proposal to hold the first annual automobile race for the Vanderbilt cup over the only roads the farmers of that section can use in taking their produce to market. . . . The Masters of the Revels have issued orders to the peasantry."[23] In the end the race was held with more than 100,000 spectators on hand. Vanderbilt and the Gold Coast reaped much favorable publicity.

And publicity was what it was all about. New mass-circulating newspapers such as Hearst's New York Journal and Pulitzer's New York World with their illustrations, half-tone photographs, and huge Sunday editions were changing how Americans, particularly middle-class Americans, thought about their world. Like the new mass magazines *McClure's, Munsey's Magazine, Harper's, Everbody's Collier's, Scribner's,* and *The American Magazine,* the glossy tabloids cultivated a personal, intimate style that played to the emotions of outrage, envy, and sentimentality. They built their circulations around sensationalistic news and feature stories that ranged from exposés of urban political corruption and corporate greed to revelations concerning the miserable living conditions of the poor.

Before movie stars emerged as the prime objects of public scrutiny, the new rich were the talk of the town, the subject of everyday conversation, icons vested with power, beauty, and status to be envied or despised. Historian Daniel Sorbin explained that

> Knowledge of what the wealthy were doing could be obtained by any person who could afford a daily newspaper and knew how to read. A current newspaper reporter remarked after considering the highly publicized affairs of the estate people that "although the feudal-like places may have been erected to keep the public out, little happened in them that was private."[24]

Once hidden behind an arrogant veil of gated privacy, the life styles of the rich were now grist for a new media-driven popular culture.

The new print media supplied its growing middle-class readership with intimate details of the private and public lives of the new aristocracy: how they dressed, what their houses looked like, how they partied, how they spent their money on European art and tapestry, and gossip of every type. Vanderbilt's auto race, flamboyant parties, and social events such as the visit of the Prince of Wales were covered thoroughly in local papers and in New York City newspapers and weekly magazines. Conspicuous consumption made for colorful stories, the more excessive the better. At one such party the Waldorf-Astoria was transformed into a replica of Versailles and August Belmont wore a suit of inlaid gold armor valued at $10,000, drawing huge press. According to historian Matthew

Josephson, "The press followed the festivals of the 'plutocrats' with a persistent fascination."[25]

Upper-class scandal was even more thrilling than the spectacle of consumption. Long before O. J. Simpson, the Thaw trial was the trial of the century. The 1906 killing of Stanford White by millionaire Harry Thaw, husband of White's former mistress, the beautiful Evelyn Nesbit, produced a blizzard of published detail. New York's fourteen papers outdid each other in exposing "the satin-lined sins of the rich."[26]

The modern media offered middle-class readers the opportunity to denounce the wealthy for their "extravagant" or "sinful" ways of life. At the same time, the new media made the lives of the wealthy leisured class part of the dream world of the American middle class. People who could not afford to live on the Gold Coast nevertheless had access to it in fantasy and popular imagination. Country havens from the city, fashionable clothes, cars and modern conveniences, and new forms of recreation, though still unattainable, had entered the middle-class perception of desire and status.

Though the idea of mass suburban living had not yet taken hold, the fantasy world that Gold Coasters created and popular media described in such detail would have a profound impact on the American landscape. While the building of suburbia in the postwar era was indeed the triumphal outcome of modern methods of production and a response to a serious housing crisis, its imaginative origins go back much further; suburbia also was the attempt to realize visions and fantasies that had been percolating for decades.

The lure of the glimmering Gold Coast persisted in vernacular language long after the enclaves the robber barons built declined. In the words of Clara Gillens, who moved to Long Island from a Harlem project in the 1970s, "When you move out to Long Island, everyone thinks you're living in the Gold Coast. After all you live in suburbia and you own a house."[27]

Chapter Two

The Second Industrial Revolution:

Mass Production Makes a Dent

The 1920s was the decade that saw the partial democratization of the "good life" in America. The conversion of a production-based economy to one defined by consumption changed everyday life. Assembly lines churned out material goods cheap enough for the middle class to afford. The mass production of cars, clothing, cosmetics, furniture, and modern appliances as well as new forms of entertainment and leisure made abundance attainable to a growing number of people. Such changes raised the possibility that the middle class might conceivably attain their dreams of a country life.

In the 1920s the class that benefited the most from these changes was a growing middle class, people who were gaining a position in the expanding sectors of lower management, service, and sales. These up-and-comers were eager to distance themselves from the industrial working class, who still lived in crowded, run-down tenements with no running water or private toilets.

Yet the promise if not the reality of abundance reshaped all Americans' aspirations. Historians generally see the twenties as a time when the social reform ethos of the Progressive era gave way to probusiness attitudes, American boosterism, Prohibition, and isolation. Even so, the flowering of a mass production economy raised the possibility of the good life, not only for the middle class but for the working class as well.

It was a decade marked by flux and mobility. Migration shaped the lives of people across class and region. There were cultural émigrés from the Midwest such as F. Scott Fitzgerald, who penetrated the world of Gold Coast parvenus and immortalized their story in *The Great Gatsby*. African Americans from the South came to the industrial cities of the North, where they found new economic and cultural opportunities and old forms of racism. Children of immigrants left the tenements of New York's Lower East Side and moved to more substantial dwellings in better though still congested neighborhoods in Brooklyn and Queens. Urban middle-class people left the city altogether, moving into newly created suburbs.

New technologies of transportation, particularly the proliferation of the automobile, had far-reaching effects on the development of suburbia. Before the 1920s, the automobile was a costly luxury, but Henry Ford's mass-produced Model T changed all this. In 1920 over nine million cars were registered; by 1925 nearly twenty million; by 1930 over 26.5 million—roughly one car for every five people.[1] Seen another way, in 1919 the number of families owning cars was less than seven million; by 1923 it was twenty-three million.[2] The automobile was becoming an essential part of daily life. In their famous book *Middletown*, written in 1929, Robert and Helen Lynd reported that a mother of nine told them, "We'd rather do without clothes than give up the car." Another said, "I'd go without food before I'll see us give up the car." A woman explained why her family had purchased a car before indoor plumbing: "Why, you can't go to town in a bathtub."[3]

During the 1920s transportation by railroad was cut in half as people took to the road in their cars. The automobile also altered people's conceptions of space and leisure as remote country areas suddenly became accessible, creating a demand for vacation homes, tourist cabins, and ultimately, the motel. Happily for the burgeoning vacation and leisure industry, access to new areas coincided with an overall increase in leisure time. Before World War I a seventy-hour work week was common. In 1920 the average had dropped to sixty hours, and by 1929 to forty-eight.[4] The Saturday half holiday was becoming part of American culture and a full day off was more common. Henry Ford had even introduced annual vacations with pay.

With more free time even less affluent, working urban people could begin to participate in new forms of leisure available in the country. Meanwhile, there were even more reasons to want to escape the city. During the 1920s New York City witnessed a rapid growth in population. Brooklyn and Queens together had 2.5 million people, a population greater than all but eight states in the union. To accommodate all these people, there was a huge burst of apartment and office building construction. Open space was quickly vanishing. Beyond the Queens border, however, lay Long Island, an area four times the size of the whole city but inhabited by less than a quarter of a million people. Long Island beckoned like a vast paradise, and its rolling surf and leaves and grass began to seem accessible.[5] People whose only access to nature had been urban parks now could pile into the family car and journey into the countryside.

Automobiles were the most visible commodities of the new system of mass production, but other technological developments in the 1920s such as electrification also changed the way people lived, worked, and played. As Marshall McLuhan noted, electricity changed people's relationship to time, to space, and even to nature. Electricity turned night into day on city streets and in private dwellings. More hours of light meant more leisure time and more time for people to take advantage of new media: the telephone, radio, motion pictures, amusement parks, and night baseball. These new commercial media linked the nation in new ways, replacing regional, local, or ethnic cultures with a common national one.

The Hollywood film industry and the new national radio networks disseminated images of the good life that centered on wealth, leisure, youth, beauty, and abundance. Borrowing from the techniques of the popular press, the movies used sensationalized, voyeuristic depictions of the life styles of the rich to attract audiences. In the 1920s Hollywood directors such as Cecil B. De Mille invented a popular formula for moviemaking: turning the sumptuous world of the wealthy into a setting for romantic comedy and drama. Movies thus provided alluring lessons in how to live a life of leisure in modern America. The movies brought the lavish interiors of country estates, the clothing, accessories, and cars of the wealthy into the experiences and fantasies of ordinary Americans. The movie theaters themselves were architecturally modeled to resemble Gold Coast "palaces," as they were then called, complete with marble staircases, lavish tapestries, velvet seats, richly appointed restrooms, and ushers dressed in livery, like servants.[6]

The media played an important role in persuading middle-class Americans that the suburban dream was within reach. The first radio commercial, for instance, attempted to persuade people to leave the lonely, overcrowded city and move to the suburbs. In 1922 WEAF (the forerunner of WNBC) broadcast a ten-minute program paid for by the Queensboro Corporation, a real estate company selling apartments in Jackson Heights, Queens (then thought of as the country). An executive of the company delivered this message:

> Let me enjoin you as you value your health and your own happiness, get away from the solid masses of brick, where the meager opening admitting a slant of sunlight is mockingly called a light shaft, and where children grow up starved for a run over a patch of grass and the sight of a tree.
>
> Apartments in congested parts of the city have proven failures. The word neighbor is an expression of peculiar irony—a daily joke . . .

The ad went on to extoll suburban living. Electricity and the car were promoted as protection against the isolation once associated with life outside the city. *Country Life* magazine claimed in the same year that radio removed "the last objection to living in the country." As media historian Eric Barnouw put it, "In its first paid-for commercials, radio helped to exploit this trend."[7] The suburbs were being turned into an object of desire. It was the beginning of a new way of life.

Electricity also was changing the nature of domestic experience. In 1910 only one in ten American homes was electrified. By the end of the 1920s most urban homes had been wired. Electricity was cleaner, safer, brighter, and healthier than gaslight. Gas fixtures required the removal of soot almost daily and soiled wallpaper and fabrics as well. Gaslight consumed oxygen and released water and carbonic acids into the atmosphere. Rooms and rugs needed frequent airing. Even if a house had adequate ventilation, the combination of smoke, humidity, and acidity destroyed furniture and books.[8]

Electrification was hailed by progressive feminists such as Charlotte Perkins Gilman, a prominent social thinker and popular writer who argued that new electrical products—vacuums, refrigerators, washing machines—would free women from housework, creating the possibility for women to enter the work force and participate in civil society.[9] Christine Frederick, Ellen Richards, and Lillian Gilbreth, more conservative in their thinking and founders of the scientific housekeeping movement, thought electrification would turn homes into efficient work stations akin to assembly-line factories. Women would become managers of their households, elevating the status of wife into a profession but still keeping women at home. Scientific housekeeping, otherwise known as home economics, was by 1920 a required course for schoolgirls.

In general, ready-made clothing, canned food, washing machines, radio, the automobile, and the electric light changed the activities people did at home and how they did them. In a 1949 retrospective on the history of modern housing, the influential *Architectural Forum* observed:

In our specialized, mass-production culture, home is no longer the center for both work and relaxation. Factory or office has long claimed the master of the house for most of his waking hours. Now, with the increased speed of electrical housekeeping, the mistress, too, may hold at least a part time job. Daughters no longer need to stay at home to help with the spinning, weaving and baking; they go to business school, college or start immediately to work. The supermarket and the department store, supplying food, clothing and furniture which formerly took long hours to make at home, have created more leisure time for all. But again, modern mass entertainment, from movies to baseball games, from the juke joint to the Lion's Club dance lure families away from home to enjoy this leisure. The automobile, symbol of the twentieth century, speeds the family into town or away from town for an evening or a weekend.[10]

Electricity changed the way new homes were designed and constructed as well. Most home builders welcomed electricity because it made construction simpler. Electric wiring is flexible and can be placed anywhere, whereas gas pipes require intricate planning. Electric lighting lends itself to houses with more open floor plans, fewer doors, and more fluid living areas. Dark Victorian color schemes that camouflaged soot and grime could be abandoned for lighter wall and ceiling colors, making rooms bright and airy.

Builders tried to design these homes with a middle-class market in mind, making an effort to keep prices down. The *bungalow*, a generic name for the simplified house, contained open spaces and was built with new efficiencies in housework in mind. The cheapest bungalows could be ordered from Sears Roebuck or Montgomery Ward and came in a do-it-yourself kit with lumber, doors, windows, and porches, mailed precut and ready to assemble.

Even more upscale bungalows, no cheaper than houses in the Victorian era, were designed to be entirely different from Victorian homes. Floor plans no longer included specialized rooms. By 1910 new houses contained only three downstairs rooms—living room, dining room, and kitchen—and two upstairs bedrooms. No longer was there a distinction between family space, private space, and work space. There were no separate areas designated for sewing, laundry, pantries, formal parlors, servants rooms, libraries, window nooks, reading corners, or other private hideaways. This merger of public and private space disturbed some eminent Victorians. Henry James, for example, noted with regret,

> We see systematized the indefinite extension of all spaces and the definite merging of all functions . . . the house with almost no one of its indoor parts distinguishable from any other . . . this diffused vagueness of separation between apartments, between hall and room, between one room and another, between the one you are in and the one you are not in, between the place of passage and place of privacy, is a provocation to despair.[11]

In spite of the new streamlined interiors James so disliked, architectural design reflected the extent to which the Gold Coast emphasis on European aristocratic features shaped middle-class ideas of style. Most new middle- and upper-middle-class houses had facades that imitated European styles, with Dutch colonial, English Tudor, and Spanish stucco the most popular. *Architectural Forum* pointed out that consumer magazines "worshipped the cult of the antique and [drained] nearly dry the European fountainhead of French chateau,

English manor houses, Mediterranean villas and Spanish patios. Even the more modest Cape Cod cottages and bungalows were being designed with brick fronts, stone fronts, pergolas . . . fake gables over the doorway . . . dormer windows, picture windows of Spanish type plaster."[12]

Some, like the department store owner Edward Filene, found these emulative tendencies in direct opposition to the new principles of mass production, which he argued required a new simpler form of design:

> Standardization, without which mass production is impossible, implies a search for simplicity of design and manufacture. In nearly everything we use today we are paying a high price for complexity that seldom adds one whit to the beauty of the product. . . . The standardization that will really pay is not the standardization that begins by trying to cheapen the cost of production, but the standardization that takes something that the largest number of people already like and then tries to eliminate everything that does not add to its beauty, its quality, or its usefulness.[13]

Lewis Mumford, prominent in architectural criticism and a contemporary of Filene, discerned a similar contradiction "between the imitative European style and modern machine production. American taste by a paradox has become antipathetic to machinery and tearfully sentimental about ages which did not boast our technical resources." Mumford claimed that Americans, rather than celebrating the modern machine miracle and looking to the new technological landscape for aesthetic inspiration, were flagrantly "imitating certified brands of European or early American culture" and building "the whited sepulchres that began to parade as the seal and hall of sound aesthetics, the dull porticos, the feeble massive pillars that support nothing and express nothing . . . the French chateau in New England and the Spanish palace in the midst of the prairie."[14]

Mumford extended his critique to trends in interior decoration as well, decrying "the absurd, non-functional imitations of European furniture and ornamentation, like such manifest idiocies as dolls' dresses to cover telephones . . . and radio sets made to look like Florentine or Georgian cabinets." Ironically, this imitative and derivative style was made possible by the mass production system itself, which turned out such knick-knacks more cheaply than ever before. Like Filene, Mumford believed the era of mass production called for creating a new American machine-based aesthetic. Instead of draping the products of mass production in outmoded clothing, the machine should unveil itself in all objects of consumption:

> None of our arty decorations and adaptations can approach for sheer beauty of line and color a modern automobile or a simple tiled bathroom or the fixtures of a modern kitchen. In motors and in porcelain bathroom fixtures we have, by designing steadily for beauty through the imaginative modification of useful instruments, produced objects of art which stand on the same plain as the handicraft production of earlier ages. If our taste were well formed, our chief effort would be to make all our interior fittings—our furniture, our walls, our carpets, our lamps—with the same spirit as we design our automobiles and bathtubs.[15]

The American architect who most embodied modernist ideas and incorporated indigenous landscapes into his designs was Frank Lloyd Wright. Lewis Mumford approvingly characterized Wright houses as being "as much a part of the prairies as the corn fields themselves. . . . In houses . . . such as those of Wright . . . the buildings were too thoroughly a part of their own day to be disguised in borrowed clothes and threadbare costumes."[16]

Wright took seriously the issue of how to design middle-class homes, raising it to a place in architectural history that hitherto had been reserved for palaces, cathedrals, and other public monuments. One of his first designs was the prairie house, which embodied the principle of harmony between the horizontal house and the midwestern plains, and included electrification, open interior space, and multiple windows. Several of Wright's plans were published in Ladies' Home Journal (1901) and given the seal of approval by its influential editor, Edward Bok.

Wright's architectural plans were based on a reformulation of the Jeffersonian philosophy that land ownership was the basis of democracy. In an industrial society, Wright believed, home ownership was the foundation of freedom. The "Citizen in his own Life in his own Home with his feet on his own Ground" he

said, is "truly a free Man."[17] Although many of Wright's houses were pricey, his
social vision included the promise of less expensive homes for the growing middle class.

Indeed, Wright's dream of popular home ownership was shared by many
Americans. The bungalow, although unaffordable, was a fantasy for working
people, most of whom still rented apartments in congested cities. This dream
was immortalized in such popular songs as "We'll Build a Bungalow, Big
Enough for Two," "My Blue Heaven," and Dorothy Parker's poem "Day
Dreams."

> We'd build a little bungalow
> If you and I were one
> and carefully we'd plan it so
> we'd get the morning sun
> I'd rise each day at rosy dawn
> and bustle gaily down
> In evenings cool
> you'd spray the lawn
> When you come back from town.[18]

But for the time being, home ownership for most people remained in the
realm of fantasy. It would take a major depression and a world war to sufficiently
shake up the housing industry and change its methods of production and design
so completely that working- and middle-class people could realize the dream of
homes of their own.

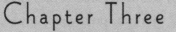

Chapter Three

Suburban Birth Pangs

When New York City folk decided to take advantage of their new free weekends by packing a picnic, hopping into a car, and heading to the country for sunshine and space, Long Island seemed a logical destination. Around the turn of the century New York City had built many bridges linking the city to the island by automobile; Long Island therefore was accessible as well as close.[1] Although the landed gentry did everything in their power to keep city people out of their private playgrounds, urban interlopers in their new, affordable Model Ts began to acquire a taste for space, sun, and sea—and some even dared to dream of owning a home on Long Island.

In 1925, for instance, Brooklyn-bred Seth and Peggy Mills inherited a dry goods store, bought a Model T, and began taking day trips to Long Island. As Peggy put it, "In those days it took a long time; the roads were so bad, the car often broke down. But still it was worth it. The sight of those rolling hills, something you'd only see in the pictures, I'll never forget it. Coming from Brooklyn, the countryside seemed endless and you could finally be alone. Even on weekends when we couldn't make the trip, we'd sit around and dream of what it would be like to live there."[2]

Clearly these dreams could not be realized on the elite North Shore, which estate owners considered their personal domain. They went to great lengths to keep it so, building huge walls around their estates and posting armed guards at the borders to prevent errant day trippers from meandering onto the grounds.

Wealthy Long Islanders also made sure the North Shore was difficult to circumnavigate. At their behest, officials in Nassau County allowed all public roads to fall into disrepair. Moreover, private estate roads were built like mazes—winding and deliberately confusing. Most of the North and South Shore beaches were marked CLOSED with large private property signs, and were guarded as well. The only beaches open to the public were rocky, unappealing, and pitifully narrow, and city residents had to pay exorbitant rates to the local towns to use them.

Opulent estate owners also made sure that the journey itself to Long Island was arduous. Northern Boulevard, a main access road through Queens to the North Shore, was the widest highway, 160 feet of macadam (a pavement of small layers of stone, bound with tar). At the city line, it shrank to 18 feet of deteriorating pavement, eventually becoming dirt and dust. Cars had to go single file and watch for gaping pot holes and unpaved stretches. Desperate families often tried to picnic at the side of the road, but the ever vigilant guards made their stops brief. The average Sunday journey of thirty-two miles in 1923, from the Queensborough Bridge to Huntington, took four hours. As Robert Caro noted, "when the families of New York City reached Long Island, they found the milk and honey sour indeed."[3]

The robber barons also insured that railroad travel to Long Island was difficult. A wealthy group lead by Charles Pratt, a partner of John D. Rockefeller, bought enough stock in the Long Island Railroad to control the North Shore lines.[4] Following the dictum of a Long Island Railroad vice-president that "population follows transportation," Pratt made sure that the North Shore branches were never electrified, because it would make for faster, more comfortable, and cheaper travel.[5]

As more city residents bought Model Ts, an increasing number of people became frustrated by the inaccessibility of Long Island's vast stretches of pristine beach lands. Mounting pressure for access to Long Island's sun and sand and the relentless intransigence of the rich combined to create an impasse.

The influential urban planner Robert Moses was one of the few men with enough power, guts, know-how, and vision to confront the estate owners and insist that they open up Long Island. Moses had worked in progressive reform organizations such as the Good Government Commission, and had the ear and respect of powerful politicians such as Al Smith, then governor of New York

State. In his capacity first as the president of the Long Island Park Commission (1924–1936) and later as park commissioner for the metropolitan area and surroundings (1936–1964), Moses wielded the political power to float special bond issues to finance and appropriate land for highways, water crossings, beaches, and parks.[6] He believed that the public had as much right to recreation and leisure activities as the wealthy.

In 1922 Moses rented a summer bungalow in Babylon with his wife and small children and fell in love "with the town, with the bay, with the whole South Shore."[7] As he commuted on the Long Island Railroad and looked out the window, he saw "thick leafy bands of wood and through the trees the blue waters of ponds and streams." Moses began to explore, looking up the property rights in local libraries and trekking by foot through vast forests and streams. His "eyes" burned with ideas, and he soon discovered that the South Shore contained 3,500 acres of empty, unused land close to the city line not owned by the robber barons or local Long Island governments. It was owned by the government of New York City, which meant that "land could be opened to the cities' people merely by turning a key." Moreover, beyond lay another vast reserve of unused land, reachable only by boat: Jones Beach and Fire Island. Jones Beach seemed remote, but Moses realized that it was a mere twenty-five miles from Times Square.[8]

Moses proposed building two connecting highways to link the city to the beach, and making the beach into a public park. The idea was revolutionary. Up to that point, most country parks originally conceived as habitats to be hiked and canoed through and kept in their natural wild state—they could not be reached by automobile and so remained unused. Yet Moses' proposal to make Jones Beach into a park transformed and domesticated the concept of the pristine nature preserve. His plan incorporated baseball diamonds, tennis courts, golf courses, and swimming pools—not exclusively for the rich but for less affluent city people.

Even though Moses wanted to see Long Island more accessible, his desire for democratization was limited. Like most mainstream progressives of the time, Moses made a distinction between the public and the common people. As Frances Perkins, later the secretary of labor under Franklin D. Roosevelt and a longtime associate of Moses, observed:

He'd denounce the common people terribly. To him they were lousy, dirty people, throwing bottles all over Jones Beach. . . . He loves the public, but not as people. The public is just the public. It's a great amorphous mass to him; it needs to be bathed, it needs to be aired, it needs recreation, but not for personal reasons—just to make it a better public.[9]

As parks commissioner, Moses had the clout to put his convictions into practice. Although he opened the beach to automobile traffic, making sure there was sufficient parking for huge numbers of cars, he vetoed any plans for making the parks accessible by rapid public transit; Moses wouldn't even extend a Long Island Railroad line to Jones Beach. He made park access to those without cars even more difficult by building bridges across the new parkways so low that chartered buses had to take slow, indirect local roads. Later on, during the Depression Moses charged 50 cents for entry to Jones Beach, in violation of the American tradition of free public parks.

Moses considered African Americans inherently "dirty" and took specific measures to deny them access to the parks. Permits required for buses to enter public parks often were denied to black groups, especially permits for Jones Beach. Most chartered trips were shunted to parks many miles away from the entrance to Jones Beach, and even in those parks buses carrying black passengers were directed to the furthest reaches of the parking areas. Blacks were discouraged by park officials from using the best "white" beaches, and the handful of black lifeguards were stationed at the most distant and least developed beaches. Moses believed that African Americans did not like cold water and had the temperature at the Jones Beach swimming pool deliberately kept ice cold in an effort to keep blacks out.[10]

Despite his undemocratic definition of the people, these actions taken by Moses were still far too democratic for the Long Island elite. While wealthy Long Islanders did not contest the construction of the Southern State Parkway, which provided access to Jones Beach but did not trespass on their vast holdings, the construction of the Northern State Parkway was another story. When the plans of the Long Island State Park Commission called for a parkway to be built in the northern part of Nassau and Suffolk counties—cutting east through their estates—the ruling class issued a clarion call to halt the highways' invasion of their territory.

Declaring that the parkway would allow the Gold Coast to be "overrun with rabble from the city,"[11] estate owners used their powerful connections in Long Island and Albany to pass legislation abolishing the Long Island State Park Commission and its authority to allocate money for construction. Moses, however, had the ear of Governor Al Smith, who considered himself one of the rabble and their cheif defender. The war was on. The state legislature favored Long Island's elite and passed bill after bill, only to be thwarted by the governor's veto.

After many years of skirmishes, a compromise was struck. The Northern State Parkway was built in spite of the estate owners' opposition, but the highway was routed far from the estates of the most powerful group of landowners. This compromise was costly both for drivers, who now had to go miles out of their way, and taxpayers, who had to finance a land purchase for the 2.3 miles of additional road. This might seem minute, but it illustrates the power of the estate owners: Drivers now had to go 839.5 miles out of their way each year.

The North Shore elite may have won the battle to preserve their dominion, but they lost the war. After the completion of the highways and beaches, an infrastructure that supported the development of housing, industry, leisure, and recreation on the South Shore sprang up seemingly overnight. In 1920 there were no highways on Long Island; but twelve years later there was a modern interconnected parkway system linking the various Long Island communities and allowing easy access to New York City. When Moses became president of the Long Island State Park Commission there was only one underutilized state park. In 1928, only four years later, there were fourteen state parks totaling 9,700 acres—parks that were automobile-accessible and outfitted with modern recreational facilities.[12]

Many people who flocked to Long Island for recreation and a temporary respite from city life decided to settle permanently, especially on the flatter, less well-landscaped South Shore, which was not dominated by powerful elites. At the turn of the century the South Shore of Long Island—which eventually would house the quintessential postwar suburb of Levittown—was still predominantly rural, inhabited by fishermen, farmers, artisans, and tradespeople. Freeport, the second-largest village in Nassau County, was a major South Shore fishing port; oystering, clamming, and whaling were the predominant industries. In 1892 Freeport became an incorporated village, which attested to its economic importance.

By the early 1920s Freeport had emerged as an open, public resort and summer haven. Located near Astoria, Queens, then the moviemaking capital of the East Coast, Freeport became a vacation center for the aristocracy of the burgeoning entertainment industry. Freeport developed its own entertainment too with summer theaters and a giant amusement park that opened in 1923 on the waterfront. Playland had numerous rides, vaudeville shows, dance halls, and a salt water swimming pool.[13] Mimicking the industrial elite, the entertainers built large and luxurious mansions and hotels, albeit on a smaller scale. This in turn attracted actors, movie stars, comedians, singers, and stagehands.

By the mid-1920s Freeport's original working population of artisans and farmers swelled to include European immigrants and a small colony of African Americans who migrated from South Carolina and Georgia to work as domestic servants for rich entertainers and a newly arrived middle class. Recruited or brought to Long Island by relatives or agencies, they settled in small, segregated enclaves, many near the railroad tracks and some in Bennington Park in the center of Freeport. These South Shore communities originally were built through family, church, and kinship ties.

Local resident Louise Simpson, who worked on voter registration forms that included information on where people were born, observed this distinct pattern:

I realized that they were all from the same area in South Carolina, a lot from Charleston. . . . Freeport was a hub, it had good transportation for people migrating to do domestic work. For domestics, it was okay, you had one day off and every other Sunday. Freeport got to be a meeting place for people who did domestic work and they were able to find work in the large homes; there were rooming houses, so when they quit a job they could find a room. This is how friendships developed, if you're from my home town, I'm going to seek you out. You felt comfortable, you knew each other. If you didn't go that route of family and friends, there was this particular family who was sort of like a personnel person for employment. She would go to where she came from in Carolina and bring people up, or tell them to get in touch and their transportation would be paid. Freeport blossomed like that.[14]

Harve Sinklar-Herring, who came from South Carolina, ran such an employment agency. Her first contact with Freeport was in 1927, when she came up with her cousin to work as a domestic servant for the summer. She also found work as a chauffeur and a caterer. Using these skills, she opened a domestic service agency, first in her home and then in a large house that encompassed an office, a dormitory, and a staff of twenty. She recruited and trained women from South Carolina in domestic work. She claims to have had "the only agency like this. I advertised in local papers. I charged employers who hired the women. I charged the domestics room and board while I trained them."[15]

Like other railroad depot towns of the South Shore, Freeport had significant real estate activity. Large tracts of land were bought by speculators, builders, and developers. Freeport participated in a nationwide suburban housing boom. Indeed, Nassau County, including Freeport, was the fastest growing county in the United States in the 1920s.[16] Planned communities and large subdivisions promoted by developers like the Freeport Land Company were aimed at upper-middle-class families, some of whom had vacationed in and around Freeport and were drawn to town life within easy access of the city.

Seth and Peggy Mills could not find a house on the North Shore, so they bought a lot and built a tudor house in Freeport. "We couldn't move to the North Shore, our original dream, but we did find a house within reach of the city with beautiful beaches, quiet streets and flowers and trees," said Peggy. "We felt like we were living rich in miniature."[17] The Mills were part of a trend of new upper-middle-class suburban home owners.

Between 1922 and 1929 six million new homes went up across the nation—twice as many as in any previous seven-year period. Well over half were single-family homes. Rising wages and falling housing prices propelled the construction industry. The suburbs grew twice as rapidly as the center cities in the 1920s; nearly one out of six Americans lived in the suburbs by 1930.[18] The increased availability of mortgages made it easier to borrow money. This growth, however, benefited only the upper and upper middle class. Three quarters of the new housing continued to be marketed to the top third of the household income spectrum, and there was no production at all for the bottom third, categorized as living below "any decent standard."[19] The 1920 census indicated that 46 percent of all American families were home owners, although in metropolitan areas—where the poor lived—fewer families owned homes. New York City had the lowest rate of home ownership, with only 12 percent. Residential patterns remained segregated along economic and racial lines.

This segregation reflected deep prejudices that were manifest in Freeport. Freeport's expansion was welcomed by many of its summer visitors and new residents, but many older local Anglo-Saxon residents felt threatened by the flamboyant entertainers and the new immigrants who had come to settle there. The Ku Klux Klan flourished in the 1920s, reflecting and inflaming local fears of immigrants, Catholics, Jews, African Americans, and ethnic entertainers. During the early 1920s one out of every eight white residents in Nassau and Suffolk counties was a member of the Klan. On July 4, 1924, 30,000 spectators looked on as 2,000 robed Klansmen marched with their floats down Main Street. In Freeport the Klan's membership included several local ministers, the chief of police, county workers, and a wide array of other townspeople—a list that would have made any civic club or organization proud; but the Klan was no Kiwanis club. It held cross burnings at Christmastime, Lincoln's birthday, and the Fourth of July. It actively tried to keep black people confined to Bennington Park and out of Roosevelt, a neighboring white community.[20]

In her 1993 book *Having Our Say*, Elizabeth (Bessie) Delany provides a rare firsthand account of a confrontation between the Ku Klux Klan and African Americans on Long Island. In the 1920s the Delany sisters had moved to New York City in search of further education and greater opportunities. Bessie was solidly middle class and one of the few female black dentists in Harlem. One Sunday she and her boyfriend were returning from the beach, heading back toward Sag Harbor, a predominantly black seaside resort town:

We came around the corner of this two-lane road, and there are about twenty men dressed in white robes, hoods and all, stopping cars and searching. You could see that they were making colored people get out of their cars! Well, my eyes popped out of my head, I said, "Aren't you going to stop?" But my friend never answered me. He stepped on the gas and drove right around them, up an embankment and everything, and next thing I knew we had just zoomed around them. . . . I believe we simply outran them.

Here, all those years in the South they [our parents] had managed to keep us Delany children out of the hands of the KKK and they'd almost got their hands on me—on *Long Island*.[21]

Racism did not only manifest itself through the organizational activities of the Klan. It was deeply inscribed into all the codes that governed who could live where. During the 1920s restrictive covenants prevented the sale of property to Mexicans, Asians, blacks, and Jews. Although the U.S. Supreme Court struck down municipal and residential segregation laws in 1917, real estate boards and property owner associations concocted contractual "gentlemen's" agreements to prevent class, religious, and racial integration. Economic restrictions such as house prices, codes that prevented the construction of two family houses and apartments, loan and mortgage policies, and minimum lot sizes all kept the suburbs closed to anyone who wasn't white, Protestant, wealthy, or upper middle class.[22] Zoning regulations also determined whether towns would be industrial and working class or residential and suburban.

Even the select segment of the population *not* excluded from the new suburbs by restrictive covenants or zoning encountered problems. The housing industry at the time was small, makeshift, local, and unregulated. At best it was a patchwork that included genuine growth in real estate sales and housing subdivisions, as well as unscrupulous promoters and developers creating speculative, profit-making schemes. By the mid-1920s large auctions of land tracts were openly promoted for investment speculation. Developers used newly conceived advertising techniques to sell both property and whole communities not yet built.

Lavish brochures and advertising folders, for example, claimed the Biltmore Shores in Massapequa had "paved streets, fine homes, a vast park, modern

shops, churches, schools, golf, tennis, yachting and riding clubs, and a splendid
fire department and complete administrative system."[23] This was all fiction.
When people bought land sight unseen from speculators, they risked getting
burned. One group of investors from Dayton, Ohio, tried to sell their Long Island property only to learn that it was nothing but worthless land. The unscrupulous activities of the "land sharks" caused one reader of the *New York
Times* to write to the editor, "My advice is to leave all Long Island property
alone."[24]

According to *Architectural Forum*, much of this fly-by-night development
was shoddy. Suburban home construction in Long Island was considered the
worst in the nation. Bradley Randall, chief underwriter for New York, did a
study of Long Island building and found that "examples of faulty construction
most prevalent were two plaster coats instead of three, no fire stopping, insuffi-
cient thickness of foundation walls, poor quality timber and flooring . . . no collar beams between rafters and other minor sins of commission and omission."[25]
One writer in *Architectural Forum* observed that "no phrase more aptly conveys
the thought of miserable home development practice than the brand, 'cheap
Long Island.'"[26]

Although there was a housing boom in the 1920s—albeit mainly shoddy and speculative—by 1925 it had peaked, followed by a rapid downturn in construction. By
1929 residential housing had dropped 46 percent to 509,000 units. In dollars this
meant a decline from $4.5 billion in 1925 to $2.45 billion in 1929.[27] The breakdown of the housing market was the bellwether of the Great Depression.

Suburban housing had accelerated in the early 1920s, but its financing had
become increasingly precarious. Single-family dwellings typically were purchased through an unsound web of first, second, and even third mortgages, generally of short terms and without any built-in orderly system for repayment.[28]
As the depression deepened and people lost their jobs, they were sitting ducks
for defaults and foreclosures.

With the onset of the Great Depression, credit was frozen and no capital was
available for speculation in housing. Upscale 1920s housing based on specula-

tion by unscrupulous promoters failed. The widespread failure of real estate and bond scandals resulted in the loss of new high-priced city apartments and suburban developments. By 1932 the housing decline reached epic proportions. As one scholar noted, "In 1930, total housing production receded to a point 60 percent below the 1922–28 average; by 1931 the rate had descended 69 percent below that average. . . . In 1932 foreclosures reached the disastrous level of 250,000 homes."[29]

Unlike European countries, the United States had never developed strategies to deal with the issue of housing on a national level. It had no federal housing programs or policies, no public housing for low-income and working-class families, and no financial guarantees to aid the middle class in case of bank credit or mortgage failures. The federal government's lack of housing policies reflected the American belief in individualism, private enterprise, and individual home ownership, an ideology eloquently expressed by President Herbert Hoover, who claimed with confidence, "The sentiment for home ownership is so embedded in the American heart that millions of people who dwell in tenements, apartments, and rental rows of solid brick have the aspiration for wider opportunity in ownership of their own home."[30] The sentiment might have been there, but sentiment alone could not build houses—especially when the fledging housing industry had already collapsed.

Part Two

New Thoughts, New Deals

Chapter Four

Housing the Masses: Ideas and Experiments

If the housing industry was only interested in building houses for the upper middle class and the wealthy, who would consider the housing needs of the masses? During the suburban boom of the early 1920s and the later housing bust, a range of social critics—socialists, utopians, communitarians, social workers, progressive architects, members of the arts and crafts movement, trade unionists, and enlightened businessmen—argued that housing was the burning social issue of the era. Whether people had decent places to live, they felt, was the true measure of whether the economy could live up to its promise of endless bounty, mitigate the old misery of the working class, and lay to rest the class conflict that haunted the industrial age. As part of their larger social and aesthetic agenda for the machine age, visionaries in the 1920s sought to put into practice inventive ideas about housing working- and middle-class people, advocating methods of mass production and innovative designs.

The ideas of Edward Filene had a great impact on social thinkers and planners of the period. Filene was a progressive department store magnate who pioneered radical employment practices such as good wages, a profit sharing plan, a forty-hour work week, and medical benefits. His famous department store, Filene's, in Boston was a model of the new consumer economy, open for all classes—who shopped on different floors depending on their wealth.[1] Filene was also a writer and social thinker. In 1925 he wrote a highly influential book, *The Way Out*. From his vantage point as both businessman and progressive, Filene recognized that a capitalist society that retained the conditions of what he called "the first industrial revolution"—that is, a society marred by class conflict and a growing disparity between rich and poor—risked massive social unrest. Filene argued that the benefits of the "second industrial revolution" should be extended to the working class. He believed that an enlightened, humanitarian consumer capitalism could content the masses, thereby defusing working-class militancy and discrediting socialist ideas.

Filene's vision stemmed from Frederick Winslow Taylor's scientific management ideas and entrepreneurs such as Henry Ford, who put these ideas into action, making mass production possible and profitable. Taylor's labor method reorganized the workforce and the workplace by allowing management to control production. Assembly lines that broke down labor into simple individual tasks no longer required skilled workers as old industrial factories once did. Managers were trained to plan and supervise, increasing speed and production.[2] Ford showed how the application of Taylor's method could speed up production and pay workers higher wages simultaneously. Filene argued that the challenge to American businessmen of the 1920s was: *"Fordize or fail. . . . We can repeat the causes or reverse the results of the old Industrial Revolution."*[3]

How would Ford's assembly line make this second industrial revolution different from the first? "The business man of the future must produce prosperous customers as well as saleable goods," asserted Filene. "His whole business policy must look forward to creating great buying power among the masses. The business man of the future must fill the pockets of the workers and the consumers before he can fill his pockets."[4]

Filene argued that workers needed higher wages, shorter hours, quality machine-made products, new housing, and mass education—in short, more economic freedom—before they could become consumers. He also predicted that a consumer society, with its perpetual cycle of abundance, of mass production that fueled mass consumption, would be a peaceful society:

Economic freedom [would] actually change men's interests and motives. Today the minds of the masses are centered on the getting of economic necessities. If we can make getting the necessities of life a much smaller part of men's lives—as we can under a regime of mass production and mass distribution—men's minds will inevitably turn to other higher issues. . . . Most of the social and economic issues that now keep the world on edge will disappear. Men who can take care of the whole material side of life by working, say six hours a day, simply won't be interested in socialism or communism.

Instead, workers would "have a wider margin of money and leisure, and as their taste and sense of values grow in that freedom, we shall see a new competition for beauty and refinement."[5]

Filene believed that modern workers would express their new sense of freedom in the consumer marketplace, citing the automobile industry as a perfect example. Henry Ford's assembly line workers were paid at the then incredible wage of five dollars a day. Workers in turn poured their money back into the economy, buying cars, taking vacations, going to the movies. Mass production made cars and the leisure pursuits they encouraged affordable for the masses, even for auto workers. Filene thus redefined democracy as people's freedom to consume. What was important for citizens, he thought, was not the right to vote or participate in politics, but rather a democracy consisting of vast choices of mass-produced goods—including houses. "Make houses like Fords," he insistently urged. Filene's slogan drew immediate attention from housing reformers and innovators, eventually making its way into business thinking, New Deal goverment philosophy, and ultimately the popular press.

The Regional Planning Association of America (RPAA), a small, informal but influential group based in New York City, took Filene's ideas seriously.[6] The organization brought together visionary intellectuals, activists, architects, planners, and financiers interested in creating democratic communities based on social rather than commercial principles. The group included Lewis Mumford, housing author and activist Catherine Bauer and social architects Henry Wright and Clarence Stein. The RPAA exerted considerable influence, directly shaping the policies and priorities of the New Deal and indirectly inspiring the emergence of postwar suburbs, especially Levittown.[7] In particular, the RPAA believed in the necessity for the modernization of housing, basing their theory and practice on the idea that the machine age had fundamentally altered the relationship between people, houses, technology, and the environment. The group proposed building communities with well-made, efficient, affordable houses and space for both pedestrians and cars, where civic life would be structured around new forms of work and leisure. [8]

The RPAA had a broader vision of housing for the modern age, criticizing past urban housing reform movements for concentrating only on legal reform of overcrowded tenement dwellings. As Mumford argued in a 1911 article in the *Nation,* "Housing reform by itself has only standardized the tenement. City planning by itself has only extended the tenement. . . . It is fatuous to suppose that private interests will correct this condition, for it is for the benefit of private interests that it exists."[9] The group also criticized the earlier municipal housing reform for restricting its vision to the slums of the city. Henry Wright argued, "The housing problem could not be kept in the slums; it has become universal." The twentieth-century dream of home ownership seemed to be bankrupt, Wright observed:

> In housing we are torn between an intolerable reality and an impossible ideal. All the while we are lulled by the fancy that we will someday be able to realize the home of our dreams. We see it pictured in the house and garden periodicals and in our Sunday magazine sections. We hear it praised and boosted in Better-Home Weeks and in Own-Your-Own-Home Drives. It is the dream of a picturesque house standing free and independent on its own plot—a whole country estate if we have any luck, but at any rate an independent and isolated plot.

Wright argued that this dream had come to nothing but an advertised illusion based on Gold Coast fantasies. The real suburban homes being constructed delivered neither freedom nor independence nor happiness:

> Within the limits of New York City no less than 50 miles of new small framed houses have been built, in long monotonous rows with a single repetitive design, closely crowded together on poor land, usually without proper public facilities or fire protection, and often with the barest provisions for health and sanitation. Practically no recreation areas have been set aside in these districts. The houses are of the flimsiest construction and the cost of up-keep will be excessive and will fall on purchasers just when they are least prepared for it.[10]

Some were not quite as somber. Mumford, for instance, agreed with Wright's critique but still believed that the idea of suburbs held great promise. Suburbanization, he argued, was the most recent migration spurred by America's great social and technological transformations. The first—westward expansion—had dispersed a farming population across the continent. The second—industrialization, propelled by water power and railroads—carried people from farms to small factory towns. The third—urbanization—was the migration of people from small towns to large industrial and financial centers. Suburbanization was the fourth migration, made possible by new technologies and giving working- and middle-class people the opportunity to move from congested cities to spacious suburbs. Mumford believed electricity to be an essential prerequisite for this current migration. Unlike coal or water, electricity can be dispensed anywhere relatively inexpensively. People no longer were forced to reside near former sources of energy for work. The automobile as well made it practical for people to live in this new decentralized society.[11]

Like Filene, Mumford believed that such changes represented progress. The second industrial revolution, he argued, was

An attempt to spread the real income of industry by decentralizing industry. . . . Far sighted industrialists like Dennison and Ford are already planning this move, and business men like Edward Filene feel that business is at an impasse unless decentralization is followed as "The Way Out." Regional planning is an attempt to turn industrial decentralization—the effort to make the industrial mechanism work better—to permanent social uses. It is an attempt to realize the gains of modern industry in permanent houses, gardens, parks, playgrounds and community institutions.[12]

The fourth migration would be qualitatively different from the previous ones. A regionally dispersed population could reap the benefits of the city and the country, living a life both cosmopolitan and planned, democratic and healthy. Communities would be built on a human scale, surrounded by the beauty of nature. Mumford believed that community planning would bring to the suburbs "a more exhilarating kind of environment—not as a temporary haven or refuge—but as a permanent seat of life and culture, urban in its advantages, rural in its situation."[13]

As articulated in the press and in academic, government, and business circles by Mumford and other members of the RPAA, this vision was ambitious, requiring a massive restructuring of society. As historian Carl Sussman explained, "Instead of working in the name of pragmatism on meaningless civic improvement projects, [the RPAA] argued for a dedication to a new social order where people have decent homes, a stable community life, a healthy and varied environment, and a genuinely urban culture."[14] Or as Mumford said, "A full realization of our ideas required a complete reformation of our dominant personal incentives and social objectives, a change from a Money Economy to a Life Economy."[15]

Clarence Stein, an influential architect and planner, described the goals of the RPAA and how they represented a radical departure from the past. "To build a substantial setting for neighborhood and family life, rather than to control and regulate, requires a completely different kind of planning. That is why I intend to call it community development or *new town planning* to differentiate it from the procedure that is generally called city planning in America." Because the RPAA believed in building real communities in the suburbs and not merely containers for living, they argued that parks, woods, hiking trails, baseball diamonds, tennis courts, and swimming pools were as important for communities as stores and houses. Creating community centers and tenant associations was equally vital.

Stein argued that creating these kinds of communities meant abandoning market-driven building for building based on the principle of community. He explained the distinction: "There is actually an antithesis between the two procedures. The prime objective of one is to assist in the marketing and protection of property, of the other to create communities. The latter deals with the realities of living rather than with trading. The two are at cross purposes: preserve and protect, in contrast with devise and produce." Four principles defined the building of non–market driven communities:

Coordinated, not disorganized

Communities, not lots or streets

Contemporary, not obsolete

Dynamic, not static.[16]

Mumford saw new town planning as the integration of people, land, and industry. "The housing problem, the industries problem, the transportation problem, and the land problem cannot be solved one at a time . . . they are mutually interacting elements and they can be effectively dealt with only by bearing constantly in mind the general situation from which they have been abstracted."[17] Thus, the RPAA believed, planning should reflect a multidisciplined approach coordinated by professionals, activists, and ordinary people working together.

RPAA members promoted their ideas through books, articles, exhibitions, and most important, by building real communities. These were, as economist and Consumer Union founder Stuart Chase said, "definite achievements; something you could kick with your feet."[18]

The first experiments in planned housing on a national level took place during World War I, when the government created the first federal housing institutions—the Emergency Fleet Corporation and the United States Housing Corporation—to deal with the lack of housing for munitions workers and shipbuilders living in new military towns. The question was, how to do it? Inspiration came from Raymond Unwin, cofounder of the English Garden City movement. The federal government hired RPAA member, architect, and writer Frederick Ackerman to go to England to investigate Unwin's new housing approach, which had attracted international attention. Back in America Ackerman and Henry Wright worked under government auspices to design 176,000 low-cost, substantial, attractive housing units. The wartime housing communities they generated, such as Blackrock in Bridgeport, Connecticut, and Yorkship Village near Camden, New Jersey, were models of enlightened architecture and planning, proof that government planning and funds could produce modern, livable communities.

Political leaders insisted adamantly, however, that these developments should not set a precedent for government-financed, low-cost, modern public housing. As they would for years to come, politicians and the real estate lobby argued that the government should not compete with private builders, and that any mass housing projects the government undertook definitely should not waste resources on aesthetic concerns. In 1920 the Senate Committee on Public Buildings and Grounds declared that "Congress certainly did not intend . . . to enter into competition in architectural poetry with any nation or private organization. . . . We do not believe that this was necessary for the mechanics who were to be housed." In response to these attacks, influential housing reformer Edith Elmer Wood proclaimed that public wartime housing "proved that government housing could be produced and administered in the United States without scandal, without the sky falling, or the Constitution going on the scrap heap."[19]

After the war, to avoid criticism that the government was constructing mass housing, reformers refined an old philanthropic idea first developed in mid-nineteenth-century England that arrived in the United States by the end of the century: the limited-dividend fund or cooperative. Early housing experiments relied on philanthropic investments but had no stockholders and paid no dividends. The issue facing reformers in the 1920s was how to expand the limited-dividend model to increase the supply and diminish the cost of capital available for nonspeculative housing. To do so the RPAA proposed that limited-dividend companies sell shares but limit dividends to 6 percent and remain exempt from state and local taxes. This would eliminate speculation—the bane of the private housing industry—and allow investments to come from private businesses, charity organizations, labor unions, and individuals.

Clarence Stein was pivotal in these efforts. He served as the first and only chairman of the New York State Commission of Housing and Regional Planning from 1923 to 1926. Stein was instrumental in passing the inventive New York Housing Law in 1926, based on the RPAA limited-dividend concept: restricting dividends on housing projects approved by the State Housing Board, exempting those approved from state taxes, and authorizing municipalities to free such projects from local taxation. The New York State Board of Housing, established to administer America's first limited-dividend law, engaged in extensive research on housing design and costs to demonstrate the superiority of large-scale developments. It defended its research based on the chronic shortage of decent housing whose rooms rented for under $15 a month.[20]

Using limited-dividend companies, housing now could be built on a nonprofit basis. Designed by socially concerned, well-known architects such as Ackerman, Stein, and Wright, new communities based on limited-dividend societies and financed either by progressive businessmen such as Marshall Field, Julius Rosenwald (owner of Sears), and Henry Buhl, Jr. or by progressive unions such as the Amalgamated Clothing Workers, provided an alternative to both tenement slums and slipshod, speculative suburban homes.

One of the best examples of such well-made, modern planned housing is Chatham Village in Pittsburgh. Built for people of moderate means, the village was constructed complete with garages and stores. At the same time, its layout reflected the notion that houses should blend in with the natural surroundings: houses climb gracefully into the hills. Similarly, successful developments included the Rosenwald apartments—Marshall Field's mammoth low-cost garden apartment houses in Chicago—and the Metropolitan Life Insurance housing in New York City.[21] A few housing experiments were built specifically for African Americans: the Paul Lawrence Dunbar apartments in Harlem (financed with Rockefeller money), Rosenwald's Michigan Avenue apartments in Chicago, the Douglas apartments built by Prudential Life Insurance in Newark, and the Cincinnati Model Homes.[22]

Most of the new housing developments were located in and around New York City. New York was home to many housing reformers, labor unions, and enlightened capitalists, and it housed a huge tenement population. Moreover, the New York Housing Law ignited interest in large-scale nonprofit housing projects. New York City was the only city in the state to take advantage of the new law. In 1927 the city enacted a measure that exempted from taxation new buildings or improvements approved by the state board.[23] The Amalgamated Clothing Workers were the first to jump in. Between 1927 and 1931 the Amalgamated Clothing Workers built two cooperative apartment complexes, one on Manhattan's Lower East Side and the other in the north Bronx. Contemporaries praised these cooperatives as, "a first step in remaking the entire Lower East Side, replacing dank, crowded tenements block by block with modern housing for the working class."[24] Unlike older tenements that were built up against each other with only narrow airshafts in the center, the Amalgamated dwellings were built around a large landscaped courtyard. Elaborate brickwork patterns marked their exteriors, while interiors contained three to five ample rooms with modern bathrooms and kitchens. Each building also included a library, nursery, roof deck, gym, and auditorium. The apartments were affordable to working- and lower-middle-class employees.

Other builders also made use of the limited-dividend housing concept. Progressive real estate tycoon Alexander Bing, working with Clarence Stein, joined to form the City Housing Corporation (CHC). The CHC was capitalism with a socialist face: it sold $100 shares to teachers, social workers, and others in the same moderate salary range as well as to wealthy capitalists who believed that profit and humanitarianism were compatible. The CHC board of directors exemplified this combination of social reform and business. It included Felix Adler, founder of the ethical culture movement; Richard Ely, progressive educator and economist; Henry Wright and Frederick Ackerman; settlement house directors Mary Simkhovitch and Lillian Wald; Eleanor Roosevelt, whose husband was then serving as governor of New York; and philanthropic capitalists such as William Sloan Coffin, John Agar, and V. Everit Macy.[25]

One of the most significant communities CHC financed was Sunnyside Gardens in Queens, one subway stop away from Manhattan's bustling streets and business districts. Finished in 1928, Sunnyside Gardens was intended to provide low-cost, low-density housing for urban workers seeking a more countrified refuge from crowded tenements. Although close to the city's employment, recreational, and cultural opportunities, the well-constructed homes were priced substantially lower than other newly constructed houses built in New York City at the time.[26]

This was possible because Sunnyside was a large-scale operation built with efficient mass-production methods on a large tract of underdeveloped land bought at a reasonable cost. It was these Fordist principles, CHC head Alexander Bing argued, that made moderate home prices possible. Unlike other construction projects, building at Sunnyside continued on a year-round basis, creating additional savings. Planners made sure labor practices maximized efficiency: when a construction worker finished one job he went on to another, assuring a steady wage and contributing to high productivity.[27]

Handsomely designed by Ackerman, Stein and Wright, the Sunnyside community consisted of traditional row houses—with a twist. Still constrained by the urban street grid, "Each house was given broad frontage and constructed only two rooms deep. Instead of pushing the design into the interior of the block, the designers turned the frame 90 degrees and stretched it along the perimeter of the street."[28] This allowed for more air and light and a large interior courtyard. Unlike conventional subdivisions courtyards were not cut up into little backyards but were left open for residents' use. A common green where children could play and neighbors could socialize was a welcome change for people used to cramped, gridiron streets. The necessity for residents to decide together how to use the courtyards fostered the creation of block associations and civic spirit generally.

Sunnyside apartments cost more than planners would have liked, but still attracted a cross-section of working- and middle-class residents.[29] A 1927 survey discovered that its denizens included skilled or semiskilled mechanics (20 percent), office workers and small shopkeepers with moderate incomes (24 percent), and a smattering of restaurant workers, domestic servants, and chauffeurs (3 percent). Businesspeople (32 percent) and professionals (17 percent) made up the rest, including, "a sizeable proportion of young artists, writers and liberal intellectuals who were fascinated with the concept of a planned community and found Sunnyside both an exciting and convenient place to live."[30]

Lewis Mumford himself lived in Sunnyside for eleven years.[31] He recalled proudly the economic diversity of the residents: "In the block where I lived, there was a grocer's clerk who earned $1,200 to $1,500 a year and a physician who earned $10,000. . . . So this effort at an acceptable minimum in housing achieved something even more important; a mixed community, not the economically segregated kind that the higher costs of a well-planned middle class suburb demand."[32] Indeed, one principle of new community planning was that planners themselves would live in the community. As Clarence Stein explained, "The planner cannot discover the needs of people merely by asking them what kinds of home and town or community they want to live in. They do not know beyond their experience. However, with their assistance—not their guidance—he must discover their requirements. . . . He should live in the places he helps to create."[33]

In the late 1920s the CHC, again under the direction of Stein and Wright, undertook their next and more ambitious project: the town of Radburn, New Jersey, a suburb of New York City. Unlike Sunnyside, Radburn was not built on a city gridiron and therefore presented new design possibilities. Built again on a large scale—1,300 acres of land that would house 1,500 residents—Radburn was designed as a suburban community of single, unattached modernized homes, complete with shopping centers and schools, advertised as "a town for the motor age."

In 1920 Frederick Lewis Allen tried to imagine how life dependent on auto-mobility would alter the shape of physical space from its vertical, urban lines—marked by the skyscraper—to new, horizontal, flat, sprawling suburban contours. The car was the medium for this alteration; it became the connective tissue between home, work, play, and most important, consumption. The prob-lem was that cars required much more space than people. The designers of Rad-burn offered an answer.

Using Central Park as a model, Wright and Stein planned a two-road system for Radburn—one for pedestrians and another for vehicular traffic. The large roadways, called *super blocks*, contained narrow cul-de-sac streets that led to houses facing large interior parks and a footpath system.[34] Each house was turned so that kitchens and service rooms faced the street and living rooms faced inward toward the garden. The Radburn idea, said Stein, "was to answer the enigma of how to live with the auto: or if you will, how to live in spite of it. . . . We met these difficulties with a radical revision of the relation of houses, roads, paths, gardens, parks, blocks, and local neighborhoods."[35]

Radburn was designed for middle-income, white-collar families with a car and children. It provided its residents with twenty acres of parkland, swimming pools, tennis courts, baseball fields, basketball courts, and summer houses. The CHC encouraged recreation and cultural activities such as nursery schools, play-grounds, sports and day camp for the children and amateur theater groups, courses in psychology, current events, and literature for the adults. New resi-dents were urged to participate in the town's many activities by Citizen Associa-tions.

In 1929 author Geddes Smith described Radburn as "a town built to live in—today and tomorrow. A town 'for the motor age.' A town turned outside in—

without any backdoors. A town where roads and parks fit together like the fingers of your right and left hands. A town in which children need never dodge motor trucks on their way to school. A new town—newer than the garden cities, and the first major innovation in town planning since they were built."[36]

Limited-dividend housing experiments such as Sunnyside, Radburn, and Chatham were important because they demonstrated that middle- and working-class housing could be affordable, innovative, and livable. They also showed that large-scale housing could be socially conscious, civic-minded, and planned. However visionary, these developments could not solve the greater problem: one-third of a nation remained ill-housed in tenements and slums.

Mumford noted the limitations inherent in these utopianlike experiments. "To improve the housing of the workers while preserving intact the institutions that infallibly produced slum housing was impossible. All that could be done, at best, was to produce demonstration samples which partially showed what might be achieved on a larger scale if the entire economic basis were radically altered." The institutions that blocked this radical alteration, Mumford argued, were "free enterprise, private land speculation, and building slums for profit." The solution lay in a dramatic reversal of priorities:

> Modern housing is a collective effort to create habitable domestic environments within the framework of integrated communities. Such housing demands not merely an improvement of the physical structures and the communal patterns. It demands such social and economic changes as will make it available to every income group. In the larger processes of reconstruction, housing, sustained by public authorities and supported by public funds, is a means for overcoming gross inequalities in the distribution of wealth, for producing more vital kinds of wealth, for restoring the balance between city and country and for aiding in the rational planning of industries, cities, and regions.[37]

If Mumford was interested in the underlying political and economic causes of the housing crisis and understood that the experimental communities he helped to create were inadequate to address these concerns, Catherine Bauer saw the enemy in more concrete terms:

The jostling small builders in the front foot lots and the miserable strangling suburbs and the ideology of individual Home Ownership must go. And in their place
must come a technique for building complete communities designed and administered as functional and constructed by large scale methods. And finally, that
only government can make the decisive step and set up the new method of house
production as a long time social investment to replace the wasteful and obsolete
chaos still prevailing.[38]

Although they differed in their analytical approach, both Bauer and Mumford understood that the housing crisis could not be solved in a piecemeal, philanthropic manner. Like Filene, they argued that capitalism had to produce a new
social consciousness in order to deliver the benefits promised by the second industrial revolution. Yet it would take the Great Depression to make this apparent. The housing projects of the RPAA—isolated experiments in the
1920s—proved to be critical models for New Deal policies and programs. As
Mumford said, "Without this [RPAA] leadership, the Roosevelt administration
would not, in all probability, have been able to evolve the comprehensive national housing policy that it actually embarked on with such readiness."[39]

Chapter Five

The New Deal:

One Third of a Nation Still Unhoused

When the Great Depression hit in 1929, the housing crisis moved into the national spotlight for the first time. The nation was not only ill-fed and ill-clothed, it was ill-housed. With wages and salaries plummeting, unemployment skyrocketing, and the national credit system on the verge of collapse, the housing problem no longer was confined to the tenements. Just as Henry Wright had predicted, the emergency spread everywhere and it affected all classes. In the cities families doubled up and moved back into old slums. The foreclosing of farms and suburban homes forced owners out of substantial housing into flimsy bungalows and other substandard housing. At the same time, thousands of new houses in the higher-priced category remained unoccupied.[1]

Unlike the 1920s, the economy of the 1930s forced the government to make low-cost housing for the working class and poor an urgent priority. Housing the masses never before had been part of the national agenda. In face of the breakdown of laissez-faire capitalism, faith in private enterprise dwindled. The housing needs of the majority obviously could not be addressed by theories of rugged individualism. Government and private studies emphasized that without a national housing policy there would be "a continuous process of greater and greater overcrowding of people and families in the lowest third of the income scale."[2] Some clung to easy explanations and solutions. The building and real estate industry and other advocates of private enterprise claimed that the problem was simple: since there had been so little housing built since 1925, there was merely a backlog of demand. To remedy the situation, contractors and builders needed to start producing new houses as quickly as possible.[3]

Members of the RPAA and other housing reformers disagreed. They believed that the housing crisis was rooted in the ideology of individual home ownership and the peculiar workings and speculative practices of the housing market. Frederick Ackerman, who helped design Sunnyside Gardens and Radburn and served as technical advisor to the Housing Authority of New York, argued "Under our economic system, use or occupancy depends upon the relation between individual incomes and the cost of occupancy or rentals charged. Our industrial capacity has no direct bearing in the case, nor has the quantity of houses available." The problem, said Ackerman, was that "the market settles the question as to whether there are too few or too many houses; it is the final arbiter and there is no appeal from its decisions."

The housing boom of the 1920s, Ackerman observed, was based on the expansion of debt and

> was much the same as would have been the case had the physical foundations of structures crumbled. It swept away the incomes which had supported the debt upon which the physical structures had been built. Without people with incomes sufficient to cover operating costs, fixed charges and amortization of the debts, habitations became vacant and were of no more use to those whose incomes had vanished than had the houses been built upon the moon.[4]

If the nation left the issue of housing to the market, then it would never be able to build decent housing for the masses.

The housing crisis and the New Deal provided social and cultural critics such as Ackerman, Stuart Chase, Catherine Bauer, and others a rare opportunity to test their new garden city conceptions on a national scale. The New Deal made it possible to address housing as a social issue, a matter of government concern, and challenge the hallowed assumptions of the private housing market and its commercial and political publicists.

Despite a political climate receptive to reformers' ideas, there were obstacles to implementing them. Home building at the time was not yet modernized, based on small business and handicraft, and thus an excessively expensive proposition. Echoing Edward Filene, theorist of neighborhood planning and RPAA member Clarence Arthur Perry argued, "Modern industry has put motorcars, radio sets, and refrigerators within reach of a majority of American families, but it has done little to reduce the cost of dwellings."[5] Stuart Chase added to this argument,

> The home building entrepreneurs do not constitute an industry, but a group of shoe string capitalists animated by speculative hopes. They proceed in a manner opposite to the motor car industry. They have worked out some excellent new conveniences like hide-a-way breakfast buffet bars, but their assembly system is little improved over that of the Hopi or Maya. This method . . . is too costly for 90 percent of our people at present income levels.[6]

In addition to being costly and outmoded in its production methods, these businesses continued to operate through small, local networks of realtors, contractors, builders and lenders. Seeing themselves as the last bastion of the traditional middle class that embodied "the true spirit of American free enterprise," the home building entrepreneurs resisted big business practices. They were reluctant to try modern building methods or better construction materials.[7]

Reformers and modernizers, however, continued to advocate assembly-line production as the key to delivering housing for the masses. One of the few groups with some experience in building affordable housing using these methods was the RPAA. Despite their confidence that houses could be constructed like Fords, they understood that mass-market housing remained far more complicated than producing cars, and that such housing was economically and legally in a different category from any other type of manufactured merchandise. Housing required an assemblage of diverse components: land, the shelter itself, mechanical equipment such as plumbing and heating, finance, and maintenance. Proximity to schools, highways, public transportation, and recreational facilities also were important considerations. As Thomas S. Holden, president of the New York Building Congress, said in 1938, "All these elements create cost factors which must be brought under control if the announced objective of the Ameri-

can nation, better homes and more civilized living for all the people, is to be at-
tained."[8]

Many government officials began to suspect that mass housing could become
the linchpin of economic recovery. A quarter of the workforce was unemployed
in 1934 and the building trades were hit especially hard.[9] Building homes could
stimulate stalled industries and create a ripple effect through the economy.

It was no accident that the rallying cry of President Roosevelt and the New Deal
became "Get Building Going."[10] Harkening back to historian Frederick Jackson
Turner's turn of the century argument of "the closing of the frontier" and evok-
ing a somewhat nostalgic vision of the past, Roosevelt insisted that the conditions of modern life mandated a new outlook:

> In a simple and primitive civilization, homes were to be had for the building. The
> bounties of nature in a new land provided crude but adequate food and shelter.
> When land failed, our ancestors moved on to better land. It was always possible to
> push back the frontier, but the frontier has now disappeared. Our task involves
> the making of a better living out of the lands that we have. . . . In pursuing this
> policy we are working towards the ultimate objective of making it possible for
> American families to live as Americans should.

The depression, Roosevelt believed, demanded that the government take responsibility for the social and economic life of the nation, and made it clear that a
democratic society was predicated on a healthy economy. This idea found a large
and receptive audience. Speaking from his fireside the day before Labor Day in
1936, President Roosevelt articulated the underlying ideas of a new conception
of democracy. "The 4th of July commemorates our political freedom—a freedom which without economic freedom is meaningless indeed. Labor Day sym-
bolizes our determination to achieve an economic freedom for the average man
which will give his political freedom reality."[11]

In other fireside chats Roosevelt clarified the meaning of economic freedom, echoing ideas Filene and others espoused in the 1920s. In the twentieth century,

> There is neither logic nor necessity for a third of our population to have less of the needs of modern life that make for a decent living. . . . We seek the security of the men, women, and children of the nation. That security involves added means of providing better homes for the people of the nation. That is the first principle of our future program . . . and . . . to use the agencies of government to assist in the establishment of means to provide sound and adequate protection against the vicissitudes of modern life. In other words social insurance.[12]

Roosevelt's call for government activism challenged a deeply entrenched belief in laissez-faire capitalism, it also drew on a tradition as old as the republic. As historian Allen Brinkley observed, "In the past governments' subsidies had almost always promoted the productive capacities of the nation."[13] Just as federal funds and policies, for instance, helped to build the great rail network of the nineteenth century, so the New Deal would build an infrastructure for the consumer age.

Within the ranks of the New Deal, among politicians, social workers, economists and policy makers was a consensus that government intervention would be vital to jump-start the economy. Alvin Hansen, one of the first American economists to promote the teachings of John Maynard Keynes, argued that consumption was to be the frontier of the future, the key to the nation's prosperity. As FDR saw it, it would cure one of the nation's main economic problems, "a lack of buying power."[14] This meant that larger segments of the society had to become active consumers. The American dream had to be opened up for a new class of people and revitalized for segments of the middle class.

Members of the New Deal coalition agreed that it was crucial to create consumer demand but disagreed on how best to do this. First, there was a need to save people in the middle class who had lost their homes to bank foreclosures. Some believed economic stimulation could be accomplished through new fiscal policies. The government would actively guarantee the viability of banks, stability of loans, and household mortgages. An example of this "commercial Keynesianism, as some scholars have called this approach" was the Home Owners Loan Corporation (HOLC), established in 1932 by the Hoover administration (through the Federal Home Loan Bank Act), but its power was greatly expanded by the New Deal.[15] Financed by federal capital and bonds, HOLC set up twelve regional federal home loan banks, which lent money to savings and loan associations to purchase defaulted home mortgages and refinance low-cost loans to middle-class home owners.

From 1933 to 1936, HOLC sent $3.1 billion to regional federal banks to refinance over one million homes, or one tenth of all owner-occupied nonfarm residences in the United States. HOLC's long-term loan and mortgage repayment scheme provided a more stable system than the crazy quilt of multiple short-term loans characteristic of the 1920s. Indeed, this agency prevented a wholesale collapse in home financing. As historian Arthur Schlesinger, Jr., pointed out, HOLC was critical in consolidating public support for the New Deal. "By enabling thousands of Americans to save their homes, it strengthened their stake both in the existing order and the New Deal. Probably no single measure consolidated so much middle class support for the administration."[16]

The Federal Housing Administration (FHA) established by the National Housing Act of 1934 was another highly influential example of commercial Keynesianism. Far more ambitious than HOLC, the FHA was designed to revitalize the construction industry and stimulate a moderately priced private housing market. Its policies were far-reaching: the FHA mandated financing and construction standards and determined where new housing could be built. It was the first federal agency to actively encourage the construction of new, single-family houses in suburban areas. Contemporaries felt the FHA "was the death blow to old time speculative building" and the passport to modernizing the housing industry:

> Gone, they feel, is the day when a man may clip a photograph and a couple of floor plans from a magazine and take them to the bank to get a loan. Gone also is the day when a man can buy up land cheaply, cut it up into small lots, price it high,

build flimsy houses, sell them at exorbitant prices, with fancy financing. Further than its rules for land development there will be strict examination into the character of the builder. They will demand that he be experienced, of sound financial standing, that he have at least a 20% equity in his property.[17]

Like HOLC, the FHA promoted stable growth in home ownership and provided low-interest, long-term (twenty-five to thirty years) mortgages, loaning up to 80 percent of a home's value. Commercial banks that agreed to FHA terms were guaranteed money from the government in case of default. The FHA issued mortgage commitments on groups of unbuilt houses in suburban development called subdivisions. It gave low-cost mortgages to "operative builders" (as opposed to speculators), who agreed to present a plan of development to the FHA that took into account land, building cost, income level, race, transportation, and provisions for playgrounds and stores.[18]

Although the FHA reflected the government's new commitment to creating affordable housing, its policies—like the restrictive covenants of the 1920s—deeply inscribed prejudices into the nation's blueprint for development. The FHA created national standards for what constituted "neighborhood stability" and explicitly advised potential investors and builders to concentrate on particular markets based on age, income, and race. The FHA's racial policies encouraged all-white suburban developments and discouraged investment in urban areas populated predominantly by racial and ethnic minorities. FHA handbooks codified communities by color and ethnicity. The least desirable neighborhoods were "redlined"—meaning they were marked to signify "dense, mixed and aging" areas not approved by the FHA.[19] These guidelines lasted for decades, long after laws were passed officially dismantling this kind of segregation.

The FHA certainly was more fair than old speculative real estate practices, but HOLC and the FHA still neglected the ill-housed, who could not afford or qualify for single-family dwellings—new or old. Even the ill-housed, however, had forceful advocates in the New Deal. Opposed to the limited vision of the commercial Keynesians, social Keynesians such as Mumford and Bauer argued that the only solution to the housing crisis was that the state, not private industry, do the actual building. The government should play a fiscal regulatory role not only in the modernization of the housing industry but also in funding and building housing for the poor and working class. Commercial Keynesians called for fiscal guarantees and commercial regulation to help the middle class, while social Keynesians demanded that the federal government initiate improvement of working and living conditions of a third of the nation.

The social Keynesian vision had its roots in part in New York City, at that time home to the most extensive low-cost housing projects. A broad coalition of reformers and trade unionists had been working for decades on housing issues to improve the living conditions of tenement dwellers. This alliance included the well-known social researcher and author Edith Elmer Wood, Greenwich House settlement director and writer Mary Simkhovitch, Clarence Stein, Frederick Ackerman, and the liberal director of Catholic Charities, Father John O'Grady. The coalition's largest constituency—organized labor, led by the American Federation of Labor (AFL)—had long demanded government subsidies for low-income housing.[20] Yet most housing reformers shied away from calling for a federally funded housing program until the 1930s, fearing they would be maligned as Socialists. The failure of private housing and the new climate of government activism encouraged the coalition to argue for direct, large-scale housing initiatives led by the federal government.

During the 1930s reformers found powerful government support for the idea of a federal housing program. Newly elected progressive politicians—Senator Robert F. Wagner, Sr., of New York (who authored much of the New Deal social legislation), Senator Edward Costigan of Colorado, Senator Robert La Follette, Jr., of Wisconsin, and Mayor Fiorello La Guardia of New York City—joined with New Deal administrators such as secretary of labor and former social worker Frances Perkins, longtime champion of the limited-dividend corporation and Secretary of the Interior Harold Ickes, and Rexford Guy Tugwell, Columbia professor and head of the Resettlement Administration to advocate for public housing.

The social Keynesians maintained that public housing did not compete with the private housing market, since it would house people that the private sector ignored. Senator Wagner argued that private housing was "unable to provide decent housing for families of low income at prices they can afford to pay." Mayor La Guardia argued this point persuasively:

> We agree that ideally there should be no families with incomes too low to permit
> them to pay for adequate housing and purchase the other goods and services for a
> decent life. Until such time as our economic system provides such necessary income, it is a clear function and duty of the government to see that no family has to
> live and rear its children in surroundings which are a disgrace to what we refer to
> with pride as the American standard of living.[21]

In 1930 public housing advocates won a major victory when the National Industrial Recovery Act was passed and federal money was appropriated for public housing and slum clearance. To the chagrin of realtors, lenders, and builders, the Public Works Administration (PWA) Housing Division was established under the leadership of Harold Ickes. The PWA was a temporary agency restricted to giving federal grants only to limited-dividend corporations, such as labor unions. Nonetheless it accomplished a great deal in a short time. Between 1933 and 1937 the PWA built 22,000 new units in fifty-nine communities for low-income working-class families.

One of the most significant of these new communities was the Carl Mackley development in Philadelphia sponsored by the American Federation of Hosiery Workers and directed by Catherine Bauer, then executive director of the AFL's Housing Committee; Oscar S. Stoneorov, architect; and John Edelman, head of the Hosiery Workers. Built on the principle of civic participation, the Mackley housing included tennis courts, swimming pools, library, laundry buildings, rooftop playgrounds, and numerous meeting rooms. Residents in the 284 units were encouraged to organize forums on socialized medicine and political issues. Subsidies to the Mackley housing led to the creation of a democratic and informed community, just as Bauer had hoped.[22]

The public housing movement believed in the importance of attractive design. The PWA Williamsburg Houses in New York City, for instance, were graced with elegant modern facades, copper roofs, doorways, and entrance

courts decorated with friezes done by agency sculptors. Inside thick walls, tiled
halls, large windows, and modern appliances made for more commodious living.

Geared to provide jobs, the housing programs had few restrictions on cost or
wages. PWA housing in general was of better quality than most private housing
and this particularly angered builders. Realtors argued in the press, trade journals, and Congress that public housing would discourage home ownership by
making "tenement occupancy so attractive . . . the urge to buy one's home will
be diminished."[23] Builders also complained that the PWA had "disrupted the
economic tranquility of many a town by starting construction at wage levels
which have drained the best workmen away from private industry."[24]

Government-built public housing was intensely controversial. Four major commercial organizations led the attack on the PWA: the Chamber of Commerce, the
National Association of Real Estate Boards, the United States Saving and Loan
League, and the National Association of Retail Lumber Dealers.[25] These groups
supported the New Deal's HOLC and FHA because they helped the private
housing industry get on its feet, but the lobby insisted that government-built
housing was a threat to private enterprise.[26]

Social Keynesians and commercial Keynesians battled over these questions
during the New Deal. Ickes, administrator of the PWA, was the primary advocate for public housing, while James A. Moffett of the FHA (and scion of Standard Oil of New Jersey), was the spokesman for private housing. In 1935 this
conflict became public when Moffett declared to the press that through private
initiative the FHA should relieve the PWA of the burden of public housing.
Ickes responded, "I have seen no evidence that the holders of private capital are
ready to use it. But we can't afford to sit around indefinitely waiting for private
capital to get going. I subscribe to the theory that a very large amount of public
money should be put out so that industry can be pepped up in a hurry." The next
day Moffett retorted, "The minute the government sells direct to the people generally you compete with private enterprise and it couldn't be done. It simply
can't be. If the National Housing Act is a real act and Congress meant it, you
can't do that. It was intended to provide liquidity so that private capital would

come in. People are not going to put up their money in mortgages if the government is competing."[27] Seeking a compromise, FDR announced that the FHA and PWA were not in competition. The FHA, he explained, was designed to stimulate the private housing market, and the PWA was intended to build homes for those who could not afford privately built homes.

While the private housing lobby protested the existence of the PWA, the progressive coalition pushed for legislation that would institutionalize many features of the PWA. In 1935 they began to fight for the Wagner-Steagall Act, which called for the creation of a new permanent housing agency. Vital support for this bill came from organized labor, the National Public Housing Conference, and the Labor Housing Conference. FDR's 1936 landslide reelection, in which he carried every state except Maine and Vermont, also boosted support for the bill. The economic collapse in fall 1937 further reinforced public support for government taking a permanent role in building decent housing. The Wagner-Steagall Act was passed by an overwhelming margin in the house and senate and signed into law by Roosevelt in September 1937.

The act went even further than the PWA, stating that "the provision of good housing for the poor is a *perpetual social obligation*. . . . The most spectacular goal was signalized by the fact that the executive body created by the act, the USHA, was specified as a body of perpetual duration." Unlike the PWA— whose primary goal was to reduce unemployment—the Wagner-Steagall Act embodied a new social vision: "the provision of decent, safe, and sanitary dwellings for families of low income and the eradication of slums."[28] The United States Housing Authority (USHA) replaced the PWA Housing Division.

To head USHA, Roosevelt chose Nathan Straus, Jr., son of Nathan Straus, Sr., the owner of Macy's department store who had been deeply involved in philanthropic work in New York City until his death in 1931. Although Straus, Sr., had wanted his son to go into the department store business, young Nathan was more interested in journalism and politics. In 1919 he ran for the New York State Senate as a Democrat, where he served for the next six years and joined forces with Franklin Roosevelt. In 1933 he sponsored a limited-dividend housing project, Hillside Homes, whose 118 modern buildings provided 1,415 apartments for low-income families. In 1926 Mayor La Guardia appointed Straus as special housing commissioner. This liberal administrative record impressed both Roosevelt and Senator Wagner, and Straus accepted the job because it "called for action and very little talk."[29] Knowing that USHA would need to be an agency of persuasion against the enemies of public housing as well as to build housing projects, he gathered together a knowledgeable and enthusiastic staff that included Catherine Bauer and Leon Keyserling, Wagner's legislative assistant.

The legislation empowered USHA to develop public projects by funding local housing agencies, lending up to 90 percent, and subsidizing construction and maintenance (the Housing Authority made up the difference between the tenant's rent and actual operating costs). The law stipulated that tenants come from the poorest third of a given locality, having lived previously in substandard housing. For every slum removed a new dwelling unit was to be erected on the same site. Since tenements were in cities, public housing was built in urban centers rather than suburbs or outlying areas. By 1939 over 50,000 public housing units were under construction, more than double that in the four-year PWA housing program. Built cheaply and without the same degree of innovative design, these low-rise projects were nevertheless sturdy, functional, and included outdoor playgrounds.[30]

Although Republicans attacked these new projects as corrupt and wasteful and built for Democratic party constituents, USHA planning was based on extensive research into building materials and labor. In order to build the Tennessee Valley Authority housing projects, for instance, Department of Labor statisticians "started with a look at the labor involved in the production of basic raw materials, continued through mills and plants, followed materials over railroads to the site. [They then] unearthed the man hours required per unit in producing, manufacturing and transporting."[31]

In 1939 Paul de Huff built a public housing project in Victorville, California, employing three inventive production methods: complete rationalization of the product and its parts before work has started; smooth-flowing assembly involving a minimum of waste, effort, halts, and hitches; and tab keeping of work as a continuous check on efficiency. Parts were precut and delivered to the site of each house. Workmen were divided into small crews, given limited and repetitive operations to perform, and last, but high in importance, "Builder de Huff clocked the progress of his job with the enthusiasm of a tyro efficiency expert, [and] ended up with a detailed record of the man hours of work needed to complete every part of every house. These records took the guess out of time saving methods and kept de Huff's finger smack on the pulse of construction."[32] Taylorism—the combination of managerial decision making concerning materials and direct supervision of workers—and government housing seemed a perfect match.

First Houses, the nation's first housing project, was a model of modern research and production methods. Built on the Lower East Side of Manhattan in 1936, it was constructed on the site of eight dilapidated and gutted tenements on land given for a pittance ($3.50 a square foot) by Vincent Astor. The project was built with oak floors, brass light fixtures, sunny rooms, and a landscaped courtyard. Amenities included built-in bathtubs, overhead showers, electric refrigeration, gas stoves, and incinerators.

First Houses was conceived as the archetype for public housing, with its well-built, low-rise apartments and mixed tenancy. The rent was the lowest in urban U.S. housing history, an astounding $6.05 per room. First Houses tenants were all working people: garment workers, taxi drivers, and barbers who had lived in run-down apartments without heat or private toilets. Before moving in the new residents' belongings were fumigated by the city. As one resident explained, "As we were all coming from the tenements, they feared we might be bringing in insects with us."[33] The project had a communal atmosphere, an active tenants association, recreation rooms, and courtyards for children to play in safely. This project was the pride of the New Deal Housing program; Eleanor Roosevelt even came to its inauguration.[34] Nevertheless it had its critics, who insisted that the project was too costly and extravagant to waste on cheap rentals for the lowest income group. Yet Mayor La Guardia and the New York City Housing Authority insisted that First Houses was built to show that decent housing could use the finest materials. As the mayor metaphorically retorted, for First Houses we "had decided to bake cake, not bread with its dough."[35]

All the New Deal's housing programs contributed to the steady recovery in housing, but USHA's public housing made the critical difference. Historian

Nathaniel Keith estimates that "by 1939, starts of new dwellings had recovered
to about the 1929 level, but with the help of 56,000 publicly financed units which
were unheard of in 1929. In 1940, there was the further expansion of 16%, including 73,000 publicly financed units."[36]

In spite of USHA's success in reviving the economy and housing large numbers of
citizens, opposition to direct government intervention—particularly government-built low-rent housing—was extremely vocal. Much as the home building
industry disliked the PWA, they had the consolation that it was temporary,
based on emergency relief legislation. USHA, however, designed as a permanent
institution, was seen as a major threat.

The private housing market would have been content had the government
stuck to programs like the FHA, which they benefited from, but they felt that
USHA was going too far. Charles F. Lewis, president of a large realty company,
summed up this argument in the *Nation's Business* in 1938: "Unfortunately, in
housing, the national administration seems committed to a policy of undoing
with its left hand what it does with its right. Against the elaborate machinery of
the FHA, set up to encourage private capital, the government has established the
still more elaborate machinery of the Wagner-Steagall Act to compete with private capital and to frighten it out of the field of housing." Lewis feared that

> Millions of families who do not live in slums and who manage to pay their way
> would find themselves not nearly so well housed as the dependent families in the
> lowest third of the population, who would enjoy life in the new subsidized hous-
> ing. The political pressures would mount rapidly, irresistibly and ruinously. Leg-
> islators would be called upon to provide new billions to provide new homes by
> subsidy, for ever higher and higher income groups.[37]

In fact this was exactly what social Keynesians hoped would happen. The New
Deal created an alternative to the private housing market, proving that government could build attractive and decent public housing and that cost alone need
not determine quality of housing. The political consequences of Lewis's argu-

ment were summed up in the *American Builder*, a magazine of the private housing industry, in 1939:

> The philosophy underlying the present trend towards subsidized public housing
> appears to be that every man, no matter what his economic status is, is entitled to
> a decent, healthy place to live—just as it has become an accepted part of American
> thought that every child is entitled to a free education no matter what his parent
> income.[38]

What the real estate industry feared most was that decent housing would become an entitlement—a right every American shared, regardless of economic status. The lobby believed that this would threaten their economic and social interests by encouraging people to remain renters instead of becoming home owners.

One solution proposed by the real estate lobby rested on a commercial Keynesian assumption that individual widespread home ownership would guarantee a stable and patriotic citizenry. Advocates argued that the barrier to providing the masses with homes in the past was the speculative market; with the FHA underwriting projects, however, private capital could build large-scale communities on sound long-term investments:

> If subsidies *must* be granted to housing, better results will be obtained by paying
> such subsidies to the "ill-housed $1/3$ in such a way to encourage them to buy
> small, individual homes, *through the regular channels of private building and fi-*
> *nance.* In other words, make the subsidies *help private* building and encourage *pri-*
> *vate* home ownership rather than *hurt* private building and discourage home
> ownership in favor of renting.[39]

Such critiques only strengthened the position of New Deal social Keynesians and the progressive coalition. In open opposition to the real estate lobby, the latter maintained that spending public monies on decent public housing was as necessary as expenditures "for public health, for education, for roads, for national defense, for maintaining public buildings, for social security, or for any of

the activities in which civilized and enlightened governments must necessarily
engage."[40] Moreover, builders (although they claimed otherwise) had zero interest in developing a private housing market for the lowest third, even with the
help of FHA; their ideological emphasis on home ownership was incompatible
with producing low-ncome housing. Senator Robert Wagner pointed this out to
reassure private developers that USHA was not trespassing on their turf:
"[USHA] will serve only those in the lowest income groups. . . . It will be strictly
non-competitive with private industry, which, by the universal admission of
businessmen and builders, cannot make available, safe, and sanitary housing at
rents which people with such low incomes can afford to pay."[41]

Despite such assurances, the private housing industry feared that public
housing presented unwanted competition and was a sign of creeping socialism
that would "eventually destroy the entire building industry"—dealers, financing
institutions, and builders. Public housing, they argued, was "the first step in the
socialization of our country—the destruction of our democratic, free enterprise
system. Unfortunately like so many evils, a first step and a small dose is appealing and popular—only by fully recognizing the social political and economic disaster which will come with its growth, can one properly gauge the eventual
result." Joseph E. Merrion of the National Association of Home Builders
bluntly stated, "We do not concede the need or the right of the federal government, either directly or by subsidy to local housing authority, to enter the housing field by building, owning, or operating permanent housing projects."[42]

In spite of the complaints of private builders and their allies, social Keynesians in the New Deal, with the help of RPAA members and the progressive
coalition, continued to operate on the philosophy that decent housing in America was a basic right, not just a privilege for those who could afford it. In advocating a new vision of housing for the masses they articulated a more inclusive
version of the American dream, an alternative to a class-bound past that would
have an impact on postwar suburban development.

Chapter Six

The Common Good: Public or Private

The battle over public and private housing was more than theoretical. The 1930s brought both publicly and privately funded housing experiments. In Greenbelt, Maryland, for instance, the federal government constructed a multi-family experimental community for renters. At the same time, the Levitt family built a private upper-middle-class, single-family development on Long Island's Gold Coast. Both provided important lessons for the postwar master builders, progressive housing groups, politicians, and the enemies of government-sponsored housing.

Greenbelt was built on the ideals of community planning advocated by the RPAA reformers. Designed and planned as carefully as Chatham Village, Sunnyside Gardens, and Radburn had been, Greenbelt had the additional advantage of a wholesale commitment from the federal government in the funding and supervising of its construction.

Historian Joseph Arnold appraised Greenbelt in this manner:

> Greenbelt in the 1930s was the premier example of a community planned and administered for the enhancement of wholesome human relationships. The creation of the municipal government, the heavy investment of services for community life, the excellent community facilities—all provided fertile soil for the pioneer residents when they moved into the town in 1937. These residents did not disappoint Greenbelt's creators. They quickly established a community life so active and intense that it has passed into the realm of legend.[1]

Greenbelt was part of a New Deal initiative by the Resettlement Administration, an agency established in 1935 to create, maintain, and operate communities for the resettlement of destitute or low-income families. Unlike USHA, the Resettlement Agency built new towns in rural and suburban locations, not housing projects in urban centers.[2] It was headed by Rexford Tugwell, a member of President Roosevelt's brain trust and an advocate of modern planning and cooperative communities. The board of advisors included Clarence Stein, Henry Wright, and Catherine Bauer.

Just as Robert Moses had fallen in love with the Jones Beach peninsula and envisioned it as a people's park, Tugwell fell in love with a piece of vacant land near Washington, D.C., envisioning how he would build a suburb on a hill. "One day in the fall of 1934," Tugwell recalled, "I asked the President if he'd go for a ride in the county. I brought him out here on what roads there were then and asked him what he thought of it for a housing project. He, too, fell in love with the place. So we got started right off."[3]

The site, thirteen miles from downtown Washington, D.C., met the planners' wish to build near a city that had a large number of moderate-income workers who could not find affordable housing. The agency acquired 12,000 acres of land in a relatively undeveloped area not yet allocated for expensive new suburban developments. Unencumbered access to land was crucial, because private industry otherwise would have blocked the government development. Instead, planners and builders were able "to work on a clean slate because [they] got there before the zoners and sub-dividers and the municipal highway engineers."[4]

Buying up large tracts of land made it possible to build a large-scale model community. With government funds, unemployed workers were hired to build the town, providing many jobs and stimulating the economy. More than 1,800 skilled and unskilled workers worked on site; the major components of houses were precut and then brought to the site to be assembled one after the other.

Total physical, environmental, and social preplanning was an essential part of the project. The benefits, Clarence Stein insisted, "must be built in—houses, roads, walks, parks, gardens—and a definitely determined reality must be created that will fit a desired way of living."[5] Greenbelt was designed to resemble Radburn. Like Radburn, Greenbelt featured neighborhood units defined by superblocks with interior parks and walkways, separation of pedestrian and vehicular circulation, and houses facing inward to the parks.[6] Landscaping was a distinctive ingredient in the creation of this garden city. Angus MacGregor, who had worked for J. P. Morgan, the Duchess of Albany, the Earl of Durham, and the Earl of Mansfield, was director of landscaping and groundskeeper, imparting the same elegance to Greenbelt that he had to the properties of his previous employers.

As in Chatham, the row houses were arranged one above the other on the rising ground, blending into the landscape. The whole community was shaped like a crescent with curvilinear streets. The town center, located in the bowl of the crescent, had cooperative stores, a school, a theater, and recreational facilities. In its center was a man-made lake. The most arresting feature of the community was the green belt that encircled it, used for recreation and gardening. It also provided a buffer between the community and any future haphazard development along its borders.

Planners experimented with construction materials and methods. As Chester Draper, a building supervisor at Greenbelt, explained, "Business was very competitive in those days and different companies were always coming up with new products to try out. Lots of things that became common in the construction industry were first tried out here."[7] Innovations included prefabricated houses, copper piping, new ways of building lathes and concrete roofs, brass plumbing, and decorative glass blocks. All materials used in construction were of high quality because, as Clarence Stein's planning study argued, "The communities will consist mainly of low income families. Therefore, they must be planned, constructed, and managed so that operation and maintenance cost will be as low as possible."[8]

To identify the needs and desires of potential residents, Greenbelt's research department sent out thousands of questionnaires. "Research was particularly important," Draper recalled, "because most architects had previously designed homes only for the well-to-do."[9] The survey revealed that attached town houses, preferred by 45 percent of respondents, were the most popular design. Popularity of this style seemed to confirm the planners' belief that town houses were the kind of housing people of modest income thought of as economically feasible.

People also were queried about the kinds of kitchens they wanted, size of families, the use or nonuse of a living room, and were asked what kind of community amenities they believed were important. All wanted a library, athletic facilities, public swimming pool, shops, and a theater. A community hall was also high on the list.

By 1937 Greenbelt had 574 town houses, 306 low-rise apartment units, five single-family detached houses, and 375 garages. From the outside the town houses all looked alike, built of either brick or painted cinderblock, but inside there were 71 different floor plans, including one-, two-, and three-bedroom units with either flat or pitched roofs. Over a third of the units were efficiency apartments intended for couples without children. All homes had copper gutters and downspouts, steel casement windows with screens and window shades and wooden doors, and bathrooms had tubs, toilets, sinks, and medicine cabinets. The kitchens had built-in enamel cabinets, a threeburner electric stove with an oven, a refrigerator, and a double sink—all modern for the period. Low-cost, sturdy wooden modern furniture, designed by unemployed artists, could be bought on credit from the Resettlement Administration.

Greenbelt's town center was particularly striking. Its school–community building, which housed a library and large gymnasium, was built in art deco style, its streamline form complemented by large windows and sculptured panels by WPA artist Lenore Thomas. The panels depicted scenes inspired by the preamble to the U.S. Constitution. On either side of the town center were two large commercial buildings, similarly art deco, that housed stores, town offices, garages, a post office, theater, police–fire station, and auto service center. In the center of the commercial mall was a monumental sculpture of a mother and child, also by Lenore Thomas. Behind the commercial center stood the recreation area, complete with swimming pool, tennis courts, baseball diamonds, picnic areas, and trails for horseback riding or hiking.[10]

A total of 885 families of various religious faiths and incomes of between $800 and $2,200 a year were selected as residents. All were white. Some were government workers and some not. The average age of adult residents was just under twenty-nine. Most of the family wage earners were men.

New residents made Greenbelt their home and appreciated the difference between a planned community and the urban slums from which they had come. Louise Steinle Winkler from Washington, D.C., for instance, remembers:

> My father had been out of work for three years and we had been living on what he could make from odd jobs and the kindness of relatives and friends. I remember taking what seemed like a forever drive to Greenbelt to look at the model home. It was furnished in 'Greenbelt furniture,' beautifully simple in the Danish style. The colors were bright and I remember even the dishes on the dining room table were in different colors for each place setting.
>
> It was nothing to compare with the cramped quarters we had in our upstairs rooms in Washington, where my brothers and I slept on army cots which we folded under our parents bed during the day. Best of all, we would no longer have to share a bathroom with three or four families. The house was so clean—we had been living with roaches and mice. Then I had my own room and a brand new bed. . . . I remember feeling the excitement my mother felt at having her own clean place.[11]

Residents' cooperative, energetic spirit helped ensure the success of the fledgling town. As Mr. Sherrod, Greenbelt's first mayor pointed out, "Greenbelt was a beautifully planned town, but it was the people that made it work."[12] Planners had counted on exactly this civic willingness, and indeed tried to foster it by design. As Stein explained, "A neighborhood community is a group of people with common interests in which they actively participate. Greenbelt, from the beginning, was such a community."[13]

People saw themselves as pioneers creating entirely new kinds of communities. Resident Mary E. Van Cleves captured this feeling in an article she wrote for the *Greenbelt Cooperator* in 1937:

> We did not arrive in Greenbelt after long tiresome miles by covered wagon: nor did we cut down trees in order to build our homes. Nor is it necessary to clear the land to plant our crops that we may eat, nor dig a well that we may quench our thirst.
>
> Yet we are pioneers—of a new way of living. We are the sculptors handling the soft yielding clay of a new community. What form shall we mold out of it?

This project has given most of us an opportunity we'd never anticipated. We
are in the process of creating homes! Our families and our children will live under
laws of our own making. Only in our fondest and most youthful dreams have we
imagined such a chance.[14]

Ethel Rosenzwieg, another resident, remembered how refreshing Greenbelt's communal ethos was: "There was no hierarchy here, no rich people looking down on the peasants. We were all equal."[15]

Not only did Greenbelt residents experience social equality, they also shared
in the mission of starting a town from scratch, creating a cooperative model of
living. As town biographers Barbara Likowski and Jay McCarl point out, "The
concept of the cooperative, as an enterprise collectively owned and operated for
mutual benefit instead of for profit, was new to most of the people. It began with
the businesses."[16] All commercial enterprises in Greenbelt were established as
cooperatives, as stipulated by the policies of the Resettlement Administration.
The Consumer Distribution Corporation, a cooperative founded by Edward Filene, underwrote Greenbelt businesses. The first commercial venture in town
was the shopping center, a forerunner of the modern, self-service supermarket
equipped with shopping carts and low-priced, good-quality merchandise. Cen-
trally located and within walking distance of all the dwellings, the shopping center became the informal gathering place for the community. "Here," said Stein
proudly, "is where one hears the news, discusses town politics . . . tickets are sold
for town gatherings, dances or lectures to support common town activities such
as the day care center."[17] Buoyed by the success of the supermarket, other cooperatives soon opened: a gasoline station, drugstore, barber shop, movie theater,
valet shop, beauty parlor, and tobacco shop.

The community building was the center for civic activities, served as a school
during the weekdays, and was used for meetings, adult education classes, and
recreation at night. It also functioned as the town hall. Greenbelt's school curriculum, unlike the more traditional schools of neighboring Prince Georges'
County, reflected its progressive attitude. As principal Catherine T. Reed explained in the local newspaper, The Cooperator, "Our course of study is tending

to become a course of living. . . . The school is evolving its own philosophy day by day."[18] Students undertook collective projects, such as theater productions and running stores. Reading, math, history, and other subjects were learned in the process of participating. Before a PTA was organized in 1937, the students formed their own cooperative to sell school supplies and candy. The Gum Drop co-op, as it was called, was so successful that it made the national news. Greenbelt residents also organized kindergartens and nursery cooperatives.

Cooperation encompassed every aspect of town life. Greenbelt residents overwhelmingly voted for cooperative and preventive medical care. They organized transportation, created citizen's associations, founded a journalism club that put out the local newspaper, and established baseball teams, a dramatic club, and a credit union. Meetings took up so much of people's time that in 1938 residents passed a town motion declaring a meeting moratorium from Christmas to New Year's Day.

The press, along with prominent and ordinary citizens, were fascinated by Greenbelt from the beginning. Some, like Eleanor Roosevelt and Sir Raymond Unwin, the father of town planning in England, admired Greenbelt. Others— particularly the press—scoffed at what they called "the socialist experiment." The Chicago American announced that "the first communist towns in America are nearing completion." Other newspapers poked fun at community rules, like the one requiring residents to take their laundry off the line by 4 P.M.[19]

Thousands of curious visitors flocked to Greenbelt to watch the natives. As Bernice Brautigam, a local resident, observed, "We were on exhibition all the time. People would come out to see Greenbelt, maybe interested, maybe curious, I don't know. You'd be sitting at your dinner table and they'd be peeking in the windows just like you were in a fish bowl. No one dared to mess it up, it was too precious to mess up."[20] In fact, more people came to visit Greenbelt than any national monument in Washington.[21]

In spite of all the public attention it attracted, however, Greenbelt was ignored by those in the private housing field, a neglect that prompted Architectural Forum to devote almost an entire issue to the accomplishments of the Resettlement Administration, arguing that:

The facets of the Housing Problem are as numerous as those of a coronation jewel, but they somehow fail in the strong light of publicity to shine with comparable brilliance. Occasional examples point the way to a solution. Thus may be classified the communities designed by the technicians of the Resettlement Administration. In presenting a portfolio of these recently complete houses, *The Forum* is twice motivated—once to record a significant contribution in housing; again, as a pattern which private [builders] may well study for clues to [help them] simplify and therefore generally improve, standards of planning, methods of design and construction.[22]

Greenbelt illustrated how a model community built with government funds could serve the needs of the working class and poor and encourage a democratic, cooperative way of life. It also paved the way for private developers. At the same time that the federal government was building Greenbelt, private interests also were experimenting with mass-produced suburban development. Many private builders suffered losses during the depression, but the firm of Abraham Levitt and Sons still had the resources to build suburban housing. *Architectural Forum* was so impressed with the firm's work that it remarked that the Levitts' "phenomenalistic depression doings have made many an onlooker blink. Suburban home buildings comatosis is a myth to them; they have made a million at it in no time."[23]

The Levitts—Abraham, Alfred, and William—began their building business in 1929, hardly a propitious time, when anyone "even mentioning building a home for sale was ripe for the booby hatch." Abraham Levitt, a wealthy Brooklyn attorney, decided to do something with the scattered plots of land he had bought cheaply in Rockville Center, a thriving commuter community on Long Island's South Shore. With plans designed by his eighteen-year-old son Alfred and the able assistance of his older son William, he built a six-room two-bath $14,500 home, at the time a rather expensive and perhaps rash move, yet he sold it at a profit.[24] By 1934, Levitt and Sons had built 255 houses in Long Island and sold them for a total of $2,725,000. That year Abraham and his sons launched their first full-scale suburban development, Strathmore-at-Manhasset, located on the Gold Coast fifteen miles from downtown Manhattan.

William was the family decision maker, and he decided that Levitt and Sons would conform to the restrictive unwritten codes of the real estate business at that time. That he was the grandson of a rabbi didn't stop him from barring Jews from his North Shore development. As his public relations manager, Paul Townsend, recalled, "Sure, he went along with the local practice of real estate agents not selling to Jews. History should show that Levitt was part of the ugly gentleman's agreement."[25]

Levitt and Sons built Strathmore-at-Manhasset for upper-middle-class families, characterizing it as "swank at low cost."[26] The firm controlled the same things in the Strathmore development that the government controlled in Greenbelt: land acquisition, architectural design, landscape, building materials, furniture, appliances, mortgaging, and sales. Like the Greenbelt planners, the Levitts used high-quality building materials: poured concrete foundations, brass plumbing, Richardson and Boynton heating systems, oak flooring, fenestra steel casement windows, Kohler plumbing fixtures, Johns-Mansville's insulation, Armstrong linoleum, built-in kitchen cabinets, cabinet-type gas ranges, General Electric exhaust fans, and copper leaders and gutters. The emphasis here was on using brand-name products that customers would recognize and appreciate.

Harkening to Henry Wright's critique of suburban development where buyers would purchase a lot and hire particular builders, Levitt's policy was to sell no vacant lots. Instead, as *Architectural Forum* observed, "Every house originates on Alfred Levitt's drawing board and every house is crammed with the same goods Bill Levitt brings in carloads from his store rooms."[27] No two houses looked exactly alike, but their construction followed strict guidelines. They had to be English or Colonial in design; Spanish architecture was taboo. The Levitts also had their own furnishing department through which perspective home owners could buy furniture, rugs, draperies, and household appliances at considerably less than retail prices.

As in Greenbelt, houses were built on-site in assembly-line fashion, twenty at a time, with workers moving from house to house. Because efficient construction methods saved money, Levitt was able to offer custom-built houses at reasonable prices. Unlike Greenbelt, where homes were rented, Strathmore houses were for sale with prices between $8,000 and $20,000 and averaging $11,000.

Whereas life in Greenbelt was governed by civic participation, Strathmore was run by rules and regulations stipulated by Levitt and agreed to by any prospective resident. These regulations embodied ideals of middle-class propriety combined with a mimicry of turn-of-the-century estate life. To maintain the private estate appearance, lawns had to be cut at least once a week between the first of April and the first of November. Failure to do so meant that Levitt and Sons cut the lawn and charged the owner. Dog kennels had to conform architecturally to the design of the house. Wash poles or wash lines were not permitted. No laundry could be exposed on Sundays or legal holidays.[28] Unlike Greenbelt, Strathmore had no sidewalks; wich Levitt felt they would mar the estate-like beauty of the landscape.

Levitt, who saw himself as a progressive builder, gave residents questionnaires like those used in Greenbelt. Although these were supposedly "to maintain an informative and enlightened attitude," their real purpose was to help him target his market. He asked, for instance, which newspapers and magazines potential inhabitants read. Based on his questionnaires, Levitt was able to pioneer a distinctive and consistent advertising campaign, placing ads in the *New York Times* or the *Saturday Evening Post*. Each ad told a pithy, human sales story illustrated by a picture of a house and an individual coat of arms.[29] They were his single most effective means of selling houses.

Levitt was extraordinarily successful, but he was not the only private developer to test out building new kinds of housing during the depression. William Burke Harmon, for instance, built housing particularly geared to industrial workers in Chicago. "Observing that they were mostly first and second generation immigrants," *Architectural Forum* wrote in one piece on the project, "he set his theme as the Americanization of the worker." Harmon's Colonial Village, consisting of single dwellings for 285 families with a choice of design of either Dutch Colonial or Regency, were priced between $7,500 and $10,500.

Contemporaries noted that in order to stress his Americanization theme, "builder Harmon and his publicity man have capitalized on the attention accorded Robert S. and Helen M. Lynd's *Middletown in Transition,* the study of Muncie, Indiana as an average American town." Harmon used public relations tactics designed to appeal to second-generation American workers, betting that this group would be drawn to housing that promised an "American" lifestyle. He organized a contest, run in the *Muncie Evening Press* to choose one "typical"American family from that typical American town. This family of four was flown to Chicago on a Friday and taken to Colonial Village the next day, where the "typical" mother cut a ribbon across the front door of one of the model houses. The model house had been supplied with the latest in electrical equipment by Commonwealth Edison and was furnished by a Chicago department store.[30]

Although Harmon and other private interests built developments smaller, less pathbreaking, and more expensive than Greenbelt, they nevertheless prefigured the mass postwar suburban development in many ways. They represented the first attempts at private mass-produced communities. Although they were as carefully planned as the new government housing, they lacked the core of the Greenbelt experience: publicly financed, inexpensive housing and cooperative living. Greenbelt posed a real alternative to individual private home ownership, and embodied the ideal that democratic government should ensure the right to a decent dwelling in a livable environment. Unfortunately this part of the legacy of the ambitious government developments of the 1930s was not duplicated later on. Although there would be tremendous political struggles over public versus private housing, the future belonged to the private developers.

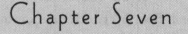

Chapter Seven

World War II: Baptism by Fire

Although the depression spurred new types of housing initiatives, World War II had an even greater impact on the housing industry in the United States. The war demanded mass mobilization of resources, technology and people, and even before the United States had officially declared war, the government allocated vast sums of money for expanded military production, including defense plants, military bases, and new aerospace industries—many of which were located in undeveloped suburban areas. The huge numbers of workers in these bases and plants would require housing.

As it had done during World War I, the government acted quickly. President Roosevelt used his war powers to consolidate all federal housing functions into a new National Housing Agency (NHA) under a single administrator who wielded total authority. The NHA concerned itself with all aspects of housing: building materials, labor, construction methods, financing, and land acquisition. The Landham Act, passed in 1940, authorized 700,000 units of federal housing to be built for defense workers.

By the end of the war 7,443,000 units had been constructed using assembly-line building methods and prefabricated parts, panels, and components. Much of the housing was government built, although some was provided by public–private cooperation financed by FHA loans, long-term low-interest mortgages, and erected by the soon-to-be master builders of the postwar period. During the war, the private housing industry became "a semi-public enterprise."[1]

World War II also gave the private housing industry the opportunity to learn how to build on a mass scale. According to housing historian Joseph Mason,

In a few short years the housing industry was torn from its slow, handicraft ways and projects into a fast-paced new world of industrialized production in huge planned projects. . . . For the first time, builders have an assured market and ample funds, plus a patriotic motive to get the job done quickly. . . . This was the combination that enabled builders such as William Levitt, David Bohannon, Barret and Hilp, Gross-Morton, Fritz Burns, and a thousand others to construct mass production lines and pioneer new pre-fabrication and panelized systems.[2]

The war spurred private builders to discard antiquated building methods. It also fundamentally reshaped their methods of obtaining construction materials and labor's relationship to mass-production methods. According to the National Resources Planning Board in 1942:

The very pressure for production forced out many of the old restraints. The rigidities in the materials supply system were often broken down, and centralized buying direct from manufacturers, either by the producers or the government itself, became accepted in the trade. Labor's hostility decreased, and instead of opposing the spread of factory methods, labor turned to organizing the workmen in the factories. Instances have occurred where union labor has installed plumbing stacks and wiring in panels before erection—procedures almost unheard of before the war.[3]

The private developers' strategy was to deliberately take on huge housing developments to prove "that private builders could produce war housing better, faster, and cheaper than public housing could." Bohannon described building 1,500 houses in San Lorenzo, California, for the U.S. Navy in four months.

We broke all production records. At one period we were completing one house every 40 minutes. We produced the 1,500 on schedule and built a complete planned community with curvilinear streets, a neighborhood center, recreation areas and a shopping center. . . . We and other private builders tried to create war housing communities that would continue to be livable and attractive after the war emergency.[4]

Although the builders freely copied public housing ideas and methods, such as those used in Greenbelt, they insisted that public housing was flimsy and would only last for the duration of the war. Their own developments, they boasted, were designed to last forever.

William Levitt got his first experience with low-cost housing during the war. Levitt built 2,350 rental units for the navy in Norfolk, Virginia. The four-room slab-based units were built by factorylike methods adapted to the construction site. Although most private builders had opposed modern construction products—particularly prefabricated house components before the war—government-built projects like Greenbelt and war housing proved that experimental products and techniques worked. Moreover, competition to out-produce government housing necessitated mass-production techniques. Both Levitt and Bohannon recognized that building large-scale developments demanded new methods. As Bohannon explained, "I studied the work of other big builders and of prefabricated-house builders. . . . I came back to the principle of precise organization, pre-cutting and streamlined site production. We brought products, components, and materials to the site and fabricated them for fast erection."[5]

Although much war housing was temporary and makeshift (frequently just barracks), some government wartime communities were intended to last, combining modern production methods, communal features, and an aesthetic appeal. One such community was the Channel Heights Housing Project in San Pedro, California. Designed by the prominent architect Richard Neutra, Channel Heights housed 600 shipyard workers and their families, with only 3.6 units per acre, one of the lowest densities ever achieved in public housing. Built with redwood and cement, all the homes faced the ocean. There were four different models: one with one bedroom, another with three, and a choice of one or two stories. More spacious than the usual project unit, many had balconies, ample closets, horizontally sliding windows, and a pleasant kitchen–dining room area with a vista. Low-cost modern furniture designed by Neutra was made available to tenants.

Channel Heights boasted a gardening building in which tenants could learn landscaping, a nursery school with a spray pool, community center, assembly room, stationery store, laundry, drugstore, and modern supermarket. Artificially illuminated underpasses, like those in Radburn and Greenbelt, made it possible to reach communal facilities by foot, without crossing traffic-filled streets. In 1944 *Architectural Forum* declared, "For those who claim that mass housing can have no individuality, that all housing projects must inevitably look alike, Channel Heights is instructive."[6]

Despite positive response to the burst of wartime building activity, defense housing also stirred up old controversies. Many New Dealers welcomed the opportunity to promote further the idea that decent housing was a basic right, something the government should provide. As John Blandford, head of the National Housing Administration, stated: "Decent housing is vital to the health, safety and welfare of the families of the nation. All American families should get decent housing."[7] Blandford's position attracted widespread support from labor unions, ethnic and religious groups, the League of Women Voters, the Parent Teacher Organization, the American Association of University Women, as well as progressive capitalists.

Private builders felt threatened, even though they benefited from the wartime housing demand. In 1940 the real estate lobby rallied in opposition to public housing and succeeded in having the Landham Act amended to specify that all the units had to be either sold or demolished after the war and could not be converted into low-income housing. The government quickly responded to this new threat. In 1941 the War Production Board proposed closing down private defense housing and turning all of the building work over to public housing agencies.

Stung by their defeat at the hands of the government, the private housing sector mobilized to form the National Association of Home Builders (NAHB), which soon became an extremely powerful real estate group opposed to any form of public housing. The NAHB was a coalition that included industry newcomers, such as Levitt and David Bohannon, president of the NAHB, and older voices for private housing, such as Chicago real estate lobbyist Hubert Nelson, the U.S. Chamber of Commerce, the United States Savings and Loan League, the National Association of Retail Lumber Dealers, and the Mortgage Bankers Association. The new coalition successfully blocked the proposed order of the

War Production Board to give over all defense contracts to public housing agencies. The NAHB was so powerful that 95 percent of war housing was built by private real estate developers underwritten by the FHA.

The war provided fast training in mass housing for the private housing industry.[8] Between 1940 and 1945 the United States created as much new industrial capacity as had existed in the country prior to 1940. The massive growth of the defense industry reshaped Southern California and Seattle as well as Long Island's South Shore, where defense contractors such as Grumman, Republic, Fairchild, and Liberty built huge factories. Workers and their families flocked to these industries and found well-paying jobs.[9] This in turn gave the private builder new opportunities for producing low-income housing on a large scale.

By 1943, however, there was general concern about the transition to a peacetime economy. Would mass unemployment, industrial stagnation, and an inflated housing market return to haunt the nation? Would people keep their jobs in the suburbs or would the defense bubble burst, returning people to the city? On Long Island this worry was expressed in a 1944 editorial in *Newsday* warning:

> During the postwar period we will doubtless see an increase in our population.
> Men coming home from the wars to young wives and new babies will want to settle down in the country so that their children may play on the grass instead of on the pavements of New York City. Many of these men will look for work. We sincerely hope there will be work here for them to find. Unfortunately hoping isn't enough. . . . If we don't plan now, we may find that after the war our airplane factories instead of turning out automobiles or prefabricated houses or flivver planes or quick freeze refrigerators will be turning into ruins.[10]

The war heightened the desires of both soldiers and civilians for peace and prosperity. After a decade and a half of depression and war deprivation, Americans hungered for a world of plenty, the wonders of modern technology, and a home of their own. Popular films, magazines, comics, radio shows, and postcards all promised soldiers that the good life awaited them:

All the fighting power of their nation is directed towards securing, for them and their children, the one thing in life they value most: a happy and livable home. . . . The home is the sound and constructive force, the builder of national character. . . . And what, for them makes up such a home? Love, freedom and human kindness of course. But also a host of *little* things—a new and better room for Junior, a den for dad. New furniture for the living room. A glassed in porch. . . . A housewife's faith that gay flowers can continue to bloom, year after year, in a little garden forever safe from the violation of a conqueror's boots.[11]

The happy, secure, commercial vision of the postwar world extolled by *Better Homes and Gardens* coexisted with a more social and communal vision of postwar prosperity. Many continued to put their faith in public housing in Greenbelt and other New Deal garden cities. The Armed Forces newspaper *Stars and Stripes* for instance, featured ads with illustrations of Greenbelt housing and the prediction that "the post war world may bring more modern communities like it."[12] These two competing ideals, commercial and communal, would shape postwar housing politics and policies.

Part Three

Who Would House the Masses?

Chapter Eight

Postwar Housing Politics:

The McCarthy Hearings on Housing

At the end of World War II, Americans were filled with visions of a new and better way of life, promised as the fruits of victory. Crammed into relatives' apartments or living in makeshift army barracks, returning veterans tuned into the pledge of postwar abundance that came from every radio and magazine. Most alluring was the promise of a new, fully equipped, affordable dwelling for every American veteran. The power of the dream was so persuasive that a *Saturday Evening Post* survey in 1945 revealed that only 14 percent of the population would be satisfied to live in an apartment or a "used house."[1] Yet how would these dreams be fulfilled?

In 1944 public support for special benefits for veterans was widespread. As a result, Congress passed the Serviceman's Readjustment Act, which included the GI Bill of Rights. The bill had two components: a free college education and an interest-free home mortgage with little money down. The GI Bill enabled veterans to borrow the entire appraised value of a house without a down payment. Unfortunately, there weren't enough houses to meet the demand of the returning soldiers.

Despite the GI Bill and people's fantasies, living conditions for many worsened. Millions of veterans and civilians continued to be ill-housed. In 1946 Chicago reported 100,000 homeless veterans. In Atlanta 2,000 people answered an advertisement for one vacancy. A classified ad in an Omaha newspaper read, "Big Ice Box 7 by 17 feet. Could Be Fixed Up To Live In." Senate investigations found hundreds of thousands of veterans living in barns, garages, and chicken coops. The most conservative reports from the government's national housing agency estimated that the country needed at least five million new units immediately and a total of 12.5 million over the next decade.[2] Who had the capacity to build housing on such an unprecedented scale?

The New Deal had convinced the majority of ill-housed people that they had a right to decent housing, and the federal government would protect that right. But the powerful private housing industry was busy pressing Congress to deny this right and get government out of the housing industry. This was a hard case to make. In the past, private builders (except for a few during the war) by and large had failed to provide substantial housing for the masses. This was precisely the reason why government stepped in. The private home-building industry had to prove to government and the public that it could quickly deliver low-cost homes for a new mass market in peacetime conditions.

William Levitt understood the stakes: "Housing," he said, "is in an emergency state today. It is a serious problem and the challenge has been thrown to all of us to help solve it. It cannot continue to remain in an emergency state much longer. If we, the builders, do not produce sufficient housing to cover all income levels the government can, will and should do it."[3]

Levitt's fears were well-founded. The government already had foreseen the emergency housing shortage and begun planning as early as 1943. Buoyed by public support from the AFL, the CIO, the Conference of Mayors, veterans organizations, New Deal housing reformers, and housing experts, a broad bipartisan bill was introduced in the Senate in 1945. The bill's sponsors were Robert Taft, a powerful Republican from Ohio; Allen Ellender, a Southern Democrat; and Robert Wagner, Sr., Democrat from New York and a key figure in the earlier Housing Reform Act. The Taft Ellender Wagner Act (TEW) was based on a number of New Deal assumptions, one of which was the recognition

> that there is an area of housing at the lowest rent levels which private industry
> cannot afford to serve and which local government is not fully capable of serving.
> Therefore . . . the importance of a well conceived comprehensive housing policy
> cannot be exaggerated. . . . From the social point of view, a supply of good hous-

ing sufficient to meet the needs of all families is essential to a sound and stable democracy. Every family must have a decent home in which to live.[4]

Supported by President Truman, this comprehensive bill contained a national housing policy, expanded lending powers for Home Loan Banks, relaxed FHA insurance terms, and improved home loans for farmers. It included housing research, slum clearance and the construction of 500,000 public housing units over a fourteen-year period for low- and middle-income families as well as subsidies for veterans cooperatives.[5]

TEW was a cogent and popular response to the housing crisis, but old issues surfaced immediately. After the Senate easily passed the bill, politics intervened. When it got to the House Banking and Currency Committee, Chairman Republican Jesse P. Wolcott of Michigan declared it dead. Wolcott, a major foe of public housing, was emboldened by the congressional election of 1946, which had been a victory for Republicans and enemies of public housing. The Republicans had campaigned on a platform of "had enough": high taxes, high prices, shortages, labor disturbances, and Democratic leadership. Now Republicans were in control of both House and Senate for the first time since 1931. They seized the opportunity to roll back New Deal social programs. Republicans, in alliance with businessmen, wanted a quick "return to normalcy" with a reliance on private not public enterprise. Among the leading lights of the new Republican majority was the nation's youngest senator, Joseph McCarthy, the junior senator from Wisconsin.

Most people associate McCarthy with the Cold War crusade to ferret out so-called Communists in the schools, government, Hollywood, and the labor movement. Demolishing many of the New Deal's social guarantees was also an important part of his agenda. High on his list of targets were the right to employment, a decent home in a livable community, social security, and a safety net in case of illness or disaster. Owing to McCarthy's actions, 1947 proved a watershed in the domestic war to redefine the meaning and scope of democracy.

Fought on many fronts—political, economic, and social—the war over housing became a central battleground. All sides saw the home-building industry as key to economic recovery, crucial to employment, consumer goods production, stimulation of industry, and modernization of transportation. The fight over

public versus private housing occurred in many arenas: Congress, local government, the courts, labor unions, veterans organizations, the real estate lobby, the
public housing lobby, building trades, the construction industry, the prefabrication business, the banking industry, the popular press, business publications,
and public relations firms. Long Island's South Shore in particular played a star-
ring role in this unfolding drama.

The most important housing battle took place in the public hearings of the U.S. Senate Joint Committee Study and Investigation of Housing. Presided over by Senator McCarthy, the hearings went on for five months in 1947 and 1948. The
creation of the committee itself provided opponents of public housing and TEW
with a public forum to attack the New Deal's commitment to a comprehensive
federal housing policy. Powerful political maneuvering, some of it barely legal,
revealed the goals of the new conservative forces as well as their increasingly
demagogic political style. The junior senator from Wisconsin in particular understood that housing was a lightning rod.

Senator Charles Tobey, a liberal Republican and strong supporter of the
TEW bill, should have chaired the committee; but through a complex manipu-
lation of Senate procedures, McCarthy managed to get Congressman Ralph
Gamble, a timid but outspoken opponent of public housing, elected chairman.
He then got himself elected vice-chairman. Furious, Tobey accused McCarthy
of bad faith and duplicity, charging that McCarthy was a known advocate of "a
sinister group carrying out its instructions from the real estate lobby."[6] Mc-
Carthy prevailed.

Formal hearings were held in thirty-three cities; 1,286 witnesses testified. To
insure that the hearings favored the real estate and banking interests, McCarthy
mounted a well-coordinated publicity campaign. He used a hefty cut of the committee's $100,000 budget to hire a staff from the New York public relations firm
of Bell, Jones and Taylor, whose other clients included, not coincidentally, the
National Association of Home Builders, the U.S. Saving and Loan League, and
the National Association of Real Estate Boards.[7]

From the very first hearing, McCarthy took control of the committee, and for the next five months he wrung all possible publicity from its investigations. As one historian, Richard Davies, observed, "In his role as Vice-Chairman of the committee, he underwent an apprenticeship as self-appointed inquisitor developing the sledge hammer techniques that he later used so effectively while seeking to exhume communist conspirators from the depths of the state department."[8]

Officially, the investigative committee was supposed to explore the reasons for the housing shortage. Its real goal, however, was to discredit the TEW—especially those sections that called for government-subsidized public housing and slum clearance. Early in the hearings McCarthy scored a public relations victory when he toured the Rego Park Veterans Housing Project in Queens, New York. With press in tow, standing in the midst of the site, he declared the project to be "a deliberately created slum area, at federal expense . . . a breeding ground for communists." Clearly he was not concerned with the tenants' views, who understood that McCarthy's visit was politically motivated. As one tenant told the press at the time of the visit, McCarthy was "interested not so much in seeing to it that the veterans are provided with a place to live, but with arousing sentiment against continuing the very vital program of public housing."[9]

Oddly enough, one of the committee's main obstacles to the elimination of public housing was the state of the private housing industry, which long had taken criticism for its outmoded methods and inability to provide mass housing. The home building industry needed an incentive, however, to give up antiquated methods and expand its market. The government was experienced in building low-income housing, and the public (and most members of Congress) assumed that the government would continue to provide public housing for working- and middle-class renters. Despite private experiments with mass-produced housing in the 1930s and during the war, it seemed logical to some that private industry would continue to build for the wealthy while the government constructed housing for poorer America.[10] In order to modernize, the building industry as a whole had to be transformed and shaken down to its foundation. Material shortages had to be overcome. The price of a single-family house had to be reduced. Middlemen who controlled supplies needed ferreting out. Modern large-scale corporate structures had to be introduced, and methods of financing streamlined and simplified.

Some, like William Levitt, saw mass-produced housing as a golden opportunity for private industry and warned private builders and bankers to beware:

> If the public is adequately clothed and fed and housed through the operation of our
> great system of private enterprise, I think it is safe to assume that we shall see less and
> less government directing of our activities. But if on the other hand, we don't ac-
> complish these objectives, then just as surely as there will be a tomorrow, you can bet
> your bank buildings that Uncle Sam will step in and tell us how to do it.[11]

McCarthy's hearings raised difficult questions: How was mass housing to be built, and by whom? Why was there as yet no mass housing despite huge demand? Could private builders create affordable housing, or was the New Deal approach still preferable? Underlying these debates was the understanding that housing would be the steam engine for economic recovery. In his opening remarks, McCarthy articulated this consensus:

> Experience has shown that it is impossible to have real prosperity in this country
> without a stable healthy building industry. . . . This industry not only provides
> jobs for millions of our citizens, but also the factories, plants and buildings in
> which they work and the homes in which they live. When healthy, the industry has
> a favorable effect on virtually every segment of our economy. More people are
> needed to work in the transportation industry, which ships building materials to
> all parts of the country, more men are needed in the forests to cut the lumber. More
> men are needed in the steel mills which furnish basic products for building. More
> workers are needed in the service trades which furnish heating, plumbing and
> other facilities for housing. . . . The first step toward maintaining such a healthy
> industry is to provide steady production of an adequate number of homes neces-
> sary to meet the needs of the American people, priced within their pocketbooks.[12]

McCarthy argued, as Filene had years earlier, that housing thus was the primer for mass production, and that conversely, a revitalized economic system would meet the housing needs of ordinary Americans. Like Levitt, he worried about the state of private housing but maintained the sepremacy of private enterprise over government projects, which were deemed socialist and thus inherently bad. In McCarthy's view, "There are those who maintain that because private enterprise has not solved the entire problem we should scrap private enterprise and socialize housing. But it seems only logical that instead of attempting to scrap private enterprise we should furnish the necessary aids to make it work."[13]

According to this logic, public housing and socialism therefore were identical. He blamed New Deal reformers for leading the nation down this unsavory path:

> The aim of professional public housers has been presented by Nathan Strauss, a former United States Housing Administrator. In his book *The Seven Myths of Housing*, Mr. Straus predicted with approval, a future in which one third of the population might become housed in public housing, thereby creating such a tax burden on the remainder of the population that the middle income group would also demand public housing. If two thirds of the population were housed in subsidized tax exempt projects the economy would not be able to stand it. The ultimate aim of such professional public housers is to socialize all housing under the guise of providing public housing for the underprivileged.[14]

The key to McCarthy's attack was to brand public housing with the stigma of poverty and remove it from the realm of average working- and middle-class Americans. Conservatives wanted public housing to be viewed as a last source of refuge for the destitute rather than as a guaranteed right for all. If government continued to build public housing, conservatives feared that housing would be perceived as a right similar to public education and everyone would demand it. From 1941 to 1955 the conservatives and their real estate allies used the media to campaign against the "socialist dangers" of public housing. They operated on both the federal and local level, attacking public housing as a Communist conspiracy.

This highly influential lobby helped defeat many local attempts to create public housing. In an anti–public housing blitz, leaflets, pamphlets, cartoons, and petitions gave the false impression of a grassroots groundswell against public housing, though the campaign was national, well-organized, and well-funded, with materials supplied by the U.S. Savings and Loan League and the National Association of Home Builders. A leaflet distributed to the citizens of Lubbock, Texas, proclaimed in big bold letters, "Do You Believe in Socialism? **No!** Is Public Housing Socialism? **Yes!**" The leaflet went on to explain that public housing would destroy America, veterans, labor, and the churches. The leaflet ends by stating, "unless you want Lubbock to sell its birthright for this **Mess of Public Housing Potage, Vote No April 4th.**"[15] Real estate propaganda used racism as another fear tactic, specifically pointing out that "certain undesirable persons— i.e. Negroes or Mexican-Americans—would be eligible for public housing and would therefore become neighbors of the established residents."[16]

Public housing also was attacked as a Democratic party conspiracy to give housing to people along party lines, while taxing the public-at-large for their operation and maintenance. In the 1930s public housing developments were diverse, containing various religious and ethnic groups, the working class, professionals, and the unemployed. This diversity—once part of the appeal of public housing—came under assault in the hearings. John Nicklas, Jr., of the Pittsburgh Real Estate Lobby, elaborated this new charge in his testimony to the committee: "I shall present witnesses who are prepared to swear that government housing in Pittsburgh is rented, not only to the worthy poor, but also to city employees earning good salaries and to people of various professions. Government housing is nothing more than a political football. About 85% of the tenants are Democrats." Nicklas also argued that private housing was better for the economy. The private housers "Certainly have a better plan than public government . . . we believe in home rule. . . . Government housing should not tap resources further. . . . We don't want government built houses; we don't want government owned homes. We don't want government managed homes. We don't want government tax free homes. We think the city is surrendering to a vicious economic political system."[17]

Committee proceedings were stacked against defenders of public housing. While witnesses such as Nicklas were given ample time and treated with respect, advocates for public housing were either summarily dismissed, cut short, or publicly denounced, receiving little press coverage. One exception was Anne Alpern, solicitor general for the City of Pittsburgh, who refused to be silenced and used almost all of her ten minutes arguing with McCarthy about the palpable need for more public housing in a city dominated by slums.

> Senator Mc—Your 10 minutes have expired.
>
> Anne Alpern—I think you are in error as to the time.
>
> Senator Mc–Your 10 minutes have expired.
>
> Anne A—I would like to note an objection on the record.
>
> Senator Mc—Will the officer remove the witness.
>
> Anne A—I would like to note an objection on the record; I have looked at the time and I have not had 10 minutes. I do not think it is a fair way to conduct the hearing. He will not have to remove me I will leave.
>
> Senator Mc—How much more time would you like?
>
> Anne A—10 minutes to make my statement.
>
> Senator Mc—10 minutes more?
>
> Anne A—You give me whatever time you desire.
>
> Senator Mc—Would 5 minutes be alright?

McCarthy continued to bait Alpern, taking the anti-government position used by Nicklas. Alpern hit the nail on the head when she responded:

> I think of Washington not as some foreign power, but as a part of our democracy; and by working together we can establish a better government. . . . We require central planning and that's what we have in Washington. . . . I believe in a democracy. People are entitled to the right to live and in that is the right to live decently . . . I feel it's necessary everywhere that all children be given a right to live under decent circumstances.

Alpern also made an important rejoinder to people like Nicklas who argued that government housing was a political football:

> There were some very unfair, untrue, malicious statements made about [our housing] authority today. Naturally, people in low income groups belong to certain parties and members of the real estate group belong to other parties, and no-

body in the real estate board has applied for admission into the housing authority because their income is such that they could not.

This was more than the senator could tolerate. At this point he abruptly stopped her testimony.[18]

The campaign against public housing was not enough to convince the ill-housed that public housing was not in their interest. The contemporary press observed: "Many people believe that public sponsored housing is the answer, not only in the slums, but for all modest income groups."[19] But, claimed *Fortune*, the substitute for public housing and socialist demands was an efficient housing industry:

A house is the most urgent, most valued, and most studied demand of an American family; failure by capitalism to satisfy this elemental want will do more to undermine free institutions than 10,000 Union Square orators. . . . And the lesson for the industry should be clear. No one gets far in proposing public ownership for the automobile industry, the steel industry the farm machinery industry, the milk producers or the oil industry, not even socialists hope to socialize efficient, up and coming industries.[20]

Although the committee was violently against public housing, it was less than clear what they believed the solution to the overall housing crisis should be. Generally, McCarthy was in favor of mass-produced, single-family homes. Without revamping the outmoded small-scale home building industry, however, there could be no moderately priced homes for those clamoring for housing.

By the late 1940s the housing industry was criticized by conservatives and liberals alike. From the *Wall Street Journal* to *Fortune* to *Reader's Digest*, criticisms formerly made only by the RPAA and New Deal supporters were now launched by the mainstream business community. Almost like a mantra, "Make houses like Fords" was in the air. *Fortune* ran a two-part series arguing that housing was "the industry capitalism forgot." *Reader's Digest* picked up the series and condensed it for its readers, and more and more people wanted houses to be produced on the assembly line like autos, shoes, and radios. This was not so simple, given the shaky state of the industry. Even the most conservative members of the real estate lobby agreed that the federal government, with its vast resources and housing know-how, should underwrite mortgages and loans through the FHA and the Home Owners Loan Corporation (HOLC). The building industry and its lobbyists drew the line, however, at government's actually building homes.

Serious political forces joined the fray. The newly powerful labor movement, including both the AFL and CIO, openly endorsed and agitated for the passage of TEW. Veterans organizations and social welfare groups as well as progressive government officials also supported the bill. Even McCarthy realized that "A great mass of the people seem to consider federal aid and public housing as one and the same thing . . . ," although he went on to say that "though it may be determined that the great group of your low income people need federal aid to be properly housed, . . . it does not of necessity follow that aid must come through public ownership and control of housing."[21]

A key motive behind the housing hearings was to undermine the credibility of this broadly based New Deal labor–reform coalition. Conservatives tried to accomplish this by pitting the house-hungry public against workers, blaming the housing shortage on labor and labor unions. The private housing lobby argued that old-fashioned, lazy, overpaid, underworked construction workers were blocking people from acquiring their dream house. This labor bashing happened both inside the committee hearings and in the popular and business press.

As Richard Gray, president of the Building and Construction Trades Department of the American Federation of Labor, testified to the committee: "In the course of the last two years a widespread campaign of propaganda has been conducted in an attempt to discredit unions in the Building and Construction Industries, and to persuade the public that labor is responsible for either the high cost of housing or the housing shortage itself. These charges have appeared in newspaper articles, in special columns, in magazines, and in every other medium of publicity."[22]

Gray was right. In articles in Look, Collier's, the Saturday Evening Post, the Wall Street Journal, and the newsreel series The March of Time construction workers were blamed for the slow pace of production and resisting new technology. The media castigated bricklayers for not laying enough bricks, painters for painting with too small a paintbrush, plumbers for refusing to install new fixtures, and masons and plasterers for refusing to do work for which they were not trained. Older, skilled craftworkers, the argument ran, refused to accept modern methods and stuck to slow, old-world ways.

Many of these charges were patently false. For example, "the big burly bricklayer" was constantly accused of slowing down, limiting production to 400 or 500 bricks a day compared with the prewar record of 1,200 a day. Yet according to Richard Gray:

> One of the most unfair and malicious pieces of propaganda was a newsreel type of movie produced in 1946 by *The March of Time*. This particular release of the film showed what purported to be a shot of an actual construction job, with two brick layers working on a wall. The older man turns to the younger one, waving him to slow down. "Take it easy, Bud," he says, "you will live longer. 500 bricks a day is plenty!"
>
> Millions of movie goers seeing this picture naturally thought it to be a shot of an actual occurrence illustrating a widely prevalent practice. But the trained eye of a brick mason could readily see that the scene was a deliberately and expensively staged hoax. Evidently the producers could not find a real brick layer to do the scene and those who knew enough could readily see that the actor hired for it had never held a trowel in his life; he was clutching it in his fist, holding it straight up, the way no real brick layer would.[23]

Actually, brickmasons changed their practices because the mode of production changed from solid walls of brick to a brick veneer with cement and cinderblock with a heavy mortar fill. According to Gray, "The work on this new type of brick veneer construction was in sharp contrast with the daily output on a solid brick wall, on which the number of brick laid may easily be more than twice as great in a day. Any responsible masonry contractor will testify that even 400 bricks a day on brick veneer construction on a typical single family house is a good record of the bricklayer's performance."[24]

A similar smear campaign was run against painters. As Gray explained,

> The charge has been made in many cities that union painters either refused, or are
> forbidden by union rules to use the spray gun on home building. It is made as a
> flat assertion with the idea of conveying the impression that a modern technologi-
> cal improvement is being held back by unions intent on perpetuating the slower,
> less efficient and more costly methods which would yield greater earning [power]
> to them.

Listing a number of national magazines and newspapers in which this charge appeared, Gray concluded, "The layman not familiar with the facts is likely to feel
indignant about the obstacles being placed in the path of progress by labor
unions."[25]

Actually, the alleged culprit, the International Brotherhood of Painters
(IBP), had initiated a comprehensive study of the uses of the spray painting machine as early as 1944. By 1946 the IBP convention adopted a national program
of standards to govern the use of the spray painting machine in the United States
and Canada. These standards reflected a study showing that the spray gun exposed workers to considerable amounts of lead and other types of poisoning, but
that much of the danger could be prevented by using modern protective methods. Workers refused to use the spray gun only when such protective devices
were lacking—which made the gun a menace to health and safety. Although the
spray gun had wide use in industrial construction, where painting on large flat
surfaces is more efficient than the paintbrush, the study found that at least 50
percent of work in residential construction required paintbrushes because of
molding, trim, sash, and different colors. "In the case of single family houses,"
the study reported, "it is doubtful that any substantial economy in cost can be
achieved."[26] The spray gun was yet another red herring used to assail unions and
workers.

Conservatives also attacked customary craftworkers' practices of training
journeymen, hiring apprentices, and making decisions about production. When
the home building industry had been a small-time operation, those traditions
and methods made sense. In the era of modernization, conservatives argued,

such old-fashioned ways stood in the way of progress. In one hearing McCarthy said:

> I received a letter this morning from a contractor in Chicago. I don't know any-
> thing about his background and don't know how authentic this is, but he made
> this comment. He said that he couldn't have a carpenter put on a piece of wall-
> board; that the wallboard had to be put on by a lather; that the lather couldn't
> work under a carpenter boss, that he had to work under a lathe boss; that the lathe
> boss couldn't work under a carpenter boss, he had to work under a plasterer boss.
> Because of that, he had to take three men to tack on a piece of wallboard and take
> them off of a job where they were needed. If that sort of thing is true, it is rather vi-
> cious.[27]

McCarthy and his real estate and media allies sought to exclude outright the organized skilled workers from the new, lucrative mass-housing market because they were used to high wages, guaranteed benefits, overtime, and pensions. Claiming that these workers were in short supply and too demanding, McCarthy and others in the building industry called for unskilled non-union workers to meet the demands of the housing crisis. If some of these claims against skilled workers were justified, the alliance clearly was not interested in working with trade unions to sort out the problems the new methods caused. As John Nicklas, Jr., put it, "Private business interests are proceeding well in the building of homes today, but they could do a much better job if they were not hampered by intolerable labor practices."[28]

The committee turned a deaf ear to the union's national codes and standards, but they were open to hearing about the necessity of establishing new standardized build-ing codes and practices. Local building codes had not changed for decades and were a major obstacle to mass housing. Ostensibly intended to insure health and safety, these codes in fact protected the interests of contractors and manufactur-ers who produced certain materials and wanted them used.

Many of these building codes came from an era when homes doubled as workshops for home industries such as carpentry, shoemaking, and steel. Thick walls were required to keep in the heat, and solid wood floors were needed to support materials for home manufacturing and storage of foods. Local codes also reflected the political clout of particular regional industries. For example, heavily wooded Arkansas and Tennessee allowed only wood-framed constructions, while in brickmaking Denver, wood-frame construction was outlawed. In glass-making Newark, New Jersey, and Toledo, Ohio, codes encouraged the use of structural glass blocks. In all, there were over 2,000 local codes blocking modern construction methods.

Senator McCarthy, who had made himself quite knowledgeable about impediments to mass housing, explained:

> I had a gentleman who is in the automotive industry in the other day, and he was talking about the consideration his company was giving to the mass production of homes, and he made a comparison which I thought was rather good. He said, the situation today, as far as mass production of homes is concerned, is pretty much as it would have been twenty years ago if in one town you had to have automobiles with rubber fenders and in another town you had to have a wheel base of five feet and in another town you had to have a wheel base of four feet eight inches. In another town a certain sized tire and in another town a certain type horn. . . . It was his position the codes more than anything else act as an absolute bar against any intelligent low cost of mass production.[29]

Local codes also prevented the introduction of innovative building materials. Many of these—plastics, asbestos, gypsum (plasterboard, more commonly known by its trade name, Sheetrock), fire-resistant plywood, copper tubing for toilets—first tested in Greenbelt and then during the war, now were seen as essential for construction of cheaper housing. According to an article in *Collier's*, "to catch up with the inventions and discoveries of recent years in both materials and building practices, most of the existing codes require review and revision." In the opinion of Robert R. Wason, former president of the National Association of Manufacturers, "every municipal building code in the country is obsolete and ready for the junk pile."[30]

In addition to attacking existing codes, the committee criticized the industry's dated methods of obtaining building materials. In a *Look* article Thurman Arnold summed up the problem: "The Henry Fords of housing can't get started, [because] building material producers were fixing prices through private arrangements or through trade associations. . . . Some material distributors were trying to raise the price of their services by secretly agreeing on price mark-ups. Others were trying to make sure that all business passed through their hands and that no new methods were introduced on which they could make no overcharge."[31]

Moreover, mass builders could not order materials directly from the manufacturers, instead they had to purchase through a web of middleman procurers. According to Levitt, "The building materials companies, United States Gypsum, . . . General Electric, Johns-Mansville, every single plumbing manufacturer, every company that I know of . . . says that they will not sell Levitt, they will not sell Burns, they will not sell Higgins, they will not sell anybody else."[32]

The housing hearings brought all of these issues to national attention. What did not come out in the hearings was that big manufacturers of building materials, such as Johns-Mansville, Celotex Corporation (the largest producers of asbestos), and U.S. Gypsum, were not merely backward: they were making it difficult for Levitt and other mass builders because in principle they opposed mass housing developments. These manufacturers made money by supplying materials for traditional expensive homes at high cost. The new Levittlike developments meant supplying a mass market at lower costs. Consequently, both Johns-Mansville and U.S. Gypsum conducted publicity campaigns aimed at debunking the low-cost postwar dream house.[33]

Conservatives found an important ally in Levitt, who objected to the current system because it required buying supplies from a middleman rather than from the manufacturer himself. Levitt testified to the Senate committee, "The markup for what I call a parasitical function—and I use the word 'function' very advisedly—ranges somewhere between 20 and 55% for somebody doing nothing but billing us. I admit it requires stationery and a three cent stamp."[34] Levitt made national news by contending that gray marketing—the buying practices of middlemen—increased the retail cost of a house from $5,500 to

$7,500. He argued, "Unless you can get a semblance of economic, sane thinking in the building industry, you will not attract talent, you will not attract know-how. Nobody wants to enter into a business and risk capital on a catch-as-catch-can basis."[35]

Yet neither Levitt nor McCarthy attacked the corporate giants who were truly to blame. Instead they focused on easier targets: the middlemen. Isidore Ginsberg, the well-known gypsum middleman mogul, became one of the committee's scapegoats. He was a Jewish, "pugnacious, articulate, 310-pound, New York attorney," who McCarthy dubbed, "the most vicious of the gray-marketeers."[36] The battle between Ginsberg and McCarthy was high drama, covered daily in the *New York Times*.

McCarthy demanded that Ginsberg turn over his records and building contacts, threatening to hold him in contempt if he didn't. When Ginsberg protested, "We deal in nothing but free enterprise and take a reasonable profit, and nothing else," McCarthy, usually a sympathetic friend of private enterprise, replied, "Your enterprise is just too damn free, Ginsberg." McCarthy told Ginsberg that he would put him out of business, to which Ginsberg exclaimed, "Only in Russia could you prevent me from doing that." Although these tactics did offend many on the committee and in the Senate, McCarthy turned over his investigation of Ginsberg to the District Attorney of Queens County. Ginsberg was convicted of grand larceny and the gray-marketing practice was somewhat curtailed.[37]

Despite the committee's attack on particular individuals, there was truth in its critique of the housing industry. Clearly the industry, were it to switch over to modern modes of production, required new leadership. The "Henry Fords of housing"—men like William Levitt of Long Island, Fritz Burns of California, and Andrew Higgins, a mass builder in New Orleans—would need to embrace modernization in all its aspects.

David L. Krooth, the general counsel of the National Association of Housing Manufacturers (the prefabrication lobby group), detailed how new mass-production methods would enable the housing industry to build affordable houses:

These are the five reasons why the new industry will produce houses at less than the cost of conventionally built homes: First, the number of man hours which go into a house by machine processes is substantially reduced; second, there is a great reduction in the amount of skilled labor with the substitution of semi-skilled or unskilled labor; third, modern industrial and engineering methods will produce efficiencies that will result in greatly reduced costs compared with handicraft methods; fourth, the time for producing and completing a house is greatly reduced with corresponding reductions in financing, overhead, administrative and other costs; fifth, the profits per house will be less because this new industry will apply the same "big volume-small profit" kind of manufacturing technique which has given Americans in every field except housing the highest standard of living in the world.[38]

Still, it remained unclear even after all the political battles whether government or the private home-building industry would provide housing for the masses. But the congressional hearings on housing, together with the public relations multimedia blitz of the private real estate lobby, succeeded in reframing the national discussion about affordable housing. The housing hearings served as a public forum to attack government-sponsored public housing, alleged lazy and inefficient union laborers, local building codes, and gray marketeers. The modern private mass builders emerged from the hearings as heroes who promised to lead the country out of crisis and build dream houses for all. This new coalition forged between political conservatives and the master builders would define the parameters of suburban postwar housing. The ties between Senator McCarthy and William Levitt went far beyond the hearings. During the hearings, McCarthy made a well-publicized visit to Levittown, then under construction, and in a speech he gave in 1948 to the banking industry, Levitt praised McCarthy as a leading figure in housing. Noting that the FHA would become a permanent fixture of government, Levitt argued,

This is not idle speculation on my part. The Senator from Wisconsin, Mr. Mc-Carthy, has already delivered a major speech in which the thoughts that I have tried to express here were clearly enunciated by him. Mr. McCarthy is first a veteran, second a U.S. Senator, third a very aggressive young man typical of the type of leadership that you might expect in Washington from now on, and fourth, he exhibits a passionate interest in housing that almost amounts to a phobia. Parenthetically, I might add he is also a Republican.[39]

Chapter Nine

Home Ownership: Is It Sound?

Although the housing hearings forever transformed public discussion of how to house the masses, it left a significant problem unanswered: Would new mass housing built by private developers be affordable? The public debate over housing made it clear to many that owning a house was not just a fantasy; it had concrete advantages. Many who rented apartments looked to home ownership to free them from despotic landlords who raised the rent, refused to make building improvements, enforced restrictive rules and regulations and threatened tenants with eviction. Home ownership also offered tax breaks and the security of a lasting investment that could increase in value.

Though Americans' desire to own homes was tempered by the fear of taking on large financial responsibilities, the new federal financing agencies of the 1930s and 1940s had raised public's expectations. In 1946 many called on the federal government to help bear the financial burden of home ownership. Furthermore, less persuaded by the ideology of home ownership than by their finances, many people demanded that the government aid those who chose to rent as well as those who wanted to buy.

A 1946 *Fortune* survey discovered that "The U.S. people are strikingly in favor of positive government action to end the severe [housing] shortage. A majority of those with opinions want the government to embark on a large scale building program." The poll also found that more people, particularly in the North Atlantic states, preferred renting an apartment to owning a home. "In addition, Government construction is favored particularly by the young, veterans, by those looking for a place to live, by those living in large cities and by the poor. In short, the two-thirds of the nation that needed housing."[1] The Economic Report of the President to the Congress in 1949 also stated that "about 80% of the housing now being built is for sale, although veterans and others with families of uncertain future size and jobs of uncertain tenure would much prefer to rent."[2] If so many preferred renting, why not build rental housing? Why was home ownership so critical to the maintenance of a democratic society?

The answer is that Levitt, Burns, Lustrom, and the other master builders, along with their allies—the bank and loan associations, real estate lobby, lumber industry, media, chambers of commerce, and conservative politicians—knew rental housing would never make them money. The automobile industry, the highway lobby, and other appliance manufacturers felt the same way. Together these groups tried to persuade the government and the public that individual home ownership was crucial for preserving "the American way of life."

Of course, they were up against the national experience of hardship and depression that lasted more than a decade. In the New Deal the government stepped in to guarantee a new standard of living, changing the notion that the American way was synonymous with unfettered free enterprise and laissez-faire government. Big business naturally battled these New Deal philosophies from the beginning. The National Association of Manufacturers (NAM), for instance, mounted a nationwide campaign against government trespassing on business turf. Coopting the grand rhetoric of the New Deal, they argued through billboards, movies, radio, and so-called grassroots organizations that only business-style free enterprise could create a decent standard of living and that government intervention endangered democracy.

After the war, business groups intensified their campaign. People who feared that the capitalist system was inherently unstable and could collapse again still supported New Deal policies. NAM promised that private enterprise had learned its lesson and swore that it would provide decent housing at an affordable price. Moreover, NAM sentimentally identified home ownership with patriotism and democracy, touting it as a bulwark against Communist invasion and government interference in private lives.[3] A nation of renters, they suggested, was unstable and un-American. The master builders and their allies interpreted history through a singular and superior Anglo-American lens, conceiving of private property as the bastion of self-government. This distinctive heritage was democratic, while renters—usually immigrants—were thought to harbor anarchist and Communist ideas. Home ownership would create a barrier against these "foreign ideologies." As W. W. Jennings stated, "Ownership of homes is the best guarantee against communism and socialism and the various 'bad isms' of life. I do not say that it is an infallible guarantee, but I do say, that owners of homes usually are more interested in the safeguarding of the worthwhile things of life and the traditions of our national history than are renters and tenants."[4]

And master builder and NAM supporter Fritz Burns contended, "It is no less important now than in ages gone by for people to have their own 'vine and fig tree' their own bit of this earth, where they are at least masters to some extent of their fate."[5] People who had no vine or fig tree and therefore were not masters of their fate, he warned, threatened the very fabric of democracy:

> It is doubtful whether democracy is possible where tenants overwhelmingly out-number homeowners. For democracy is not a privilege; it is a responsibility, and human nature rarely volunteers to shoulder responsibility, but has to be driven by the whip of necessity. The need to protect and guard the home is the whip that has proved, beyond all others efficacious in driving men to discharge the duties of self-government, and from the landed barons of King John down through squirearchy and yeomanry of England to the makers of the American revolution, the men who have preserved the civil liberties of the English speaking peoples have been the men with a stake in society.[6]

Although the builders disparaged immigrant renters as un-American, they also urged immigrants to purchase a home, suggesting that the achievement of the American dream—and the acquisition of refined Anglo-American traditions the immigrants supposedly needed—would be part of the package. Builder Fred C. Trump claimed in a full-page ad in the *New York Times* in 1949,

> For generations, the Statue of Liberty has greeted newcomers to the United States of America as a symbol of our basic freedom, which has made possible the American way of life. And now a new community at the entrance of New York Harbor symbolizes this American way. Shore Haven is a new monument to the American

spirit of free enterprise. The project was conceived, planned, executed by Fred C.
Trump, acting as a free and rugged individualist to meet the basic needs for shelter. . . . And now, for generations to come, hundreds of American families will
live happily in this newly created garden apartment center, making it a living
monument to the "American Way of Life."[7]

Home ownership in the age of mass production, mobile people and modern
conveniences was quite different of course from building a log cabin on the frontier. As Nathan Straus, former head of USHA, derisively noted: "Under conditions of modern civilization, a man does not have to buy a cow because his family
needs milk. He should not have to buy a house because his family needs a
home." And the prominent social thinker Robert Lynd observed in the late
1940s, "Here is a root problem of current American democracy; our failure to redefine the conditions of 'freedom' in step with changing complexity of daily living. In home ownership, as in so many other current matters, neither the things
bought nor the conditions surrounding the purchase are so simple today as when
they were when the traditions concerning home ownership were being laid
down." Lynd worried that home-hungry veterans with money in their pockets
were easy targets for the sentimental pitch of the private housing industry:

Within the reassuring, unequivocal precepts of the American tradition, a responsible family can loose its shirt. This is complicated by the fact that not only does
business organize itself to keep alive the unequivocal sentiment of the rightness of
home ownership, but even our government lends itself to the ends of the real estate and home-selling interests. In the midst of this torrent of ballyhoo stands a
man with the family—no fool, and a man who means to be thrifty and do the best
he can by his family, but also a fellow incapable of being a specialist in everything
and having to rely at many points on what they say. His question "Ought we
buy?" receives in the main only one answer from every side; "Sure! It's the American Way."[8]

Was homeownership the American way, or was it all a scam? Whatever one's
ideological bent, the renting route was becoming increasingly difficult. New

dwelling units built for rent had declined from 41 percent during 1922 to 1928 to 17 percent during 1946 to 1950. As Straus fretted, "The people who need these homes are entitled to a free choice as between renting and buying. They are denied that choice today."[9]

Despite the decline of rental housing, a new group of housing experts came out in support of an alternative to individual privately owned houses in the suburbs. This group, which followed the lead of the RPAA, included Nathan Straus, who had come under fire in the McCarthy hearings; Charles Abrams, attorney and public housing activist; Charles Lewis, director of the Buhl Foundation that managed Chatham Village; and John Dean, sociologist and planner. Deeply suspicious of private industry's invocation of the American way as a means of selling houses, leery of builders' claims that prefabrication would produce quality housing, and concerned that the nation could fall back into another depression, they advocated in books and popular articles the building of planned communities, subsidized by the government, that offered rentals as well as homes for sale.

Supported by many veterans groups, liberal politicians, housing reformers, and civic organizations, these experts called for a government-sponsored housing program based on rent. Unlike propagandists who spoke of home owning as a time-honored American tradition of independence, reformers spoke of home ownership as voluntary servitude, especially given the change from small-town craft society to modern industrial order. Charles Lewis argued:

> It is no longer sufficient to attempt to refute these forces by singing of 'the old oaken bucket.' . . . The feeling of insecurity brings many families to realize that independence is to be had, not by attaching oneself to a lot, but by avoiding long term commitment, which can be terminated by great difficulty and great loss, or by both. . . . But it is time to recognize that changing conditions of life are making ever increasing numbers of American families want to rent their homes rather than to buy them.[10]

John Dean discerned, "In all the talk about freedom from landlords, too little is said of freedom from mortgage debt, and freedom to move as one's job and family require."[11]

Private industry realized that rather than fight public pressure to build rentals they should turn the demand to their advantage. They took heart from a 1937 Roper survey that found that if people could buy a house yet "pay for it just like rent," they would perceive home ownership as feasible.[12] Private builders reasoned that renting could be a first step in transforming renters into buyers. After 1946 most ad campaigns for new houses began calculating costs in terms of rent. One of Levitt's early ads reads, "$52 a month for veterans only."[13]

The ads made purchasing a home seem as easy as buying a toothbrush, but there were significant risks: hidden costs and future financial burdens. The Browns, as Straus described them in *Two-Thirds of a Nation*, his cautionary study of the housing market, were taken in by housing ads, like many an unwary first-time buyer. Ted was a veteran who earned $60 a week working in a factory while his wife, Peggy, took care of their children. Eager to move out of the cramped quarters they shared with in-laws, they started combing the real estate page. They hoped to rent a decent four-room apartment for $60 a month, but none was available.

When the Browns could not find a rental, an advertisement like the following caught their attention: "The irresistible ranch home that set Long Island buzzing with excitement. Set in a spacious, carefully planned community, this ranch sensation is an architect's dream come true. Automatic kitchen, fluorescent lighting, two walls of baked enamel cabinets, radiant heat. No cash for vets only $68 a month for everything." After some hesitation, the Browns bought a ranch home for "$72.60" a month. The ad claimed that the $72.60 was just like paying rent and the Browns asked few questions. "Instead they did what more than 11 million other families have done in the last decade: they bought a house—not on comparative values, but on comparative adjectives."

Why wasn't paying $72.60 like paying rent? The new home owners were unaware that before they even entered their house, they would have to pay $300 dollars in closing charges and after they moved in, the cost of gas, electricity, water, fuel, garbage collection, upkeep, and repairs brought their monthly expenses up to $100 a month, not counting the cost of Ted's commuter ticket and the car they needed. Straus concluded, "Like hundreds of other young couples, the Browns find out too late that $72.60 like rent pays all is, in the word of Theodore

Roosevelt 'a falsehood better called by a shorter and uglier word.'" The Browns
might have found out that they "did not own the house, but instead, that the
house owned them."[14]

The jump into home ownership had long-term consequences for a family.
John Dean maintained in his influential book *Home Ownership: Is It Sound?*, "If
a family makes a bad mistake in purchasing food, clothing, or rented shelter, a
correction is possible within a reasonable span of time. In the home ownership
field the market is not self-correcting, and it is especially costly to learn by experience."[15]

The real estate interests vigorously protested articles and books such as those
by Straus and Dean that questioned the ideal of home ownership. Not only was
Straus and his books denounced by McCarthy in the hearings, newspapers sympathetic to industry joined the fray. The *New Haven Register*, for instance, in an
unsigned critical review of Straus stated "What appears to me the strongest arguments for home ownership are neglected by Straus. Some things in life cannot
be measured in dollars and cents. Bringing up children on city streets cannot be
compared with rearing a family in a small town or country environment. No
matter how poor a home owning family may consider itself, it is getting more out
of life than tenancy."[16]

Real estate interests and master builders were aided in their campaign for
home ownership by FHA subsidies and support. The FHA assisted private industry in advertising designed to create a suburban home ownership market.
Through ads and billboards such as "Own a More Livable Home! Pay For It
Like Rent" and radio programs subsidized by General Electric entitled "What
Home Means To Me," the FHA circulated literature and pamphlets, sponsored
expositions, and cooperated with local realtors to promote subdivisions.[17]

Housing reformers criticized the alliance between the FHA and the master
builders. John Dean contended, "In the minds of many laymen the 'FHA'
stands for a plan whereby home ownership is made feasible for moderate income
families. But the FHA plan suggests that its main purpose has been the stimulation of the building industry, an aim which quite naturally turned its attention to
promoting home ownership."[18]

Although master builders and realtors praised the FHA building standards,

Straus and Dean argued that the FHA tolerated shoddy housing: small rooms, crackpot prefab schemes, and shacks resembling emergency war housing. In 1951 Fritz Burns boasted of having produced houses for $5,000. Investigations disclosed that these dwellings had an area of only 480 square feet—significantly smaller than the 575 square feet that the Los Angeles Housing Authority required as a minimum in its public housing program.[19]

The situation became so extreme that in 1950 the American Public Health Association (APHA) mandated minimum space standards for health and safety.[20] According to APHA member Dr. Winslow, "In most of our mushrooming suburban housing developments today you cannot tell the house from the garage. If we progress much further in this direction, you won't be able to tell the house from the letter box."[21]

Master builders trying to cut costs disagreed. From the builders' standpoint, such regulations interfered with what they felt was their right to build as they saw fit. The controversy escalated. In 1950 the *New York Times* reported:

The Long Island Home Builders Institute [was] authorized by its Board of Directors to start immediate legal action to set aside the order of the Town Board of Babylon, which increased the minimum habitable floor area of homes from 400 to 800 square feet. The Executive Secretary of the Institute said that . . . the determination of the size of homes is an improper use of the police powers of the state . . . and has no relation to the safety, health, morals, or welfare of the citizens.[22]

Meanwhile, home buyers felt standards were important for protecting their long-term interests against quick schemes and shoddy builders. The public certainly did need protection from builders who were testing new materials and methods, especially the new prefabrication industry. The Lustrom Corporation, for instance, builders of factory-produced homes made of metal, announced with great fanfare that they would produce factory-built houses at record speed. Subsidized by an unusually large government loan of $37.5 million, the corporation produced few houses, having spent the money instead on newspaper and magazine publicity, as well as a widely circulated promotional pamphlet written by Senator McCarthy, who was compensated handsomely by Lustrom. The company had boasted that it would manufacture 120,000 houses in 1948, or 125 a day; but by 1950 they only completed 2,096 houses. In the end, the government put the Lustrom Corporation on the auction block in an attempt to recover millions in loans.[23]

Such abuses certainly made prospective home buyers wish the government was as involved in constructing housing as it had been earlier. Government in fact could have continued to build housing communities had public housing agencies not been reduced to the point where their mandate was to provide housing projects for the very poor. This policy left the master builders in charge of delivering inexpensive housing for modest-income families. Straus, who had real experience as head of USHA, argued that it could have been otherwise:

> The use of government subsidies for "brick and mortar" to build up new assets and to meet social needs is . . . also in the American tradition. The railroads of the United States were not built up by subsidizing passengers so that they could pay railroad fares. Instead, a network of railroads that opened up our country was made possible by huge federal subsidies.
>
> The automobile industry in the United States became great largely by reason of government subsidy. The Federal Government and the State Government did *not* make grants to families so that the wage earner could drive over private toll roads to his place of employment. Instead, the government contributed to the automobile industry. The subsidies made possible the construction of a great highway system. This was the largest subsidy ever granted by the government in the history of our country and produced the most notable results. The average amount expended for this purpose by federal and state governments *annually* in the period from 1935–1940, was nearly a billion dollars.[24]

Private builders, Straus insisted, should not be subsidized by the government. The government itself should be building planned communities.

But the real estate interests successfully contended that the federal government should "subsidize people and not brick and mortar."[25] In other words, the real estate interests wanted federal government out of the construction end of housing, but they were happy to be eating out of the hidden hand of government subsidies. In the climate of postwar rhetoric, which equated home owning with apple pie and government intervention with the evils of communism, it made sense to be discrete about the government's role in providing shelter. As Robert Lynd succinctly spelled out, "Business succeeds rather better than government in enforcing its coercions because the coercions of business are disguised as 'choices.'"[26]

The real estate lobby liked to pretend that it held the high moral ground and had the nation's best interest at heart. This was disingenuous. Government housing was built on the assumption that it was the peoples' right to live in decent homes in a viable community and that the government had a duty to provide the services that would make this possible. Private housing was built only for profit. Government-built housing supplied a wide weave of community activities and institutions, including provisions for education, health, recreation, politics , leisure, greenbelts, cooperative shopping, newspapers, and social life.

In contrast, as sociologist John Liell noted in his thorough study of Levittown, "The Levitts knew more of real estate values than they did of community values."[27] Commercial village greens and swimming pools may have been pleasant but they were a far cry from a community in which the basic necessities and amenities of life were available and democratically managed.

Moreover, commercial builders had no interest in attracting diverse residents. By restricting mass building to mainly white veterans, the master builders insured that their developments would be racially, generationally, and economically homogeneous. These policies gave a large group of people the opportunity of owning their first house and made for communities that were integrated ethnically, but they were far from democratic. Government housing, though racially segregated, had at least tried to be somewhat more inclusive, providing homes for families, single people, elderly people, middle and working class, white and blue collar. Bryn J. Hovde of the Pittsburgh Housing Authority summed up the philosophy behind government housing:

A well planned neighborhood is one which avoids extreme stratification of family income groups; consequently every effort should be made to make the community attractive to families representing as broad a belt of incomes as possible. . . . What we want to achieve is a neighborhood to produce good Americans, not good low income Americans or upper income Americans.[28]

This vision, however, was forgotten, as private developers took over the business of constructing homes for postwar America.

Chapter Ten

The Master Builders and the Creation
of Modern Suburbia

While Joseph McCarthy and others insisted that private enterprise should assume responsibility for housing the nation, trade experts debated just how this might be done. In the late 1940s many questions remained unanswered: How would low-income homes be constructed, and how would the financing operate? The most pressing issue, though, was what economic class would have the option to buy. The answers to these issues were compelling; many eager families were waiting impatiently to be housed.[1]

Writers in *Architectural Forum* and other housing professionals had known since the late 1930s that the traditional market was "almost without exception aimed at the better-than-average income brackets; the balance of the population is dependent almost entirely on the second hand housing facilities which this group discards. . . . Similarly, because most new houses are beyond the reach of the average pocketbook, home building responds only indirectly to actual housing needs, and directly only to an increased demand from the above-average income group." The magazine contended that the way out of narrow market confines were large-scale, limited-dividend housing projects.

> In almost every instance the success of these projects depended upon an almost
> complete reversal of ordinary home building procedure. They were treated as in-
> vestment properties, were built for rent, and instead of being aimed at the shrink-
> ing market of the above-average income group, they were aimed at the growing

below-average income group: a market which probably will continue to increase for sometime to come whether by additions from above or below.[2]

Within a decade *Fortune* would go on to claim that private developers, not limited-dividend corporations, should start producing homes for the below-average income group, and that it was unlikely private industry would bother with homes for the lowest income groups. "Few industries provide products at prices low income groups can pay. The slum dweller cannot buy a new Chevrolet or a refrigerator. If it's important that he have a decent dwelling—and without doubt it is—then the state will have to help provide it. The housing industry cannot be indicted for its ill treatment of a man who everyone treats badly."[3]

Who, then, would make up the new market everyone agreed was so important? According to *Fortune,* in 1947 the "modal income of American families, the income of the largest number, was about $2,750 a year or $230 a month. If one-fifth to one-quarter is available for rent, there is a mass market for houses renting for about $60 a month or selling for about $7,000. This the private housing market can be expected to supply. It calls for solid, decent, and, inevitably, somewhat standardized shelter."[4] In other words, the working-middle classes.

Reconceptualizing the housing market was crucial for private industry to agree to house this new class of people. *Architectural Forum* reported that "a rich market for housing exists midway between the ceiling of government subsidized projects and what has heretofore been regarded as the floor for private enterprise."[5] In part, new theories of a consumer-based economy made this market visible to private enterprise. Future homeowners were evaluated not only as potential purchasers of houses, but equally important, as consumers who bought cars and appliances with savings accumulated during the prosperous wartime economy. The money they spent on the new mass-produced goods of the machine age made it clear that they could afford homes, too.

The new market—for the most part veterans dubbed Mr. and Mrs. Kilroy—represented a cross section of the skilled working class, white-collar professionals, and second-generation immigrants. If affordable mass housing was to be built for Mr. and Mrs. Kilroy, it had to be constructed with modern methods. The practices of custom craft builders of old had to give way to the techniques of corporate merchant builders. In the late 1940s merchant builders—men such as Levitt, Bohannon, and Burns, who integrated and controlled all the aspects of housing as Rockefeller and Carnegie had done with oil and steel—became pivotal figures in the building of low-cost modern houses. Their ideas drew on twenty years of debate and experimentation about how to build modern houses at a price within range for those not traditionally considered home owners.[6]

Building new modern houses on a large scale demanded design and production methods pioneered by public housing. Merchant builders in the late 1930s had begun to copy these techniques to simplify construction. In 1937 the editors of *Architectural Forum* maintained that public housing had shown that

> Besides the undeniable efficiency and economy of shop fabrication, it is proved in practice to have a good many other advantages. Most important of these has been the fact that the technique of shop fabrication has permitted the use of materials and processes resulting in better quality and lowered cost . . . such products are generally lighter, stronger, more attractive, and a great deal cheaper than their counterparts made by hand.[7]

Architects and builders contemplated smaller houses without basements, with radiant heating, an open space interior, and built-in plumbing and wiring centered in the kitchen and bathroom.[8] The only thing left was the mass production of the frame and foundation. Postwar builders took all this into consideration and would use this legacy as they pondered building affordable modern houses for a new market.

But what kind of new homes did Americans desire? In 1938 *Life* magazine, in conjunction with *Architectural Forum*

> presented for the critical examination of its 18 million readers, eight houses designed for four typical American families. The families covered an income range from $200 to $1,200 a year. For each family, one modern and one traditional house were designed. . . . Of *Life*'s readers who voted on their preferences a phenomenal

45% plumped for modern. . . . In a particularly pointed manner and on a national scale these eight houses show that that the modern house is rapidly emerging from its extremist swaddling clothes.[9]

If these were ideals in the late 1930s, by the mid–1940s they had become imperatives. During the 1940s more people married than ever before, at three times the previous rate. Stalled by the war, couples anxious to have children and looking for a place in which to raise a family demanded brand-new houses they had seen advertised everywhere. Aware of this challenge, a 1944 *Architectural Forum* article warned its conventional builders, "Even if not a single factory built house is made or sold in your entire area, the threat will be there. Your customers will see it in the advertisements, in the home magazines, in the movies—and you will have to match the results. There will be the threat within your own business from the aggressive and uninhibited group of merchant builders in your midst."[10]

Merchant builders looked to the mass-production methods that worked wonders in producing cars, but as *Architectural Forum* cautioned, a house was not "an isolated article of commerce like an automobile, but a complex social cell resisting the production line."[11] How then could modern building methods be applied to something as complex and intractable as a home?

In a 1948 *Life* Roundtable on Housing a group of merchant builders debated the relative methods of three options: the factory-built home, the prefabricated single house, and the prefabricated community. Some builders, such as the Lustrom Corporation in Milwaukee, believed they could produce complete houses in factories. They manufactured prefabricated five-room houses of welded steel using porcelain enamel for the walls. They sold the houses for $10,000. Although early experiments in this design met with many failures, Carl G. Strandlund, president of the Lustrom Corporation, was optimistic. He noted that in its early days the automobile business produced hundreds of failures for every success. Strandlund also thought that his method could turn out a new model of house every year, just like the auto industry turned out new cars.[12]

There were others like Lustrom. The Pennurban Housing Corporation manufactured factory-built houses in Syosset, Long Island (142 houses), Bayville, Long Island (40), and Pleasantville, New York (40). According to Albert Levy, one of the firm's principal architects, total prefabrication allowed for construction efficiency and individualization. Levy insisted he could install the shell of a house in ninety hours, simultaneously altering the facade of each. "You don't have to have a dinkey facade on each one down the line," he argued. He believed his technique was "more economically feasible than a lot of site fabrication by a few operators."[13]

The majority of merchant builders, however, believed that the factory method alone was too expensive and did not take into account all the challenges of home building. Such a method, they worried, could never supply enough homes for the new chartered market. As William Levitt pointed out, "No one has discovered how to prefabricate the land . . . how to prefabricate streets, sidewalks, curbs, utilities, and get the house up in the air."[14] Levitt and other merchant builders, including Fritz Burns and industrialist Henry Kaiser, decided to take an entirely different route. Kaiser and Burns bought huge tracts of barely developed land in California to build a development using modern methods. Fifty percent of the construction—precutting, prefabrication of walls, and prepainting—was done in nearby factories in Los Angeles, while the other half— the foundation, the structure, and the skin—was done on-site. "Since the [Kaiser–Burns development's] biggest raw material is land and since its one completely standardized house chassis is disguised with infinite variations . . . houses have a conventional appearance, which meets the public's prime requisite of individuality and avoids the fear of a prefabricated look."[15]

Prefabrication of the whole house or precutting in the factory and on-site assemblage were both critical for the industrialization of home building. There were two important reasons. Neither good weather conditions nor skilled labor was necessary for producing houses or housing materials. Moreover,

> prefabrication, even if limited to pre-cutting encourages more careful planning than does conventional hammer and saw carpentry. In pre-fabrication, the work is studied and completely specified by an expert, the builder or architect who know materials and their worth. In conventional building, on the other hand, many important decisions are entrusted to mechanics to whom an extra saw cut or wasted foot of lumber means nothing.[16]

Although most builders only used prefabrication to build single-family home developments, some experimented with it for building large-scale communities, continuing in the tradition of Greenbelt and Radburn. Park Forest, near Chicago, was one such project.[17] It was constructed as a planned community, with both row houses and single-family dwellings. Park Forest included parks, greenbelts, tot lots, schools, churches, and a shopping center, all in the inner core and accessible through pedestrian walkways. Built for 30,000 middle- and working-class families, its innovations included an industrial section carefully segregated from living and shopping areas. Stability was more important than profit. Operating money came from rentals and profits from the shopping center and industrial park. The whole financing was underwritten by the FHA. The point of Park Forest was to show "how private capital, if sufficiently enlightened, can apply and develop those principles of social planning which are all too often assumed to be solely the province of the state."[18]

Each of these methods had something to recommend it. Of the various options, the one that most defined suburban postwar growth was the prefabricated single dwelling advocated by William Levitt.

William Levitt would become the Henry Ford of housing. He understood that the building industry could not fully modernize unless the nation's financial practices were drastically transformed. Begun in the New Deal, this overhaul continued during World War II through HOLC and the FHA. Earlier, large-scale developers had to contend with banks only lending to builders who had a customer in tow. Title VI under the FHA reversed this policy, allowing large-scale builders to borrow money to build houses before they had buyers. In the postwar period Title VI was extended and amended at the behest of master builders. Title VI had an overwhelming advantage: ninety percent of the loan went directly to the builder. *Architectural Forum* declared, "This is *the most important change* in the character of house building finance since the appearance of the amortized mortgage and the big house builders were not slow to recognize that it yielded what their industry has conspicuously lacked: the working capital for a large scale operation."[19]

Some politicians feared that the extension of Title VI would cause inflation; many wanted to discontinue it altogether. Levitt, however, understood that the FHA and Title VI could jump-start the economy and help create a permanent mass housing market. As writer Eric Larabee argued, "Levitt is not quite the apostle of private enterprise that he seems to be at first glance. There is no way of knowing that without Title VI behind his commercial loans, or without the GI loan behind his veteran purchasers, Levitt would be able to go on building inexpensive houses at such a rate of speed."[20]

Levitt's emphasis on financing was echoed by the press. By 1948 public blame for the housing shortage shifted from unions, building codes, and middlemen to the unwieldy system governing low-cost housing loans. *Look*, for example, focused on the issue of financing through its popular series about a model, low-cost home called the Look House, designed by the modernist Walter Dorwin Teague and factory-produced by Adirondack Homes. The stories the magazine published about the Look House featured several home-hungry cases such as the former Sergeant Feeny and his new family, whose American dream was four-fifths complete; he had obtained a discharge, a wife, a college education and a job. The remaining fifth was solved by the purchase of a Look House. He was then compared to John Doe:

> His name doesn't matter, for he is typical of thousands having a different experience from Lester Feeny's. He, too, has a wife, a child, the problem of inadequate housing. But his attempts to solve that problem have been unsuccessful. For there is more to housing than designing inexpensive homes. There is still the problem of raising down-payments to obtain individual construction loans to finance building of these houses until mortgage loans apply.[21]

Title VI promised to take care of these home-hungry millions. While many small-scale and local builders didn't benefit from Title VI, the new corporate giants did, and they changed the face of America seemingly overnight. Huge, low-priced, suburban developments appeared to spring up magically from corn and potato fields. Long Island in particular provided the perfect setting for this rapid expansion: lots of unused land and farmers ready to sell, proximity to both the

metropolis and local burgeoning defense industries, pools of experienced workers, recently constructed highways, the Long Island Railroad, and families with
wartime savings yearning for peace and prosperity.

Moreover, future home owners also had Gold Coast images in their minds. In
1944 Albert Wood, the engineer who had built low-cost housing for Henry
Ford's workers in the 1920s using on-site assembly-line methods, explained the
lure of Long Island to Alicia Patterson, the editor of Newsday: "Where can you
find an environment which offers to the home owner of modest means all those
natural attractions and advantages which have so long made Long Island the favored place of residence of the well to do?"[22] While the North Shore remained the
venue of the well-to-do, the South Shore, largely inhabited by farmers and fishermen and home to the aerospace industry, was the perfect spot for postwar developers.

William Levitt also knew the attractions of Nassau County: its physical attributes, proximity to New York City, Jones Beach, the defense industries, and
the infrastructure built by Robert Moses. He also understood the workings of
the Republican political machine.

In 1950 West Coast master builder Fritz Burns visited Long Island, "the
great spawning ground of new housing," and declared, " I don't want to seem a
traitor to California, but the builders are really doing a job on Long Island. They
are not only producing a better house today for less money, but are also setting
the pace for the entire house building industry."[23] The pace setters to whom he
was referring was Levitt and Sons.[24]

In some ways, the firm seemed an unlikely candidate for the role. Both Abraham (the father) and William were trained as lawyers. Alfred liked to draw, but
was not a trained draftsman. Yet somehow the firm worked. All the Levitt home
designs came from Alfred's drawing board. Bill was "President, front man, pub-
licist and super salesman for the organization."[25] Levitt and Sons transformed
the housing industry from small scale to large scale, from an industry relying on
craft methods to one that used the latest industrial techniques. They pioneered
the shifts from union to non-union labor, from individual home owner mortgages to government subsidies, from middle- and upper-income buyers to a new
market of working- and new middle-class consumers.[26] Before Levitt neither
housing reformers nor the real estate industry and home builders believed it pos-

sible to build a privately owned home for less than $10,000. Levitt and Sons proved that it could be done.

Levitt described his enterprise as industrial, capitalist, and consumerist. Echoing Ford and Filene, Levitt insisted, "We are not builders. We are manufacturers. The only difference between Levitt and Sons and General Motors is that we channel labor and materials to a stationary outdoor assembly line instead of bringing them together inside a factory on a mobile line. Just like a factory, we turn out a new house every twenty four minutes at peak production."[27] The outdoor method was one of the fundamentals of the Levitt housing philosophy.

Levitt and Sons believed the public would purchase Levitt houses because they would come to trust Levitt products as a new national brand. William Levitt explained at the McCarthy hearings,

> I don't believe that there is a man in this room or a woman in this room who wouldn't rather buy from the A and P than the General Store. There is a very good reason. A and P is gigantic. They have taken American methods of production on large volume and small profit and have given much more intrinsic value to the customer than the corner drug store or grocery store. . . . Ask your wife whether she will still buy at the corner grocery store or does she buy at A and P. I don't propose anything. I don't have to propose it. The public will go where it gets a bargain, where ever it gets more value for its money.[28]

Levitt understood that the age of consumption called for new methods, styles, and tastes in homes just as it did in brand-name grocery stores, cars, and other mainstays of the mass-market economy. "The market for custom housing, like that for custom tailoring, no longer exits. People who want to buy that kind of thing will always be able to get it, but the real market is for the ordinary, mass-produced suit of clothes. And you can't build $30,000 houses by the six thousands."[29]

Before he could build for the millions, Levitt, like the builders of Sunnyside, Radburn, and Greenbelt, first had to buy huge parcels of land. Levitt bought 1,300

acres of potato farms on Long Island's South Shore in the town of Island Trees,
1,000 contiguous acres of farmland near Hempstead, Long Island, and 1,200
acres of the former estate of A. T. Stewart, the department store magnate. Levitt
had become a pro at land acquisition during World War II, when the Levitts
bought farmland to build naval housing. Long before crops were harvested, the
Levitts arranged for the title. When they told the farmers, the farmers said,
"Hell no!" They were incensed about wasting food during wartime and losing
profit. But Levitt, who was patriotic himself, took up the challenge and plowed
under $25,000 worth of spinach in order to build wartime housing quickly.[30]
Levitt could be tenacious and gutsy. He was a one-man economic steamroller.

With access to FHA credit, Title VI funds, and the largest line of credit ever
offered to a privately owned corporation by the Bank of Manhattan, Levitt stock-
piled building supplies from New York to California. He also had the resources to
become a manufacturer and supplier as well as a producer, making his operations
that much more efficient. He bought all his materials from the North Shore Supply
Company, a subsidiary of Levitt and Sons. The Levitts also owned the Grizzly
Park Lumber Company and acres of forest land in California. North Shore operated a $200,000 fleet of Transit-Mix trucks that prepared concrete as they hauled
it to the job; $300,000 worth of other heavy equipment, including nail-making
machines; a plumbing prefabrication plant; a woodwork prefab plant; and a cutting
mill that precut lumber to the size of the house.[31] North Shore also purchased all of
Levitt's appliances from washing machines to General Electric stoves.[32] Levitt
also used only materials prefabricated to exact specifications beforehand. The
wood was precut at the mill in California to the exact size, the copper coils for
heating were cut preshaped and bundled at the factory, and even such details as
the chrome moldings in the bathroom were precut. By cutting out most middlemen
and controlling his flow of supplies Levitt gained unprecedented efficiency.

Levitt also turned the construction site itself into a factory, using such items
as precut lumber, standardized windows, and doors that workers moved from
the foundation to the framework to the finishing. *Architectural Forum* reported:

> Levitt believes it is quicker and cheaper to apply the continuous principle of mass
> production by moving crews of men in standardized operations over the site than

que having cellars. Now, if we had come in and said that we intended to build 4 houses next year or 5 houses, I think we would still be building them with ars. But we announced a program that we were going to build several thousand d they were more or less impressed, but not completely.

However, the American Legion was impressed, and the veterans organiza- ions were impressed, and they stormed the meeting hall, and I mean that word absolutely literally, they stormed it: they overflowed it into the streets, and the town board of this particular municipality moved much more quickly than Joe Louis in his prime and they did it very, very, quickly.[40]

Levitt himself carefully orchestrated this storming of the Bastille. Using fear tactics, Levitt took out paid newspaper ads declaring any veteran who wanted a place to live should attend the meeting that would decide the fate of the base- ment build codes. Reminiscing years later about his strategy, Levitt said, "You don't think that protest meeting evolved out of thin air, do you? We told the boys that if they really wanted homes, they would have to get out and fight. We spread the news by ads and word of mouth among veterans groups. The boys did the rest at Town Hall." Levitt remained firmly convinced that he was right. "The end," he said, "always justifies the means, within the four corners of reason, of course."[41]

By fall 1948 Levitt was able to provide six thousand veterans with their dream houses for $60 a month. Levitt made about $1,000 profit on each house.[42] Levitt knew his houses represented a historic achievement, yet for all his confidence, clout, skill, and resources, it had been enormously difficult. He remembered years later: "We knew all along we could mass produce houses. All that is needed is size plus organization. But housing isn't like the proverbial 'better mousetrap.' Even if you can turn out a better product, at a lower cost, other things have to be going for you or it won't work." By 1947 those other things

were going for us; house hungry GIs doubled up with in-laws in crowded apart- ments were clamoring for homes. The government [was] faced with the decision

it is to move the house itself along a factory assembly line. This system, of course, depends on the most minute breakdown of site operations. Twenty-six major con- struction operations—starting with digging house footings and ending with painting—are further subdivided into simple standardized steps easily handled by a specially trained crew . . .

It has been estimated that the average building worker spends 25 percent of his time figuring out what to do next. In the Levitt operation this percentage must be close to zero. Levitt had all the processes down to a science: installation of radi- ant heating coils—1 man hour; caulking in rough plumbing assembly—3 to 4 man hours; pouring slab (automatic troweler)—1 hour; framing—45 man hours, sheathing—40 man hours; installation of plumbing fixture—4 man hours.[33]

Levitt applied the principles of Taylorism to his "factory," minutely breaking down tasks according to skill and speed and supervising the workers closely. All these processes were overseen by Levitt himself.

Levitt believed that the rules and regulations of craft unions would be anathema to his new construction methods. To convince workers to labor without union protection, he paid them handsomely, kept them working nine months of the year and offered incentives such as retirement benefits.[34] Only 40 percent of the work- ers were skilled, and Levitt deliberately did not observe elaborate apprentice reg- ulations. This non-union method kept home prices low and building fast.

Many workers understandably were wary of non-union shops, but the com- pany's system of extra pay for extra accomplishment provided better-than- union earnings for almost all workmen. Rate of pay was computed on the basis of minimum daily output. The Levitts figured that it should take a crew of four men not more than fifteen hours to frame a house, and this made daily earnings about the same as union pay. Practically all workers did much better than these minimum quotas and accordingly took home more money than they would have on union scale. Moreover, workers were divided into crews according to skill, and the more skilled group earned a higher rate of pay.[35] The open shop allowed Levitt to meet fixed construction schedules and at the same time avoid union ju- risdictional strikes and other work stoppages, which could delay production and cost millions.

The popular press, inclined to depict union workers as lazy laggards hemmed in by ancient guild restrictions, admired Levitt, who showed that non-union workers could build twenty-four houses a day, even in the snow. Eric Larabee observed in *Harper's* magazine that Levitt "is not dependent on the unions for his craftsmen, and the unions have not been able to break him. The Levitt plant has been picketed once by an outside union, but the attack petered out and died a natural death."[36]

Levitt's industrial methods elaborated the techniques pioneered in the 1930s, although he never acknowledged his debt to public housing innovators. With twenty-six different operations, Levitt's project was actually more complex than most industrial plants. Levitt and Sons hired sixty superintendents to supervise closely subcontractors, who generally were former Levitt employees. The subcontractor was both an independent enterpriser and a Levitt foreman—a paradox that was actually an ingenious device for relieving the Levitt organization of a great deal of the burden of cost control and labor supervision. It had the equally important effect of insuring, simply by its own momentum, the fastest possible building rate.

Many such contradictions built into this system served Levitt's interests. For instance, a subcontractor for every one of the major construction operations had complete responsibility for hiring, paying, and supervising labor for that part of the job. In effect, he was a bigger businessman than most independent house builders, but this same subcontractor was totally under the gun of the superintendents and Levitt himself. He had no written contact and knew he could only keep his position as long as he met his part of the schedule. The schedule was determined by Levitt's estimate of the number of man hours required for the operation and the subcontractors' allowance for overhead and profit. Thus Levitt had the incomparable advantage of fixed cost for the whole building job, while the subcontractor had to continually increase his production. His efficiency was carefully monitored as well. Levitt provided him with machinery and a measured amount of materials. "If he runs out of nails," Larabee said, "Levitt wants to know why."

*   *   *

Another reason Levitt was able to build houses so qu stood as a large-scale builder with a prestigious organ the media in his pocket that he could change out-o codes. In Hempstead, for instance, the building cod dwellings must be built with basements. To construct cella houses without them saved $1,000 per dwelling in addition labor. Since the 1930s, architects and builders had been experil structing homes on concrete slabs with radiant heating instead Lloyd Wright advised in 1938, "The old fashioned basement, exce heater space, was always a plague spot. . . . A concrete mat four inc directly on the ground over gravel filling, the walls set upon that, is be

Levitt faced opposition on this issue not only from town official from Nassau County Republicans, who ostensibly were worried about bility of radiant heating; in reality, they feared that if Levitt succeeded, Lo land would be flooded by veterans from New York City who migh Democrats. They also felt threatened by the prospect of a different class of p ple who would not uphold cherished upper-class values. In 1947, for exampl the Republican *Nassau Daily Review-Star* warned its readers that "We should be extremely cautious not to permit the existing shortage of houses to stampede us into junking all the precautions that have been adopted to protect individual purchasers and the standard of entire communities."[38]

But Levitt found support too. *Newsday*, a new publication that saw the issue of building codes as a way to establish its own voice and build readership, championed Levitt's position editorializing that the Levitt plan was "big, practical and ideal enough to make national news. . . . If we were prevented by the code it would make Long Island a national laughing stock."[39] Despite local opposition, Levitt was determined to build houses without basements. He appealed to the masses:

We went into and asked this municipality for a change in the code. There was not one single building expert and architect who did not agree that a slab house with radiant heating was excellent construction. This municipality [The Hempstead Town Board] decided that they had had cellars for 100 years, and were going to

of building the housing itself, or . . . making mortgage decisions such that private
industry would take the job, and mortgage money became plentiful. . . . Some
method had to be found to build housing for the typical, housing in big and profitable batches . . . the only thing missing was the product, the house. And that's
where we came in.[43]

One of Levitt's difficulties was that most of the people to whom he was trying
to sell houses had never before bought homes. Initially, Levitt rented all his
houses. Soon, however, he began to sell some, first for $7,500, then in 1949 for
$7,990. He provided compelling incentives for home ownership. Veterans who
rented and lived in Levittown for a year were given the option to buy for $7,500.
Veterans had access to low-interest GI mortgages, and a Levitt house called for
little down payment. If they bought, Levitt gave them back their $90 deposit.
The carrying charges on the loan were less than if they were paying in rent.

Levittown offered other attractions as well. Unlike other builders' developments, Levittown had concrete streets that allowed easy access for construction
materials and furniture. It was serviced by every utility found in a big city. Although Levittown lacked the schools, libraries, movie theaters, meetings rooms,
and community centers that government-sponsored programs like Greenbelt
featured, it was equipped with nine public swimming pools, seven commercial
centers or "village greens," as they were called, and baseball fields. Levitt
boasted, "Access to a swimming pool or a baseball diamond is as important a
part of what a purchaser buys as solid walls or a strong roof because he's not just
buying a house, he's buying a way of life."[44]

The first Levitt house was a simple four-and-a-half room Cape Cod, reminiscent of early-American saltboxes designed to make Polish, Italian, Lithuan-
ian, Jewish, and Catholic owners feel that they were claiming a piece of
American tradition. Inside the "early American" was a modern interior: each
house featured radiant heating, General Electric stove and refrigerator, Bendix
washing machine, venetian blinds, and an unfinished attic for future expansion.
The up-to-date amenities appealed to people coming out of old, urban run-
down apartment dwellings. Despite pleasing residents and being a commercial
success, however, Levitt's design met a fair amount of ridicule. *Architectural Fo-*

rum scoffed that "Small, squarish, built on one floor," Levitt's house, "was the true child of the depression. It never really lost its pinched, poor man's look."[45] The Cape Cod house was criticized by architects, intellectuals, and influential business magazines. Ironically, all of the people who advocated building houses like Fords found Levitt's mass-produced houses depressing. A writer in *Fortune* phrased it this way: "The basic Levitt product is a four-room bungalow. . . . No one would call them beautiful—or spacious or elegant. A number of tricks are performed with the eaves and roofline, and they are shingled and painted in a variety of colors, but they are basically as alike as Fords."[46]

Levitt was stung by this appraisal of his Tin Lizzies, but defended them, saying, "We are constantly criticized, because we have sacrificed in esthetic consideration to ease of production. But ease of production is basic in providing a house for what people can afford to pay."[47] Still, Levitt took the criticisms seriously and spent between $50,000 and $100,000 to study new housing designs. Moreover, the Levitts didn't trust blueprints. They weren't satisfied with their new model house until they'd built and ripped it apart at least thirty times.[48]

Despite its snugness, the 1949 ranch house received praise from the public and architects alike. *Architectural Forum* announced, "Never before in the history of U.S. building has one house type made such an impact on the industry in so short a time . . . builders by the dozens junked their Cape Coddled programs, switched instead to the new Levitt type."[49]

There were good reasons why the new ranch functioned as well as it did. The 1949 ranch embodied many of Frank Lloyd Wright's principles for a modern low-cost house. This was no coincidence. In 1936 Alfred Levitt had taken leave of the family firm for ten months to watch Wright, who was building a home in Great Neck, Long Island. He went to the site every day to watch the brick and glass house that contained many of Wright's modernist designs, an open-plan interior, the unity of inside and outside, and the signature fireplace that was the home's focal point.

Many of these features were included in the 1949 ranch.[50] Like Wright, Levitt's house had an open-style interior. The ranch reversed the traditional house plan, putting the living room at the back of the house and boldly opening the front door into the kitchen. A wall-size, double-glazed picture window in the living room looked out to the yard. And like Wright, Levitt placed the fireplace at the center of the house.

The Levitts saw themselves as translators of modern architectural design for the masses, becoming the arbiters of a new middle-class style of life. Alfred Levitt explained, "There is no point in trying to do something unless it can be handed out to the great mass of people as a cultural increase. The $7,999 for which we sell our house [is the means] by which a few thoughts of the progressive architects can be given to the public."[51]

With the advent of mass production in housing, Edward Filene's prediction came true. The combination of new consumer products and the modern suburban home changed the way of life for previous tenement dwellers, it also eschewed the Gold Coast style of housing in favor of designs more original, more adapted to their setting. As Frank Lloyd Wright pointed out, "to give the family the benefit of industrial advantages of the era in which they live, something else must be done for them than to plant another little imitation of a mansion."[52] By 1955 the rejection of imitative style was in full force. *House Beautiful,* which had always ignored Wright, now gushed with praise for him. An article entitled "The Man Who Liberated Architecture" claimed,

> As freemen, we can no more imitate the styles of other times in our homes than we can copy the lives and thoughts of other men. We must continue to develop new forms—new space concepts equal to the new ideas of life we have set stirring in the world. This is the meaning of Frank Lloyd Wright. Away with fake facades, false styles, all impositions on the freedom and honest expression of the individual and his home . . . Here is a new architecture for a new world.[53]

Oddly enough, the ranch house, symbolizing the modern age, also appealed to Americans by invoking the frontier. Or maybe the ranch was evocative of the new suburban frontier to which urban residents were flocking. "Of the 1.25 million houses built in the U.S. in 1950, virtually all were ranches."[54] It is interesting that "new world" ranches—with their suggestion of the rugged West and rejection of traditional New England vertical lines for the western outdoorsy horizontal aesthetic—appealed to citified East Coasters.

Just as the auto manufacturers changed models every year, so too did the Levitts. Never content to rest on his laurels, Levitt's 1950 model added a choice in facades, a built-in television, and a carport, but kept the same floor plan. Levitt, abreast of modern trends, understood that television would become central in the American home. Unlike architects and designers who proposed placing the TV in the basement or bathroom so that it would not ruin domestic life, Levitt bought 4,000 televisions from the Admiral Corporation and installed them in the living rooms of his houses. Previously, installing a TV had been complicated and expensive, buying in bulk lowered the cost. Television became the centerpiece of the ready-made Levitt house. As one writer in *Architectural Forum* noted, television completely changed how people used their time and space at home:

Where the television set has come into the home the separate dining room has disappeared. The family has begun to eat its meals where it has put its television set. It has postponed dish washing til the favorite program has faded from the screen. Some families have even taken to sleeping in relays in order to look after the large number of firmly rooted guests who have come over to look at the television.[55]

Levitt houses seemed to sell themselves, but like most other master builders, Levitt put to use modern advertising and public relations techniques. Like Fritz Burns on the West Coast, Levitt first built lifelike model homes, equipped with gleaming appliances and fully furnished courtesy of Macy's. Prospective buyers could walk through; Levitt hoped shiny new appliances and plush furniture would make them realize their own apartments were dingy and uncomfortable. Even if families couldn't afford to purchase these houses immediately, Levitt and other master builders hoped the model would linger in their minds and soften them up for future home ownership. This bet often paid off. As one Milwaukee resident remembered:

We had a nice little house. We built it back in the days when things were a lot different. We had an old-fashioned hot air furnace instead of new-fangled air conditioning. We had a kitchen with a nice old-fashioned pantry instead of these new cabinets and shelves. It was just like hundreds of other nice houses that were built twenty five years ago. We all liked it fine. One Sunday the wife noticed an ad for a new house. She kept after me to drive up there and we went through it. The old house never looked quite right after we made that inspection. We found we were hopelessly out of date. . . . Well, to make a long story short, we got the habit of visiting those new houses. Pretty soon the wife was so dissatisfied that we had to buy one.[56]

This was a seductive sales method that made house buying seem as simple and cheap as buying new clothes. The industry worked hard on this angle as in this advertisement from the Pennsylvania Savings and Loan League: "Home furnishings, washing machines, radios, refrigerators and the like would be covered by the same mortgage, making it possible for the veteran, with one down payment, to secure a home completely furnished."[57]

By 1950 Levitt completed a new twenty-two-acre sales complex with glass-walls and air-conditioning—flanked by furnished model homes. Located on a main thoroughfare overlooking a swimming pool and shopping center, the compound included a museum display of building materials Levitt used to construct his homes. Electric doors ushered customers through the model house, into the museum, and finally to the salesroom, where four uniformed attendants stood behind a fifty-foot desk and sold houses on the spot. As reported in *Architectural Forum*, "In the salesroom with its hubbub of activity, electric-eye door openers to hurry you along, people buying all around you, no money down or little money down and with all the superlatives, it was hard to resist."[58]

Levitt introduced other innovations in his sales techniques. Levitt's distaste for "parasitical" middlemen shaped his strategy. Traditionally, families purchased homes through real estate agents who charged the builder up to 20 percent in brokerage fees. The Levitts had their own sales department with a large staff on salary, which saved the builder middleman fees. Every week Levitt took out full-page ads in the *New York Times, Herald Tribune, New York Daily News, New York Mirror, Newsday,* and the *Levittown Tribune,* his own newspaper. According to *Fortune,* "It is a poor week when Levitt houses aren't featured in at least one full-column story in the New York newspapers." Levitt's flamboyant selling techniques met with disapproval from the industry. He substituted "salesmanship for craftsmanship," *Fortune* complained.[59]

Levitt knew what he was about. Although men traditionally were perceived as purchasers of big-ticket items such as cars and homes, Levitt's marketing strategy targeted women, too. During the war most women had been cooped up with relatives in crowded, decaying tenements without modern conveniences. Many worked exhausting industrial jobs on top of grueling domestic duties. A house equipped with gleaming, electric, easy-to-use kitchen and laundry appliances seemed magical and irresistible. The conventional Cape Cod design coupled with the elegantly modern kitchen "represents a well-thought-out plan for catching the most attention of the most women," mused *Fortune*.[60] *Architectural Forum* speculated: "The urge to own is based more on emotional than on financial grounds; it is more concerned with satisfactions of the ego than with considerations of economy. Which explains the widely held belief that gadgets continue to sell more houses than good construction."[61]

Levitt devised a brilliant marketing strategy for appealing to women's needs and emotions. Not only did the kitchen serve as the central room of the house, accessible by the front door,[62] it came fully equipped with shiny new brand-name appliances, in vivid contrast to old tenement kitchens that had only rudimentary, old-style equipment. Explaining this plan, Levitt said, "To include a Bendix washer in the sales price may seem frivolous and extravagant, but it is worth every bit of the cost in sales appeal and publicity. And it will sell faster." *Fortune* commented, "The $229 retail value Bendix washing machine, which, like all the rest of the kitchen equipment, goes with the house and also gets under the mortgage is worth twice its price for the way it stirs the acquisitive impulses of the average bride."[63]

Levitt made sure appliance companies used his name to endorse the new gadgets women most desired. This was easy because the big appliance companies like General Electric and Bendix did quite a business with Levitt; to them his name was gold and Levitt would elevate his rhetoric to fit any occasion. Quoted in an ad for General Electric, Levitt claimed that "a dream house is a house the buyer and his family will want to live in a long time. . . . An electric kitchen-laundry is the one big item that gives the home owner all the advantages and conveniences that makes the home truly livable." Levitt's advertisements for his dream house emphasized over and over that purchasing a Levitt house would allow the buyer "a time to live decently, time to have the better things of life without giving an arm and leg for them."[64]

This sort of joint advertising was innovative but quickly became common. As soon as Levitt adopted a product to use in his homes, the company would take out ads with Levitt's endorsement. Levitt's name was money in the bank and he reaped reams of free publicity. A full-page ad for General Electric in *Architectural Forum* announced in bold type, "Levitt and Sons select GE oil-fired boiler for entire 1949 low-cost housing program." Another full-page ad for Asphalt Company, makers of roofs and shingles, tooted, "you can't beat 100%! 10,000 roofs in Levittown and every one is ASPHALT." The ad contained an aerial photo of Levittown and a picture of Alfred Levitt with a testimonial underneath, "Combine the genius of Alfred Levitt, and the dreams of 10,000 homeowners—and you have Levittown, a Long Island dream city, that's no longer a dream—it's a reality. Mr. Levitt believes in 'dream homes' . . . but they've got to be practical. That's one reason why every home in Levittown is roofed with asphalt shingles."[65]

Thus Levitt put into practice the theory that a house was like a car, a crucial element in the new economy of mass consumption; the private home was the container for families who wanted their own new washing machines, brand-new stoves and state-of-the-art asphalt shingles. The Levitt house, in its insistence that modern homes and appliances together make up "the good life," was both a training ground and microcosm for a new economic vision.

Like most advertising, the Levitt ads left out as much as they revealed. The pictures of houses in the ads were drawings, not photographs. These illustrations depicted the house alone—no neighbors anywhere—when in reality houses were on top of each other. In the ads houses were surrounded by lush green when, "in actuality," John Liell noted disparagingly, "Levittown's trees were saplings, detracting rather than adding to its appearance."[66]

Residents of course soon discovered the ads were misleading. Where were the sidewalks, lawns, huge fruit trees, bushes, flowers, gardens, and open vistas? In *Time* Levitt jokingly protested that people who took advertising at face value were gullible. "The masses are asses," he said simply.[67]

Levitt's publicity machine did not stop at print ads. The Levittown houses were debated, discussed, applauded, and vilified nationwide, from newsreels to popular magazines, including *Life, Time, Coronet, Harper's, Reader's Digest, Newsweek,* and *Look.* Levitt answered to his critics publicly and flamboyantly, keeping his name in the news and always getting the last word. Levitt must have fine-combed the press and professional journals for items about himself. For example, *Architectural Forum* criticized the Arizona master builder Del Webb, whose housing development they considered slipshod. The magazine dared to compare Webb's operations to "a record yet to be beaten even by the notorious Levitt." Levitt responded in a detailed letter noting vast differences between his communities and the Webb development. He also objected to being called notorious. "Neither my brother, my father, nor I have ever spent a single minute in any duly authorized jail or penitentiary," he wrote. "I think you should instruct whoever wrote the phrase to smile when you say that Mr." He concluded with a long list of questions ostensibly to defend his reputation, but reading rather transparently like his famous ads:

Does the Webb community have a complete water distribution system paid for by him and reflected in the prices of his houses?

Does the Webb community have a swimming pool for each thousand families?

Does the Webb house have a General Electric refrigerator?

Does the Webb house have all-steel kitchen cabinets, with a stainless steel sink and double drain boards?

Does the Webb house contain a log burning fireplace?

Does the Webb house include complete financing charges and all recording fees?

Just for the record Levitt can produce the 3 Webb houses here in the New York area for at least a thousand dollars a piece less than the price is quoted.

Apparently delighted by the controversy, the editors of *Architectural Forum* published the letter in full with a few digs of their own:

> Does Levitt offer four sizes of houses in one development?
>
> Does the Levitt house have a carport?
>
> Does the Levitt house have the best in contemporary design?
>
> Does the Levitt community provide builder paid-for schools, churches, and movie theatres in addition to a shopping center?[68]

Despite such needlings, Levitt was fabulously successful. By 1950 Levittown had become synonymous with mass-produced housing for the middle and working class. Kilroy got his dream house and Levittown became a household name. Levitt's design was copied all over the nation and the world. So were his methods, from labor management to building techniques. Levitt set the pace and always kept in front of the competition, coopting their innovations and adding his own. No one could compete with his empire. Nobody else could match his bold publicity. Levittown and suburbia were fused forever.

Part Four

Suburban Life and Culture, Fifties Style

Chapter Eleven

The New Suburban Culture: Living in Levittown

Levittown, Long Island, was the Model T of the American postwar generation. Imitated across the nation, the same criteria governed home ownership in all the Levittown clones: minimum income, veteran status, and race. In Levittown itself families were overwhelmingly white, supported by a single wage earner, and married fewer than seven years. Most were in the process of conceiving three children. Residents ranged from twenty-five to thirty-five years of age. Forty-one percent of the men and 38 percent of women had attended college, and half of the men worked in Manhattan.[1]

Levittown was designed as the perfect American environment, immune to the dislocations and discontents of industrial urban life, for people who fit this description. Cape Cod houses, curvilinear streets called Lanes (with names like Harvest, Normal, Prairie, Cobbler), seven village greens, ten baseball diamonds, nine swimming pools, and sixty playgrounds contributed to Levittown's Norman Rockwellesque appearance. Levitt felt so strongly about this vision that in 1947 he arrogantly changed the name from Island Trees to Levittown.

Never one to be modest, Levitt felt he had really brought the dream of a small-town life within everyone's reach: "We began to dream of a low income community, complete in every phase with shops and amusements and planned houses and parks and 1,000 other things. We realized that the dream was not a new one, but the achievement of the dream would be."[2]

But mass-production methods, as critics noticed from the start, do not really lend themselves to creating picturesque places. Levittown was plagued by a dulling uniformity. Levitt recalled, "At first, we picked themes for subdivisions, like the celestial section, the homesy set, but we soon ran out of ideas and for each section we picked a letter of the alphabet and named all streets in the area of words of that letter."[3] Residents referred to the sections of Levittown by these letters: the T section, the W section.

Moreover, Levittown—like any town, no matter how idyllic—was continually wracked by power struggles. Levitt wanted to maintain tight control over the community. He hoped that residents would learn the ways of middle-class civility and manners once they had moved into his nice new homes, but the real-life people who populated Levittown proved more unruly than he'd imagined. Levitt's two newspapers, the *Island Trees Eagle* and the *Levittown Tribune* regularly issued stern decrees as to how residents should park cars, take care of their new "kentile" floors, or when they should hang out wash (not on weekends!). As they had in Strathmore, the Levitts even supervised lawn cutting, doing it themselves when necessary and sending laggard families the bill.[4]

In no way did Levitt encourage Levittowners to engage in civic-minded activities; he preferred to run Levittown himself. The town's residents surprised him, however, by immediately forming an array of organizations such as the Island Trees Tenants Council, the Island Trees Community Association, and the American Veterans Committee.

In 1947 tenant groups protested Levitt's decision to change the name of the town. He ignored them, changing it unilaterally. When asked by angry residents demanding to know why he thought he had the right to do this, he shot back, "Levitt and Sons as owners and developers are the only people with the right to name this community as they see fit."[5] He later remarked in an interview, "I wanted the new name as a kind of monument to my family. And, by gosh, I wasn't going to brook any interference."[6]

The next skirmish happened in 1948 when Levitt raised the rent by five dollars. As one resident wrote in the *Island Trees Tribune*, "We enjoyed living in our 'dream house' but I guess it was just a dream. It's just too bad that Mr. Levitt can't find some other way to meet *his* expenses. He certainly leaves us with no way to meet ours. The extra five dollars is the straw that breaks the camel's back." Levitt promptly bought the paper that printed the letter and renamed it the *Levittown Tribune* in order to "eliminate distortion of facts which from time to time enabled a small group of individuals to provoke antagonism and misunderstanding."[7]

Levitt quickly discovered that democratizing housing was great for sales but terrible for keeping people in their place. He resorted to inflammatory, anti-Communist tactics—including sending out a mysterious (most likely self-manufactured) leaflet from the so-called Island Trees Communist Party opposing the rent hikes. Then he delivered a pamphlet to residents' doorsteps branding dissenters as "communist dupes."

Despite such skirmishes, the communities in these new suburban towns like Levittown seemed to erase class distinctions. As *Harper's* observed in 1953: "Socially these communities have neither history, tradition nor established structure, no inherited customs, institutions, socially important families or big houses, everybody lives in a good neighborhood: there is to use a classic American euphemism no wrong side of the tracks."[8]

The old American dream of a classless society thus appeared to be manifesting itself in the daily details of suburban life. Outdoor barbecues, fast food, casual clothing, modern interior design, relaxed, informal social interactions, and child centeredness all differentiated these communities from their 1920s Gold Coast upper-middle-class antecedents. Instead of formal dress, *Harper's* reported, "Slacks or shorts are standard wear for both men and women at all times including trips to the shopping center. Visiting grandparents invariably are shocked and whisper, 'Why nobody dresses around here!'"[9] This new informality represented a break with the past, a moment "When porch society gave way to patio society. Where the formal dining room gave way to the barbecue and the TV dinner. Where white gloves gave way to pedal pushers."[10]

National magazines, as well as magazines such as *Thousand Lakes* (geared especially toward Levittown home owners), helped educate suburbanites in the mores of casualness. New residents also learned from observing their neighbors.[11] What people undoubtedly learned from most was what Levitt ingeniously placed in the 1950 ranch house: television.

Television became the new voice of unity and information. Culture by defini-

tion was changing, although critics were slow to catch on. The old high standards—opera, classical music, museums—could not offer what people needed
most and did not exist in the suburbs. What formerly was considered low class—
movies, television, and radio—now became the arbiters of taste and style. Moreover, the new media were accessible and affordable. Residents tuned in for
information and advice on how to live in communities in which they had never
lived before. To quote writer Harry Henderson: "These are the first towns in
America where the impact of TV is so concentrated that it literally affects everyone's
life. Organizations dare not hold meetings at hours when popular shows are on.
In addition, it tends to bind people together, giving the whole community a common experience." Television became a necessary component of everyday life.

Many couples credit television, which simultaneously eased baby-sitting, entertainment, and financial problems, with having brought them closer. Their fa-
vorites are comedy shows, especially those about young couples, such as "I Love
Lucy." Though often contemptuous of many programs, they speak of TV grate-
fully as "something we can share," as "bringing romance back." Some even credit
it with having "saved our marriage." One wife said: "Until we got that TV set, I
thought my husband had forgotten how to neck."[12]

Since television only came with the 1950 house, many older homes were
without it. Families who bought televisions became popular with their TV-hun-
gry neighbors; watching television became a block activity. Longtime resident
Dan Gossard fondly recalls the time "when there were only two televisions on all
of Saddle Lane and we would all meet on the weekend to enjoy it."[13]

If suburban life blurred social distinctions, it did not, however, eradicate economic insecurity. One Levittowner remarked, "The community is completely
mortgaged."[14] Houses, schools, screens, storm windows, automobiles, appliances, repairs, churches all had to be paid for out of residents' pockets, and unlike the city, there was little taxable industry to share the tax burden. Most
families had difficulty making ends meet. Families in which the husband worked
in local industry in a unionized, blue-collar, highly skilled job had the least trouble. Ironically, those with more middle-class city jobs in professions and busi-

nesses were more financially strapped: the price of commuting was high.[15] Many suburbanites often relied on relatives for loans.

Even though the price of life was high and exacting, new residents did not rush to move back to the city. Property, however small, transformed greenhorns into middle-class American. Moreover, the physical distance between workplace and home helped people assume their new middle-class identities. In a place like Levittown, whether a household's breadwinner was a mechanic, factory worker, low-level engineer, white-collar employee, salesman, or small businessman scarcely mattered; who cared what Mr. Kilroy did during the day? What mattered was that his home bore the trappings of a middle-class life—a new house, new car, new television. It was what one consumed—not what one produced—that was important.

Even people who were never status conscious before found themselves affected by media depictions of suburban life. One resident, Agnes Geraghty, revealed,

> Materialism is not confined to the suburbs, but it is more obvious in its display. When we came here our first goal was to buy a new car. I mean with all the traveling that we needed to do, our old car just didn't cut it. We soon realized that task was a little more complicated than we anticipated. A car was a real status symbol and hey, who didn't want to impress the neighbors?[16]

Where to consume in towns like Levittown, however, was a problem. In the experimental Radburn and Greenbelt communities, cars were parked on the outskirts: pedestrian walkways linked central shopping, schools, and leisure activities. Significantly, postwar master builders left this concept out of their designs, making their suburban residents even more car dependent. In Levittown—like other commercial communities with no centers—small clusters of stores along turnpikes became the shopping areas, challenging older local towns with Main Street shops. Given the huge influx of families in the postwar period, Main Street had little room for the new consumers and their cars.[17] Small shopping centers close to new neighborhoods were the first malls, or as they were called in *Architectural Forum*, "markets in the meadows." The shops in these centers were a combination of mom and pop stores, gas stations, and commercial chains like the A&P; but this was still not enough. Parking and access to the latest consumer goods—furniture, appliances, interior decorative products—remained elusive.

Given this large-scale market, the next step was to bring together corporate giants such as Macy's, Woolworth's, and Buster Brown Shoes in vast suburban centralized areas like Roosevelt Field, one of the earliest malls, located on Long Island's South Shore near Levittown. In 1956 real estate tycoon William Zeckendorf bought Roosevelt Field's 370 acres—the cradle of American aviation and site of Charles Lindbergh's historic cross-Atlantic flight—to house over a million square feet of retail space, an office center of 50 acres, and an industrial center of 123 acres. Macy's opened its largest branch there, a two-story building with 500,000 square feet of selling space. Underground were an air-conditioned concourse and ice skating rink. Most important, there was outside parking space for 17,000 cars.[18]

Overnight, Roosevelt Field became the supply center for suburban residents.[19] The impact of Roosevelt Field and other such malls was not only felt by the newcomers but by older residents as well. Malls made once-thriving downtown areas obsolete. As Robert Sweeney, former mayor of Freeport, recalled, "Roosevelt Field killed Main Street; it had better bargains, more parking, and was built for a more mobile society—for people who go shopping, but don't know what they are shopping for."[20] Norman Appleton, whose family moved to Freeport in 1915, observed the same phenomenon: "Freeport was quite a shopping area. On Main Street there were dress shops, specialty shops, shoe stores, and the owners either lived there above the store or had houses in town. Roosevelt Field wiped this community out."[21] Main Street was in fast decline, and a mall culture was emerging that allowed suburban residents easy access to the consumer-defined way of life.

If husbands were away earning the family bread, who took on the role of consumer? Wives, of course. The middle-class ideal included the notion that wives are not supposed to work for wages. Raising children and managing a household was a mark of leisure-class status. With their husbands at work, women were the center of home life, but with a new imperative: to become modern housewives—that is, the new consumers. This ideal is based on the division of family life into

public and private spheres, a distinction shaped by the nineteenth-century Industrial Revolution, which removed cottage industry to factories and offices in
the city. The home was to serve as a haven from dirt, grime, and chaos, presided
over by women. Obviously, some families embodied this ideal more successfully
than others. Working-class women who needed money for their families or
themselves worked to make ends meet; other women worked because they
wanted to. The ideal, however, persisted.

In the 1950s female domesticity became infused with patriotism. Women
who had gone to work in war industries now were told it was their patriotic duty
to leave the workforce to become housewives, mothers and especially consumers, to get the economy rolling again. The expansion of the postindustrial
economy after World War II was supposed to make it possible for second-generation families to realize the dream: women at home, men at work, children in
school. Suburbs in particular became synonymous with the achievement of this
new status. Given this pressure, it is not surprising that most suburban women
did not seek paid work outside the home until two decades later.

Such ideals cut deep; families who did not fit the accepted mold were isolated
and ostracized.[22] When Betty Scott, a white woman, first came to Levittown at
age twenty-six, in the late 1950s with her husband and five children, she fit into
the community well enough. Yet she and her husband—both musicians who
worked sporadically—were different from their neighbors. This proved especially painful when three years after they moved to Levittown they divorced.
Betty, who was from Michigan, had no family support and was forced to go on
welfare. She recalls her neighbors' reaction:

Generally they avoided me. The men were often hostile. I remember remarks like,
"You are draining our tax dollars, why don't you get a job?" In truth I would have
loved to work, but I had five young children and it was chaos. My kids had trouble
in school. They were constantly being singled out because they didn't have a father. I did have a lover and they didn't like that either. In fact, after Lennie, my
lover, gave me a new car, a neighbor reported me to welfare and I was cut off.

Some of this isolation was tempered by other women:

While my next-door neighbor's husband made nasty cracks, his wife secretly gave me food. I remember how she used to bring me pork chops, claiming she had extras. We both knew that was a white lie. Another neighbor gave me a used car. In a way I think they felt sorry for me.[23]

Representatives of the consumer industries, new forms of mass media, and a host of professional experts writing in the popular press did not want suburban women to emulate Betty Scott. Instead they did their best to educate families about the importance of proper female domesticity. They all had a stake in the housewife—Mrs. Consumer—who would keep the economy prosperous. Their messages, however, often were contradictory and unclear. As one scholar observed, women's suburban middle-class life during the era of the fifties represented a "tension between self-sufficiency and ineptitude."[24] Cut off from her immigrant roots and old neighborhoods and placed in an unfamiliar setting, the suburban housewife was fair prey to the agencies of communication ready to inform her everyday existence, meet her every need, and fulfill her middle-class desire through the purchase of their products. Agnes Geraghty, for instance, recalls the impact of media images of the perfect housewife in her life:

To say that media doesn't affect our lives is to say radiation has no harmful affects. Both change us, but we don't feel it when it's happening. I remember watching those TV commercials with those women so overly concerned with how the kitchen floor shined, and of course I never pictured myself that way, but I tell you, if a relative or friend stopped by unannounced and my house wasn't in order, I almost felt like a failure. There was this pressure to be the perfect housekeeper. I mean now that I had this home I "had" to be Donna Reed. These messages were so subtle, but they had obvious effects.[25]

Levitt was conscious of the necessity to stimulate consumption. He condescendingly pitched his kitchen ads to "the magazine reading, ruffled chintz housewife" and sponsored yearly decorating contests to promote competition and stimulate a desire to "keep up with the Joneses."[26] New York interior decorators judged the homes, and gave prizes ranging from $250 to $1,000.[27]

The housewife was expected to make her house shine; her work ethic was supposed to blend efficiency and relaxation. Helen Eckhoff, a Levittowner, described her system of scientific housekeeping in *McCall's* in 1948:

> The first thing I did was to arrange my kitchen so that it would save the most time and energy possible. I now have three working centers—the baby center where I keep all baby food bottles and the like, a baking center and a cleaning center for general cleaning. It may not sound impressive but it's amazing the steps you save.
>
> My greatest joy is my washing machine. I wash every other day in two loads: one as my husband leaves and the other at ten. I buy washable fabrics that don't require ironing. I save time by preparing casserole and quick refrigerator desserts. It means that Bob and I have just about as much social life as we ever did. Naturally, I don't gad about, but there's always time to have people over. On Saturday night we usually have a television party. Refreshments are simple and we don't use many dishes, so it's just as relaxing for me as the guests.[28]

Despite Helen's enthusiasm for efficiency, studies suggest that all her time-saving devices and practices probably made her spend more time on housework and the application of more rigorous standards of housekeeping.[29] Furthermore, the time she saved now was taken up with the labors particular to middle-class suburbia: consumption, entertaining, and constant driving.

What took up the most time and energy was child care, and Levittown families had children by the bushels. Pregnancy often was referred to as the town's "major industry" or "the Levittown look." The community itself was nicknamed Fertile Acres and the Rabbit Warren. As Levittown pioneer Lila Paige declared, "Our children were our major products." Pregnancy was so commonplace that nobody made a fuss over pregnant women.

> Women with romantic ideas, or those accustomed to being surrounded by doting relatives, sometimes feel that they are being neglected. As one woman put it, "I had Jane in the city. My mother and sisters used to call up daily just to see how I was. Out here you are nothing special. At first, when I was pregnant with Arleen, I really missed the attention."[30]

Caring for young children, often close in age, bound mothers together. In the absence of older relatives, the top authorities on child guidance were *Infant Care* by Dr. Benjamin Spock and *The First Five Years of Life* by Arnold Geselles.[31] Suburbia was built around children's needs: "Everything from architecture to traffic control takes into consideration their safety, their health and the easing of their parents' worries."[32]

Nothing's too good for the kids summed up the Levittown attitude. A toy store proprietor observed that business in suburbia was much better than in a rich neighborhood in the city:

> You see that toy automobile (a model car large enough to ride in). That costs $24. To sell one in my other store to rich people—what a job! They want to inspect it; they hem, they haw, they test it, they put it back and come back the next day and then 50 percent of them don't buy it. Here, if the kid sees it and wants it, they buy it: that's it. Are they spending more than they can afford? Who knows? I do know selling is nothing at all. It's strictly what the kid wants.[33]

This toy proprietor was echoing a national theme. "Never underestimate the buying power of a child under seven," Dr. Frances Horwitch, widely known as Miss Frances of television's Ding Dong School, told a Chicago advertising conference in 1954.[34] Sears and Roebuck even extended credit to young people: children with allowances were eligible for their own Sears credit card. Children thus were becoming as important to the consumer economy as their parents.

While Levittown women were home- and child-centered, they were not homebound. Indeed, being home-centered meant that much of their activity took place *outside* the home. Women were the telephoners, organizers, and arrangers of community life.[35]

This community activism can be understood as the product of two legacies; first, as a continuation of turn-of-the-century social feminism. Jane Addams, one of the best proponents of this heritage, stated, "Woman shall extend her sense of responsibility to many things outside of her home, if only in order to preserve the home in its entirety."[36] Equally important, community organizing was an adaptation of immigrant women's working-class traditions of neighborhood solidarity in a different setting.[37] Community institutions were almost nonexistent in Levittown. Most sociological and feminist literature portrays suburban women in coffee klatches gabbing about trivia, yet these women built a world for themselves, their children and their community.[38]

The first settlers of Levittown, like those in Greenbelt, refer to themselves as pioneers. Initially they felt lonely and isolated. Many women coming from the city did not know how to drive, and driving was the passport to the new frontier. Doris Kalisman, for instance, recalls coming to Levittown screaming, crying, and in culture shock:

> As a city person I wouldn't dream of living in a development where every house looked the same. But before you knew it, I couldn't find any other place and I had a baby. It was the boondocks. I didn't drive and there was nothing to walk to. I had to wait for someone to take me and it was a terrible feeling. Neighbors were wonderfully generous. There was a need we had for each other. Our need was because we were lonely and locked in our little house.[39]

Mathilde Albert moved to Levittown from Brooklyn in 1947. She was one of "the first hundred families to move into a Cape Cod rental house." She was horrified to discover how barren it was, despite ads that made Levittown appear as a community filled with shops and services. She described her initial experience:

> There were no telephones, no shops; in the blizzard of 1947 the only telephone booth blew down. There was no grass, no trees, just mounds of dirt and snow covered it all. The dirt, the house. We ran out of oil. I was stranded and couldn't even drive. It was an incredible experience, but everyone was most helpful; everyone helped everyone else.[40]

Since everyone was pretty much in the same boat, women had to depend on their neighbors for help. With few urban amenities like bakeries shopping was scarce, and knowing how to drive was at a premium. Mathilde Albert's neighbor in the W section, Clare Worthing, was one of the few women on Willowbrook Lane who could drive. She became a central figure and teacher in the community: "On Thursday we would pile up in my car and go to Hicksville [a nearby town] with the kids and come back with the packages filling up my little car. Hicksville had a bakery. Oh, how we loved that bakery. I ended up teaching my neighbors how to drive."[41]

The women's sense of isolation led to action. Since there were no institutions, it was up to women to create them. Virginia Crowther of Weaving Lane described the first informal baby-sitting arrangements Levittowners created.

> I would watch my neighbor's kids; she would watch mine. The group got bigger and we would baby-sit each other's children and we even had intercoms between houses. Out of this, a group of women started the first nursery school. We hired a teacher, but we all participated.[42]

After a while more elaborate baby-sitting co-ops developed. "In these groups one mother keeps a book—a record of how many hours you sit as well as how many hours you use. You are all allowed to go into debt 15 hours or get ahead 15 hours."[43]

Martha Mordin, a Levittown daughter still living on Whisper Lane, recalls the nurturing atmosphere: "Living here was like being in an extended family. There were lots of mothers. If you couldn't talk to your own mother, you could talk to someone else's mother."[44]

Helga Baum of Wildwood Lane confirmed this sense of living in an extended family from an adult point of view:

> I lived on a block where five families had children who were within three months of each other. One afternoon a boy not ours fell and broke his arm and his mother wasn't home at the time. When the mother got home the child had already been taken care of. Someone knew they belonged to the Health Insurance Policy (HIP) program, a cast was put on and the whole thing happened before his mother came home. It was just that kind of sense of community.[45]

Some women participated in more commercialized forms of companionship. Doris Kalisman of Tardy Lane described her encounters in the T section at Tupperware parties:

There were lots of Tupperware parties. That was the big thing in 1951 and 1952 and that was a real big event. That was the only way I got to meet people, so I would go. They used to all talk about what they used to clean the various parts of the house with. I was a very poor housekeeper. They used to talk about what they used for what and I remember one had a gadget that as she walked down the stairs it would dust the banister. I never thought of dusting the banister in my whole life. I was so miserable at these Tupperware parties, but it was a way of getting to know women, even though I was a Tupperware snob at the time.[46]

Political organizing was one alternative to Tupperware parties. Education proved the town's most divisive political issue. Within three years a school system that began as a three-room schoolhouse mushroomed into fourteen schools with 12,000 pupils. There was controversy over the curriculum, with liberals pressing for progressive education and school services funded by higher taxes, and conservatives fighting for moral training, discipline, and lower taxes. As Roberta Stim of Whisper Lane explained: "There was an absolute division. You were either right or left. There were two school philosophies, one was conservative and supported by religious Catholics and Episcopalians and one liberal supported by Jews and liberal Catholics."[47]

The conservative protest about higher taxes reflected anxieties about the unexpected tax burden suburbanites had to pay. Almost all moved from the city and did not anticipate that local taxes would consume such a big portion of their weekly wages. Moreover, home owners had little experience managing their own school systems, and there was no separate school tax. Conservatives were most upset by the tax crunch, fearing that it would cost them their "only recently acquired middle class status."[48]

Whatever their political leanings, women found that civic activity was an important way to gain influence in the community. Men also discovered that involvement could bring new status.[49] Consequently, Roberta Stim observed, "The officers were very often men and the workers were women." Despite sexism, women gained political know-how and self-confidence from school battles. As one woman commented: "Had we stayed in the city, I never would have joined anything. I can hardly believe I'm now chairman of the education committee of the PTA."[50] Often these school controversies lasted for days and late into the night. Barbara Croswell, a pioneer, reports: "When there was a big school issue, I used to bring my mother out to take care of the children. For days we would argue and sometimes the meetings ran till six in the morning."[51]

A particular high point of the struggle, many pioneers recall, was the 1954–1955 controversy over a proposal to ban "The Lonesome Train," a cantata that mourned the death of President Lincoln and celebrated the Emancipation Proclamation, written by Earl Robinson. Robinson, a popular composer of union songs and American populist ballads in the 1930s and 1940s, was under attack in the 1950s for his liberal political beliefs, and was accused of being a Communist by Senator McCarthy and other conservatives. When "The Lonesome Train" was used as instructional material in public schools, conservatives in Levittown claimed the record was "loaded up with communist propaganda and should be banned."[52] Mathilde Albert, then president of the PTA, reports:

The conservative Catholics called everything that was progressive Communist. They wanted to ban this record and most of us were opposed to book or record banning. I organized meetings and marches. The meetings were held on Friday nights and went on till early the next morning. Thank God my husband watched the kids on Saturday, for this was real important to me.[53]

Although these school controversies divided the community, Helga Baum maintains,

We were all pioneers, we were in the same situation, we all came in together. It's like the Senate. No matter what party, you don't attack another senator; it's a club. We had the same kinds of desires and need, fought the same kinds of battles; no matter what sides we were on, there was a camaraderie.[54]

Despite the cookie-cutter houses, homogeneous demographics, and Levitt's tendency toward autocracy, Levittowners had strong and sometimes clashing ideas about what sort of place they wanted to live in, and they set about trying to make Levittown that place. What Levitt left unbuilt, people partially made up for by forging new bonds among themselves. The legacy of community building was carried on by women who were at first lost in this strange world, but who then remade it. Pioneers point "with pride to the fact that with no outside help and little experience they filled in the pieces of the puzzle that Levitt left out: a school district, a Chamber of Commerce, a Little League, a library and a volunteer fire district." As long-time resident Beth Dalton says, "You know, Levitt built the houses. It's the vets that moved in that created Levittown. He just built houses. They're the ones, it's their values and energy that created this community."[55]

Chapter Twelve

America, Love It or Levitt

Suburbia was hailed by many as the realization of the postwar American dream, but just as Levittown and other suburbs had their own internal critics, so they had external ones as well. As soon as residents moved in, suburban life came under fire. Contemporary writer Donald Katz observed: "Much as the muckrakers of 50 years ago had exposed the 'Shame of the City', writers now catalogued the myriad syndromes and deficiencies exhibited by the 'cheerful robots' who lived in what sociologist C. Wright Mills called, 'the illusion of the suburbs'."[1]

In 1949, Phyllis McGintley, a leading writer of popular verse, offered an analysis of where these stereotypes came from:

> To condemn suburbia has long been a literary cliche. I have yet to read a book in which the suburban life was pictured as the good life or the commuter as a sympathetic figure. He is nearly as much a stock character as the old stage Irishman: the man who spends his life riding to and from his wife, the eternal Babbitt who knows all about Buicks and nothing about Picasso, whose sanctuary is the club locker room, whose ideas spring ready made from the illiberal newspapers. His wife plays politics at the PTA and keeps up with the Joneses.[2]

McGintley's argument is that snobbery toward suburbia was part of a literary tradition that set the stage for the "muckrakers" of the 1950s. Indeed, intellectual contempt for slow, boring, and boorish middle-class life began in the 1920s, the first decade of suburban expansion. In the suburban migration of the late 1940s and 1950s, this antisuburban snobbery gathered steam, even though the class of people moving changed.

While television celebrated the advent of suburbia, popular novelists, journalists, academics, and particularly sociologists maligned it, portraying the suburbs as conformist, consuming, profoundly dulling to mind and soul—a place to
be scorned and its residents belittled. David Riesman's *The Lonely Crowd*
mourned suburban sadness and alienation; William Whyte's *The Organization
Man* ridiculed the status anxiety of recent suburbanites; and John Cheever's
novels and short stories satirized upper-middle-class suburban life. In 1957
popular writer John Keats published *The Crack in the Picture Window,* a particularly venomous antisuburban book. His characters were John and Mary Drone,
who lived in Rolling Knolls, where "For *literally nothing down,* you too can find a
box of your own in one of the fresh-air slums we're building around the edges of
American cities . . . inhabited by people whose age, income, number of children,
problems, habits, conversations, dress, possessions, perhaps even blood types
are almost precisely like yours."[3]

Echoing Philip Wylie, misogynist author of *A Generation of Vipers,* Keats argued that suburbia "actually drives mad the myriads of housewives shut up in
them."[4] Women in particular were singled out as the mainstay of suburban su-
perficiality and blamed for everything from juvenile delinquency to keeping up
with the Joneses to producing a generation of morally inferior sons and Milque-
toast husbands.

As Donald Katz put it,

> No citizen of the American suburbs . . . was the object of more concern from
> the revisionists of the moment than the "young suburban housewife," source of
> dull children and ingrained family neurosis. The mother and wife now bore
> daily moral responsibility for everything that was right and wrong about family
> life.[5]

Interestingly, later writers such as Betty Friedan and Marilyn French would
use aspects of this suburban antifeminist critique to explain the source of middle-class women's distress. Friedan argued in *The Feminine Mystique* that suburbia created overeducated housewives who were trapped in boring, repetitive,
unproductive, isolated lives and didn't even have a language to describe their

condition. In *The Woman's Room* French also stereotyped women in suburbia with another cliché, comparing them to women in ancient Greece who were "locked into the home and saw no one but children all day. The Greek women at least saw slaves, who might have been interesting people. But suburban women have only each other."[6]

Friedan found the preoccupation with consumption and the home itself the central problem of the suburban desert, a cultural and psychological toxin for women. In *The Feminine Mystique* she argued, "Women's ambitions were supposed to be totally fulfilled through their domestic activities . . . kissing their husbands goodbye in front of the picture window, depositing their station wagon full of children at school, and smiling as they ran the new electric waxer over the spotless floor."[7]

Published in 1963, *The Feminine Mystique* became a best-seller. It struck a chord.[8] Thousands of women all over the United States wrote Friedan fan letters, poems, and hymns of thanksgiving; others took issue with her analysis. The letters generate a rich diversity of experience, allowing women residents to explore the connection or lack thereof to her argument. One of the many women who identified with Friedan's critique wrote from Raleigh, North Carolina,

> I'm probably one of the few women who planned and devoted my energies to becoming a "suburbanite." I grew up in Cicero, Illinois, as a Czech living in a factory town filled with Czechs, Poles and Italians. I wanted nothing so much as to get out—become Americanized—live in a suburban house with a white picket fence. I studied *McCalls*, went to movies—to see how to behave and tried to fit that special mold of woman. . . .
>
> One day I crawled out of bed, I looked at the split levels surrounding me, and I looked at myself and said: this stinks. These people have no substance—and neither do I. I'm living in a vacuum and there must be a way out or it's better to die . . . It must be a hard thing to face that I literally "lit candles" for years to become a nonentity in a stupid, faceless society, known as suburbia.[9]

Some working-class women, however, analyzed the suburban malaise differently. For example, one woman from Queens Village, New York, wrote:

In another part of your book you mention the Jewish and Italian woman category are the prime victims of this mystique. Since I am in this category I would like to add a few facts to your critique. In order to give her American children some of the advantages she never had, the immigrant mother often had to work, not only in her home, but outside as well, under the most harrowing conditions. For the sons, it was important and necessary to obtain an education so he could escape the sweatshop labor of his father.

For the daughter, however, the most precious legacy was an escape from the hard work and drudgery of her mother and the attainment of leisure—the very leisure the immigrant mother never knew herself and which she so desperately needed.

Very often when my sister and I would plead with my mother to teach us some of her sewing or other skills "for fun," she would look upon us with genuine horror and say "I hope to God you never have to sew." We'd get a similar response to our other requests for her know how. To this immigrant mother, education was the only necessary thing for the son to get a better job and the daughter with nothing else besides her femininity would with luck marry well, thereby achieving the leisure her mother never knew.[10]

Other women criticized Friedan for her racial and class bias. Some argued that leisure was productive rather than wasteful. One woman took Friedan to task for skimming over

a very vocal and articulate group of women today that should have given you a strong feeling of optimism and enthusiasm. . . . Bear in mind that it is only the housewife who has the necessary time to participate in [political] activities. Most activities are done during the day. . . . The non-working housewife can be more outspoken and take the daring initiative that is requested at times, that the employed woman [and man] cannot do for fear of antagonizing employer, client and other business associates.[11]

Others pointed out that Friedan neglected the question of necessity. Many first-time suburbanites were forced to move because there was simply no housing in the cities. Many remember the move as difficult and that they felt they were moving to the "sticks," leaving behind family, neighborhood, and friends. They recall city life nostalgically, though they never seem to want to return. Nevertheless, their initial descriptions of suburban isolation echo Friedan. Grace Grillo, who was raised in a Brooklyn apartment house surrounded by "her entire family" and longtime friends, recalls that in the city "There was always something going on. In our neighborhood in the early evening we would always sit out on the front stoop. In fact, all our neighbors did this. It was a sort of ritual." But when she moved to Long Island, "she was very, very lonely. I did not sit out on the front steps each evening because there wasn't anyone to sit out with. No one did this in Long Island, and all my friends were back in the city."[12]

Gertrude Shedlick captured the critical difference between city and suburban social life:

> We knew some of the neighbors in Babylon [Long Island], but it wasn't like Brooklyn; we didn't know them as well, and we didn't meet them the same way. In Brooklyn we knew the neighbors because we saw them in the hall everyday. But in the suburbs you made friends through your children. If the kids made friends, the parents would eventually meet. Otherwise we had no way to meet anybody except the families that we shared the fence with.[13]

Many women overcame their initial isolation by creating close-knit communities of women, particularly, through their children. Virginia Guarnari Brown explained,

> Although I moved reluctantly to the suburbs, the women on my block were very close because of the children, of which there were many. . . . These early years were filled with pool parties, barbecues, and block parties. The neighbors were close-knit families who were able to rely on each other for every little thing.[14]

What accounts for these divergent reports? Maybe the class of women Friedan wrote about didn't move from working-class neighborhoods and didn't need to rely on each other as much because they found commercial solutions to their baby-sitting or other needs.

Critiques of the lives of suburban women were linked inextricably to the view that suburbia was infused with a crass mindlessness. Many critics, such as Keats, singled out Levittown for their harshest criticism. In 1961 Lewis Mumford, bitterly disappointed by the defeat of public housing, joined the fray with his blistering attack on suburbia—particularly Levittown—seen by him as

> A multitude of uniform unidentifiable houses, lined up inflexibly at uniform distances on uniform roads, in a treeless command waste inhabited by people of the same class, the same incomes, the same age group, witnessing the same television performances, eating the same tasteless prefabricated foods, from the same freezers, conforming in every outward and inward respect to a common mold manufactured in the same central metropolis. Thus the ultimate effect of the suburban escape in our time, is, ironically, a low grade uniform environment from which escape is impossible."[15]

While critics accused suburbia in general, and Levittown in particular, of stifling uniformity, others viewed it as symptomatic of the widespread reach of consumer culture in the postwar period. Indeed, Levitt made this point in his own defense:

> It seems to me incredibly myopic to focus on the thread of uniformity in housing and fail to see the broad fabric of which it is a part—the mass production culture of America today. To fuss about uniformity in housing touches on only so small a part of the truth as to be without meaning. It is not just our houses that are uniform but the furniture and appliances we put in them, the clothes we wear, the cars we drive. This isn't something to grieve over. It's something to glory in—just so long as we keep in mind the difference between material values and those of the mind and spirit. The reason we have it so good in this country is that we can produce lots of things at low prices through mass production. And with mass production, of course, uniformity is unavoidable. . . . Houses are for people, not critics.[16]

Levitt continued to argue fiercely for mass housing, insisting: "The plain fact is that, for many families, the choice lies between a so called, 'tract houses' and none at all. The day has long passed—if it ever existed—when an appreciable number of people could live in individually designed and custom built homes."[17]

While many families perhaps agreed with Levitt, others sided with the cultural critics. On Long Island plenty of the established residents—wealthy home owners as well as fisherman and farmers—shared Keats's fear that Levittown would change their bucolic way of life and turn the area into a slum. Levittown pioneer Mae Brandon recounts that she too originally, had such fears:

> I read about Levittown in the paper and heard only bad things about it. In ten years, it would be a slum, the equipment will collapse. It's going to be terrible, you wouldn't want to live there. It's better to stay in the Quonsets [army barracks]. But a friend went to visit and she said the houses were nice. She couldn't see them becoming slums, and so we came out. We had tried other places but they were much too expensive.[18]

The fear of Levittown was typical of reactions to new suburban subdivisions across the country. Author D. J. Waldie wrote of Lakewood, California, in the early 1950s, "when the residents of the young suburb voted for incorporation, older neighbors retreated into the city of Long Beach. The residents were afraid they would be caretakers of the slum my city was supposed to become."[19] One antisuburban organization called California Tomorrow coined the term *slurbs* to describe a new California development, Valley of Heart's Delight, inhabited by Lockheed workers. Author David Beers, who grew up in this development, defined slurbs as "the mocking term coined to describe what my people tended to create in place of orchards. Slurbs . . . were the 'sloppy, sleazy, slovenly, slipshod, semi-cities,' where nine out of ten Californians would soon be living if my people could not be contained, if precious farmlands weren't zoned safe from us."[20]

Where critics saw conformity or future slums, however, suburban residents saw a blank canvas. The new suburbanites, many of whom were skilled workers, brought with them craft knowledge and home building and maintenance skills. If the Levitt houses all looked alike at time of purchase, within ten years they were distinct. Although some saw the Levitt house as a "starter, and planned to move to bigger houses in more upscale neighborhoods when their incomes rose, many regarded the original box as a challenge," to be added on to, extended, built out, completely remodeled. One journalist commenting on Levittown noted,

The roofs have developed so many dormers it seems like they've grown dormers on dormers. Fronts have sprouted pergolas and porches, roof lines have been raised, pitched, expanded, corniced, and cupolaed. Sides have been carported, breeze-wayed, broken out, recovered in redwood, sided in cedar shake, disguised in brick and fieldstone, transformed into ranches, splanches, colonials and California ramblers.[21]

As one female remodeler remarked, "maybe because they [the houses] all started out looking so much the same . . . that's why they [the residents] are trying so hard to be different." Or as another Levittown resident mused, "every house has a signature."[22]

Long Island's new suburbs did not turn into slums. Rather, the developments brought vitality to the region's sleepy economy. Between 1940 and 1950 the population of Nassau County increased almost 50 percent, and in the three-year period from 1947 to 1950 over 70,000 homes were built. Since the average house at that time cost between $12,000 and $15,000, owners feared that their property values would be brought down by the Levitt houses, which cost only $6,999. In fact, exactly the opposite was true: property values continued to rise, not fall. This pattern was repeated all over the country.[23] While suburbia's success, powered by the new economy of consumption, and residents' commitment to their homes stilled some objections, however, it provoked others.

Cultural critics, like wealthy home owners, did not fully understand the class concerns reflected in debates over suburbia. The lack of clarity about class permeates the harangues. From Mumford to Keats, critics noted a phenomenon, but failed to grasp it from the perspective of those who lived it. The voices of these pioneers were conspicuously absent from the critiques. Even when they spoke for the suburbanite, as Friedan did, they spoke for the privileged, not the masses. The pundits condemned the conformity, predictability, and sameness, but they would not or could not appreciate the soul of the new suburbanite—indeed, they were blind to it.

Particularly striking in reminiscences of residents and recent memoirs written by children of postwar suburbia is the desire for the *new*. This yearning was deeply connected to postwar advertising and television that depicted a new, bright and shiny, product-laden, affordable life. This desire perhaps went deeper. Most suburbanites had been crowded into slums during the depression and war; given the opportunity, they wanted to leave this world behind them. Home ownership in a virgin community is an adventure, a pilgrimage; they were moving up, from one class into another.

The voyage itself could even mean entering rough seas, because class lines were quite murky. D. J. Waldie, a resident of Lakewood, California, captured this class confusion when he explained that people thought of his development "as middle class even though one thousand one hundred square foot tract houses on streets meeting at right angles are not middle class at all. Middle class houses are the homes of people who would not live here. In a suburb that is not exactly middle class, the necessary illusion is predictability."[24]

If critics had bothered to ask David Beers, they might have found a different sensibility. He said that what his family desired most

> was a new empty space, that, my mother and father will tell you, is how they remember their brand new tract home in their brand new subdivision; as a certain perfection of potentiality. Nowadays when suburbia is often disparaged as a "crisis of place" cluttered with needless junk and diminished lives, it is worth considering that it was not suburbia's *stuff* that drew people like my parents to such land in the first place, but the emptiness. A removed emptiness, made safe and ordered and affordable. An up-to-date emptiness made precisely for us.

The Beers never "looked at a used house." Instead they roved in search of the many billboards advertising "Low Interest, No Money Down," shopping for a new house "the way you shop for a car." David Beers often asked his mother, "Didn't the sterility scare the hell out of you?" The question never phased her; she answered:

We were thrilled to death, not afraid at all. Everyone else was moving in at the same time as us. It was a whole new adventure for us. Everyone was arriving with a sense of forward momentum. Everyone was taking courage from the sight of another orange moving van pulling in next door, a family just like us, unloading pole lamps and cribs and formica dining tables like our own, reflections of ourselves, multiplying all around us in our new emptiness.[25]

Most of the Levittowners and inhabitants of other semi-middle-class suburbs didn't write about their experiences at the time or deem them noteworthy until recently. Interestingly, the defense of suburbia has come not from the intellectuals but from letters, interviews, articles, and books by the children of the pioneers, people such as Ron Rosenbaum, David Beers, and D. J. Waldie. Waldie viewed the issue from a working-class perspective. "You could say that Lakewood was the American Dream made affordable for a generation of industrial workers who in the preceding generation could never aspire to that kind of ownership."[26] Even Bill Griffith, who grew up in Levittown and created Zippy, a cartoon that satirizes suburbia, understood what it meant to his mother. Griffith recalled that Levittown was made up of

working class people . . . salt of the earth type people who saw Levittown as this dream. My mother always told me that for all the drawbacks Levittown had culturally, she still couldn't believe she owned her own house. She came from a family that didn't have much money, and so did my father, and here they were in their own house. It was a miracle to them. They thought they would never live anywhere but an apartment . . . I think they saw it through the eyes of someone who was in love, almost. They had found something and they made it even better than it was.[27]

Even though most Americans now live in suburbs, snobbery toward suburbia and its inhabitants continues. Yet suburbia was a commercial response to a long-standing social need: housing for a third of the nation. People moved to the suburbs because it was their best financial option. Some found it isolating; others found it rich in possibilities. None found it to be a changeless never-never land. From the beginning it has been riven by conflict, and so it continues to be.

Part Five

Suburbia Speaks

Rural town life: Huntington, Long Island, in 1903.

The Gold Coast invasion. William Randoph Hearst's castle—not in San Simeon but in Sand's Point, Long Island, circa 1915.

Otto Kahn's Cold Spring Harbor estate, circa 1920.

By the 1920s, the middle class began its exodus to the suburbs. The middle-class ideal is depicted here; dad returns from work, children run to greet him, as mom stands demurely by the door of her gingerbread house. This cover of a promotional booklet was distributed by the Long Island Railroad Company and the Long Island Real Estate Board in 1923.

FREEPORT

Right: The Long Island countryside was not all that bucolic, as witnessed by this Ku Klux Klan poster for a rally in Freeport in 1926.

1926

Below: A Klan rally marching down the main street of Stonybrook in 1933.

Left: Chatham Village near Pittsburgh, Pennsylvania, was another alternative designed by progressive architects Clarence Stein and Henry Wright in 1932.

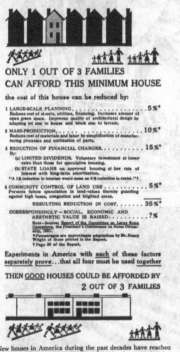

GOOD HOUSES ARE CHEAPER THAN BAD ONES

ONLY 1 OUT OF 3 FAMILIES
CAN AFFORD THIS MINIMUM HOUSE

the cost of this house can be reduced by:

1 LARGE-SCALE PLANNING...................5%*
Reduces cost of streets, utilities, financing. Increases amount of open green space. Improves quality of architectural design by adapting lot size to house and block size to terrain.

2 MASS-PRODUCTION......................10%*
Reduces cost of materials and labor by simplification of manufacturing processes and unitisation of parts.

3 REDUCTION OF FINANCIAL CHARGES...........15%*
By:
(a) LIMITED DIVIDENDS. Voluntary investment at lower rates than for speculative housing.
(b) STATE LOANS on approved housing at low rate of interest with long-term amortization.
"A 1% reduction in interest would mean an 8% reduction in rental."†

4 COMMUNITY CONTROL OF LAND USE...........5%*
Prevents future speculation in land-values thereby guarding against high taxes, congestion and blighted areas.

RESULTING REDUCTION IN COST......35%*

CORRESPONDINGLY — SOCIAL, ECONOMIC AND
AESTHETIC VALUE IS RAISED..........?%

Note–Source: Report of the Committee on Large Scale Operations, the President's Conference on Home Ownership, 1931.
*Percentages are approximate adaptations by Mr. Henry Wright of those printed in the Report.
† Page 26 of the Report.

Experiments in America with each of these factors separately prove...that all four must be used together

THEN GOOD HOUSES COULD BE AFFORDED BY
2 OUT OF 3 FAMILIES

New houses in America during the past decades have reached only the upper third income-group. With adequate planning and modern non-speculative methods of finance, most of the middle third might be reached. For the under-paid and those with no income at all there must be either higher, regular wages, or a direct housing subsidy. (This chart was prepared by the author for the traveling exhibition of Modern Architecture of the Museum of Modern Art, New York.)

Above: In the late 1920s and early 1930s socially conscious architects constructed suburban alternatives—planned, attractive communities for people who were not upper middle class. This chart by Catherine Bauer demonstrates the principles utilized to build such housing.

Above: When the Great Depression hit and Franklin Delano Roosevelt was elected in 1932, New Dealers incorporated the ideas of visionary architects and expanded them to include the working class. This New Deal poster starkly contrasts games children play on tenement streets with kids' leisure time in the government-built Greenbelt towns.

Top: Greenbelt, Maryland, near Washington, D.C., was a model suburban community that included cooperative stores, schools, movie theatres, and playgrounds—all in the interior and accessible by pedestrian walkways.

Left: In Radburn, New
Jersey, architects built a
community for the automo-
bile age. Cars were parked
on the outskirts and pedestrian underpasses connected
homes to schools, recre-
ation areas and the swim-
ming pool.

Below: Sunnyside, Queens, built in 1927, was one of the first large-scale planned
communities. With its built-in open courtyard, children could play safely while adults
socialized. Sunnyside drew a diverse population from the middle and working classes.

When most people think of government-built housing, they imagine huge prison-like structures. This before-
and-after picture shows that this was not always the case. The picture of the Irish Channel (left), a slum in
New Orleans, was taken in 1936. The one on the right was taken in 1939 after the Irish Channel became
the St. Thomas Housing Project. Both pictures were taken from approximately the same vantage point.
(Notice the position of the water tank in both pictures.)

By 1946, there was a very
powerful lobby of private
real estate and building
interests, who joined with
conservative politicians to
oppose public housing.
Here is an example of their
perspective, which links
public housing to socialism.

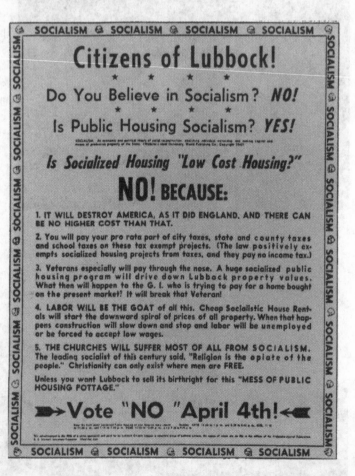

A

B

C

D

E

F

G

H

I

New master builders such as William Levitt believed they had the answer to public housing by constructing affordable houses using assembly-line methods.

A. Trenching machine digs thirty house foundations a day; **B.** Radiant heating coil installation: one man-hour; **C.** Slab poured: three man-hours; **D.** Sills are laid; **E.** Interior dry wall applied; **F.** Framing takes sixty man-hours; **G.** Four men with power saws work from each portable generator; **H.** Sheathing takes thirty-six man-hours; **I.** Road top applied.

To convince people to buy rather than to rent their houses, Levitt advertised that buying was cheaper than renting and that Levitt houses came with modern appliances and conveniences. By 1950, that meant television.

Members of the pioneer generation of Levittown.

An early picture of Roosevelt Field. Notice all the space allocated for parking.

Chapter Thirteen

Suburban Segregation

African Americans who sought to live out the postwar suburban dream on Long Island had limited options. Segregated housing patterns had been the rule long before the war and continued long after. Most African Americans in Freeport, for instance, lived in Bennington Park, which *Newsday* considered "the worst slum in New York State," despite the fact that it was a stone's throw from the new and prosperous Levittown.[1] Bennington Park had been built in the first decade of the century to house southern blacks who came to work as domestics in the wealthy South Shore estates.

By the 1940s many who worked as domestics and artisans had accumulated enough to buy their own houses and plots of land. World War II brought greater employment opportunities through the burgeoning defense industries. Even though the opportunities were not equal and most blacks were employed in the service and maintenance area, a few managed to work in the industrial sector despite ongoing discrimination.

Charles and Meta Meredy, for instance, came from South Carolina to Long Island in 1927. He worked as an artisan: blacksmith, mechanic, and all around handyman. She worked briefly as a domestic servant. For years they lived with various relatives in Hempstead, looking on and off for property they could afford. In 1940 they finally discovered a piece of land in an undeveloped area of Roosevelt and slowly built a house. Although he was a skilled mechanic, Charles got a job at Grumman as a porter and supplemented his income by driving a truck. When war broke out he was finally given a temporary job as Grumman's first black mechanic.

I worked at Grumman for three and a half years and never got a raise or was promoted. I took every course which was supposed to qualify me for a raise but I never got one. I even invented a special pliers and several other tools but Grumman took all the credit. All they ever gave me was a $25 prize.[2]

Although a few residents, like the Meredys, managed to build or purchase homes, most rented substandard housing, often in the same dilapidated buildings that had housed residents since the 1920s. After the war Bennington Park had become an "eyesore." By 1948 the Bennington Park slum contained 250 black families, "people crowded six and eight and ten to a room without sanitation, without electricity, some without even adequate ventilation."[3] Shacks that were worn out a quarter of a century earlier straddled the area that could have provided high taxes as business property.[4] Bennington Park in fact resembled the shanty towns and tobacco roads of the South, from which many of its residents had migrated in search of a better life. As *Newsday* editorialized, "A Negro who escapes the bonds of his life in the South expects to find in the North all the equality the damn Yankees boast so loudly about. Instead, he feels that at every hand the darting cat's paw of discrimination that won't admit it exists."[5]

The Village of Freeport was promoted by the real estate industry in advertising tacitly understood to be for white families only. "You've got a garden and a place to keep a boat . . . people around here take pride in their homes. It's cool in summer, too, with all the bay. All the fishing and swimming you want, complete with schools and a busy, friendly shopping area, new residents, and you don't have to go into New York for a thing."[6] Yet despite enthusiastic promotion, real estate agents knew they couldn't sell Freeport as an idyllic garden locality if potential residents saw a slum in the city center when they came to visit.

Not that others hadn't tried to eradicate the "vicious man-made jungle," as *Newsday* called Freeport's ghetto.[7] In 1941 an interdenominational group of clergymen formed the Freeport Housing Authority to petition the state for funds to rebuild the area.[8] The New York State Housing Commission studied the situation. When it completed the investigation in 1946 it declared the area the worst in the state, in need of immediate rehabilitation, and offered the village a $741,000 loan to build 100 units of new housing to replace the old. The procedure should have been simple; the loan was to be paid back by rents collected on the new buildings.

But things got complicated very fast. The Freeport Village Board, composed solely of conservative property owners committed to segregation, refused to guarantee the loan and turned to other village property owners for a referendum—the first of its kind to be held in the country. Only property owners were allowed to vote in the referendum. "None of the people most closely affected by the vote—the residents of Bennington Park—could vote. . . . Of the village's 25,000 population, only 2,676 voted on the question. They turned the loan down, 1,682 to 994."[9] Not only then did Freeport make the reactionary and racially loaded move of disenfranchising nonproperty owners, it also took the unprecedented step of refusing public housing loan monies.

The residents of Bennington Park did not give up. In 1951, the Nassau County Women's Forum and the American Veterans Committee asked the Freeport Board of Trustees to use the new provisions of the National Housing Act of 1949 "to provide decent homes for our citizens, who are now living in conditions not fit for human beings."[10] They also requested a new referendum. This time the new liberal Freeport mayor and the Village Board both decided to support public housing and a new referendum that read, "Shall the Village of Freeport take advantage of available federal and state funds to eliminate slums and for that purpose establish an authority to erect housing for eligible families in the Village of Freeport?"[11]

Despite broader support for it, public housing remained intensely controversial. Armed with propaganda and over 200 active ground forces, the Northeast Civic Association, located in Freeport's most prosperous neighborhood, led a campaign against the referendum. Employing the hallmark rhetoric that always had been effective for the anti-public housing lobby, the association argued that the referendum represented the threat of "socialistic principles and unlimited power given to an appointed committee, not answerable to the voters of Freeport."[12] They also insisted—unconvincingly—that the slum could be renovated under existing laws.

The mayor called it like it was. Village Board members, he said, were "conservative businessmen who have no use for socialism or any other ism. . . . We are however realistic enough to know that we are faced with a problem which we cannot solve alone. . . . Public housing and the elimination of slums is the best answer to communism since by it you remove one of the conditions in which communism breeds." The mayor also argued that the existing laws had proven useless: "Enforcing local ordinances to eliminate slums has resulted only in removing families and aggravating already crowded conditions."[13]

Newsday supported the eradication of the slums as it had in 1946, this time with daily articles, editorials and arguments calling for the community to approve the referendum. So much press undoubtedly made a difference. There was a good turnout for the referendum. It passed in sixteen out of seventeen election districts. Perhaps the dramatic change also was due to a recent influx of property owners who were more liberal and cosmopolitan than older residents, many of whom were actively involved with the Ku Klux Klan.[14]

Although the referendum passed, changing federal housing policy caused delays and setbacks. In 1953 Congress refused to pass a housing bill that would have made funds available for Freeport's housing project. In 1955 President Eisenhower finally signed legislation extending the Federal Housing Program, clearing the way for low-rent housing contruction in Freeport. The Moxey A. Rigby housing project, named after the first black judge in Nassau County, was completed in 1959. Although this was a small-scale skirmish in the battle for suburban public housing, it is significant that even to this day little public housing has been built in suburbia.

After World War II many African Americans believed that the war for democracy abroad would change segregated practices at home. In the postwar period, however, older, preexisting segregated suburban communities relied on "interlocking friendships, mutual loyalties and existing social pressure . . . as an adequate barrier against Negroes."[15] In suburban boom communities financed largely through Federal Housing Authority (FHA) mortgages, covenants to maintain segregation became a matter of policy, as these communities were new and custom could not be relied on. A 1947 FHA guidebook for suburban development,

Planning Profitable Neighborhoods, stated, "Protective covenants are essential to the sound development of proposed residential areas, since they regulate the use of land and provide a basis for the development of harmonious, attractive neighborhoods." In 1946 the NAACP charged that the FHA was supporting racist housing practices, and in 1948 the U.S. Supreme Court outlawed protective covenants. Yet the FHA waited two years after the Court's decision to announce that it would no longer officially issue mortgages in restricted housing developments. Unofficially the FHA accepted unwritten agreements and traditions of segregation as late as 1968, long after the boom was over.[16]

By the 1950s suburban development was open to white, ethnically diverse middle- and working-class families, but racial diversity continued to be purposely avoided by policy makers and real estate interests. Urban ghettos were reserved for African Americans and other minorities; suburbs were to remain lily white. As early as 1949 Thurgood Marshall articulated the problems inherent in this bifurcation:

> Housing in our society today is more than a shelter. It includes the whole environment in which the home is maintained. A well-built house in a poorly planned, impoverished, slum area, without adequate schools, community facilities, etc., does not provide good housing. Nor does a well-built house in a ghetto provide good housing in a democratic society.[17]

Ignoring the courts and the sound social advice Marshall offered, Levitt, who had moved mountains to shift age-old housing practices, chose to carry on age-old patterns of racism. As he explains, Levitt originally moved to suburbia in the first place to escape the black residents of Brooklyn:

> In the 17th century, in 1624 exactly, a man by the name of Captain Hawkins, an Englishman, bought the first boat load of slaves to Virginia. Up until then there were no black people on this continent. But now the black people were here, they multiplied geometrically until finally a couple of centuries later as they moved into the north, they moved onto the same street we lived on in Brooklyn. Next to

us a black assistant DA moved in. Fearing a diminution of values if too many came in, we picked up and moved out. We then got into the suburbs, into building.[18]

Levitt thus was a pioneer of white flight with both a personal and business stake in keeping Levittown all white. Some Levittown residents wanted to live in an integrated community and organized to change Levitt's policies. In 1947 they formed the Committee to End Discrimination. This organization was an especially irksome thorn in Levitt's side. It brought out all his racism, arrogance, and talent for revenge. In 1949 he refused the committee permission to meet in the Levittown Community Hall, which he could do because all applications for the hall's use had to be cleared by his Manhassett headquarters. He publicly branded committee members as troublemakers and Communists.

Newsday, the major Long Island newspaper whose fortunes were tied to building circulation in communities like Levittown, agreed with Levitt's assessment:

> It is lamentable that the Levitts have been currently under attack by local trouble-makers. Organizations which appear to be either communist dominated or communist inspired have been attempting to raise a racial issue at Levittown. The issue did not exist until it was fostered by people not immediately affected by it. Their only real motive seems to be to set race against race, and, if possible, to bog down the Levitt building program which means homes for thousands of people.[19]

Echoing the common suspicion that organizations fighting for racial justice were probably Communists, the same editorial condemned the Levittown integrationists, claiming that

> their sneaky tactics are demonstrated by mimeographed hand bills which they slip under doors at night in Levittown. Addressed to Levittown veterans, one of these rants, 'Remember how we were told that we were fighting for the four freedoms which were supposed to be for ALL? We believed in it then and we believe in it now. BUT IT'S TIME WE SAW IT IN REAL LIFE!'"[20]

Levitt cracked down on the group in other ways, too. In 1950 he evicted two white families because they had invited black children to spend some summer afternoons playing with their children; they also happened to be committee members. Even after the Fair Housing Act banning segregation in housing was upheld by the U.S. Supreme Court, Levitt continued to justify segregation on the basis of private enterprise.[21] Opening his community to blacks and other minorities, Levitt argued, would be economic suicide: "Most whites prefer not to live in mixed communities. . . . The responsibility [for this] is society's. . . . It is not reasonable to expect that any one builder could or should undertake to absorb the entire risk and burden of conducting such a vast social experiment."[22] Most realtors agreed. White suburbia made them more money.

Although liberals continued to challenge the "caucasian only" clause in Levittown, throughout the 1950s and 1960s racism remained the dominant ideology and outsiders were ostracized. The Arroyo family, for example, is one of two Puerto Rican families who moved to Levittown in the late fifties from the Puerto Rican countryside. They were different in many respects from their neighbors. Both parents worked full time, they had five children, and they spoke Spanish. They were subjected to continual harassment and racism by the community and the schools. Nancy Arroyo, the eldest daughter, recalled the situation:

Since I was so big, I knew there was prejudice. Not a day went by when we weren't called "spics." The people next door even taught their three- and four-year-old grandchildren to say racial slurs. The neighbors on the other side did incredible things. They would throw dirt onto my mother's kitchen when she left the kitchen door open for fresh air. It took ten years for things to calm down somewhat. Still after thirty-six years we are not yet fully accepted.

This harassment extended to the schools.

When I went to school I had problems everyday. I had a cousin who was darker and always in fights. My younger sister had a problem with a teacher and every morning my sister would scream. She was terrified to go to school. My mother, suspecting racism, took off work and in her broken English went to confront the teacher. My mother asked, "What is the problem that my daughter is so terrified? Is it prejudice?" After that the teacher was nicer. On another occasion the school even came to our house and told my mother not to speak to us in Spanish. What else could she speak to us in?[23]

In response to this situation the Arroyos relied on each other. Their extended family became their community. As Nancy states, "We kept to ourselves. We had a strong family structure. We maintained each other, we partied together, we were always together, we defended each other."[24] The two African-American families who slipped through the cracks and moved to Levittown left after a short stay rather than endure the daily provocation that the Arroyos lived through. Levitt's racist policy reigned. Today Levittown remains primarily a white community.

A few builders, however, began to see minorities as an untapped market. They constructed Cape Cod bungalows, six-room ranch houses, and "custom-built specials" in communities already designated for racial minorities—which on Long Island usually meant African Americans. Builder Thomas Romana, hoping to mine this marginalized market, decided to develop Ronek Park, Long Island, without "regard for race, creed or color."[25] The story of Ronek Park is a sobering story of parallels and divergences between the histories of white and black suburbia.

Romano built 1,000 houses in Ronek Park to be sold for $6,999 a piece. In 1950, when Ronek's Park's first model house was shown, most of the 3,000 people who rushed to see it were African Americans. Some had tried to buy in Levittown. Ann Gilmore and her husband, for instance, recall looking for a house there in 1948: "It was a Sunday, and when we got there . . . well, it was strange because we finally approached a salesman to ask for an application. Well, he didn't say anything, but just walked away from us. It was as if we were invisible." The Gilmores' dream home thus demolished in Levittown was restored by the purchase of a modest ranch house in Ronek Park. The Gilmores were not alone in this experience. James Merrick was living in Harlem when he saw an advertisement for the Ronek Park homes and explained his excitement over buying his first house: "We all had new homes. . . . We had never owned a home, most of us."[26]

By the 1960s integration was the major goal of the growing civil rights movement. Although the South is usually remembered as the focus of the struggle, integration battles were fought in the North, too—even in suburbia itself. A new housing crisis was brewing. This time the question was whether government would use its power to enforce residential integration. Gains had been made in integrating public accommodations, education, and transportation. The riots of that decade made clear that inadequate housing was still a major component of poverty and segregation.

In 1971 George Romney, head of Housing and Urban Development, decided that one solution to urban poverty to build low-income public housing in the suburbs. The government, however, unwilling to finance public housing, ignored Romney. As in the post–World War II period, the federal government turned to private enterprise, subsidizing the real estate industry and guaranteeing banks low-income mortgages for individual home owners, this time for minorities. President Nixon, in a speech about housing, explained the government's policy, maintained that "we will not seek to impose economic integration upon an existing local jurisdiction; at the same time, we will not countenance any use of economic measures as a subterfuge for racial discrimination."[27] In other words, the federal government would not mandate integration or underwrite new integrated housing developments in suburbia. Nevertheless, African Americans and Hispanics challenged these policies by insisting on their rights to join the great suburban migration.

Between 1940 and 1960 three million African Americans left the still mostly rural South for the cities of the North hoping to find industrial jobs that would let them share in postwar prosperity as well as relief from oppressive and often lethal southern racism.[28] These hopes were kindled by civil rights activism from the late 1950s to the 1970s. At the same time, white people left the cities for the suburbs. Cities became more segregated, crime-ridden, and impoverished. The suburban migration absorbed enormous amounts of federal aid for housing and highways, draining the cities of resources. Meanwhile, however, the civil rights movement inspired new local and federal policies in education, health, social welfare, housing, and law enforcement. These government programs, together with the vast expansion of the civil service sector, helped foster the growth of a new black middle class. From 1960 to 1976 the black middle class tripled in size.[29]

Middle-class black families who sought better housing, schools, and integrated neighborhoods were drawn to the suburbs. Hazel Dukes, a longtime Democratic Party and NAACP activist, explains:

They didn't think they were escaping, they were looking for something better for their children. They wanted backyards and frontyards, they wanted a garage for themselves, they wanted comfortable spaces. They didn't want apartments, they wanted houses. People then were getting a salary that wasn't being eaten up in taxes. They could afford a car and could drive back and forth to the city, if they worked there. They wanted good schools for their children, they wanted a better life for their children.[30]

Long Island's South Shore, particularly the Roosevelt, Freeport, and Hempstead areas, had special allure for black suburbanites. Located close to New York City, convenient to jobs in both the city and the suburbs, the South Shore offered less costly houses and an attractive place to live. Like white suburbanites, some African Americans traded a familiar community for a suburban home. Jean Wyatt, who worked for the motor vehicles bureau, and her husband, who worked for the post office, lived in a deteriorating housing project in Brooklyn. They thought of moving to the suburbs when their son reached the first grade. Jean explains:

We thought our son would have a better life in suburbia. We began looking in the newspapers and found a place in Freeport. I transferred my job to Long Island. We were both city kids, but we thought we'd give the suburbs a try. We'd live the suburban dream. We tried it and it was a bit of a dream and a bit of a nightmare. I loved my house, not having to come into an elevator. But I was lonelier here than in the city. The projects were an automatic community, here it was more difficult to make friends and generally people didn't need to be as supportive here.[31]

Helena White, a schoolteacher, and her husband, an accountant, also lived in the city but felt their children needed more space. They moved into a modern house in Freeport. Her husband wanted to move there because

he wanted a house with push buttons and a garage you drive into. . . . He considers himself a successful black professional. Along with that image and a successful self-esteem, there has to be this life style that justifies a reason for going to work every day. It has to have a certain look. That look is a green manicured lawn and a modern house with push-button facilities. My image is different, living in an old house in a more ritzy community like Garden City [an exclusive, segregated North Shore community]. But it's his lifestyle ideas that were important when we moved.[32]

Turner Bond moved to New York City from North Carolina. First a sharecropper's son, he moved from the cotton fields of Carolina to the opportunities of the city in the early 1960s. After many years he earned a degree from City College. After several years doing odd jobs, Turner got a job at Con Edison. One dream lingered—his desire to own a house on Long Island. Long Island was portrayed as "the place to be. It was a place where you could raise a good prosperous family, just like on television. The home, the picket fence, Long Island was the epitome of the American dream." After living for years in a housing project in Queens, in 1985 he finally bought a house in Freeport.[33]

Such dreams could be realized only in those suburban communities that had a sizeable black presence. Levittown was closed to African Americans, but the older communities of Roosevelt and Freeport drew African-American families and single people through word of mouth, family ties, and job opportunities. In 1967 the New York Times reported that Roosevelt was becoming a racially mixed community where "houses sell anywhere from $15,000 to $50,000. Many of the Negroes who have moved in are college graduates who are teachers, personnel managers and other professionals. Another group is made up of such workers as truck drivers and gardeners."[34]

*   *   *

The new black middle class originally regarded Roosevelt as a place where integration was possible. John Rice, Jr., a Harvard graduate in 1950 and an Air Force major in the Strategic Air Command in the 1960s, moved into a split-level house in Roosevelt in 1968 with his wife and three children. At the time, all his neighbors were white. He felt he had arrived. Yet within ten years all his white neighbors had moved and his block was inhabited solely by African American families. Parts of Roosevelt, once well-off, became impoverished. One would not know this by looking at his house, his two Jaguars, or his extensive gardens. All his life he sought a place among the American elite, yet in many ways this prospect still eludes him.[35]

John Scott grew up in Roosevelt. He remembers that when he was a boy, "the town was mainly white and most of his friends were white," although he recalls an incident when a white mother refused to let her five-year-old son come out to play with him. "At first I was confused, but came to realize it was due to my race. I was extremely upset because before this incident I was absolutely color-blind." By the time he was in high school, "more and more black people started to come to Roosevelt, there were almost as many blacks as there were whites." After Martin Luther King, Jr., was murdered, "the whites began to notice the many blacks coming to town. Then whites started to leave in great numbers." Scott left too, married, and had four children. Since the couple both had college degrees, they obtained work in the city at the Department of Social Services in 1967. John and his wife wanted to move to Long Island, but in an integrated community. They were turned down for a house in Baldwin and shown a place in a poorer part of town. Ironically, the Scotts now own a house in Roosevelt, where in his own lifetime he experienced the community change from white to integrated to segregated.[36]

In part the transformation of Roosevelt had to do with whites' fears about integration—in the town in general, and the schools in particular. As African-American families moved to Roosevelt, they were steered to the southeast section of town, where a small number of black people already lived. These families enrolled their children in the Theodore Roosevelt elementary school. As black children began attending the school, white parents withdrew their children and enrolled them in the Centennial school on the largely white northeast side of town. By 1965 this led to de facto school segregation. As a result, the Education Department of New York State ordered the integration of the Roosevelt school system by March 1966.

While some white parents accepted integrated schools, others enrolled their children in private or parochial schools, as had been done in the South. By 1967 For Sale signs began to appear in larger numbers. The school integration plan, while somewhat successful, in the end backfired. Even parents satisfied with integration were moving out of Roosevelt. In 1967 Dr. Daniel Terry, superintendent of the Roosevelt school system for eighteen years, told a *New York Times* reporter that while integration had gone very smoothly, "We have no feuds in school, no gangs against the Negroes. It hasn't reached the parents. Many parents have said to me that their child is getting along just fine, but 'we' are going to move anyway. Negro and white children play together on the sidewalks and the community had had no racial disturbances. Still, there will be quite an exodus again at the end of this year."[37]

At the same time, journalists were busy writing sensationalistic stories about Roosevelt that focused on the threat of school busing, the "dumping" of welfare families, and the fear of lowered property values. The media added fuel to white flight. Stories with headlines such as "The Making of a Black Ghetto," "Harlem Comes to Long Island," and "Negroes Invade Roosevelt" played on racial stereotypes and created constant fear on the part of white home owners. To this day local Roosevelt residents blame the media for what happened to their town, particularly what they call "the yellow journalism" of *Newsday*.[38]

To a large degree white flight was helped by a hidden hand. Recognizing that quick money was to be made from these residents and available federal mortages, real estate brokers, agents, and speculators also moved in, employing two strategies that deeply affected black suburban migration: blockbusting and racial steering.

By the early 1960s the South Shore of Long Island was a prime target. Roosevelt is an excellent example of a successfully blockbusted South Shore Long Island community. It is a small, unincorporated village in Nassau County without a local government, train station, or sizeable commercial center. From 1920 to 1960 Roosevelt was a predominantly white middle- and working-class town with a small black community. Then suddenly, overnight, it fell prey to block-busting and racial steering.

Blockbusting is a tactic real estate agents use to create an unstable housing market through fear and intimidation. Their strategy is to create a climate in which long-term residents sell their houses at lower prices, and agents then can resell homes at higher prices. Blockbusting was used far and wide: the suburbs of Boston, Philadelphia, and Cleveland, for example, all were targets of these campaigns. Through the use of telephones, leaflets, and word of mouth, families were told that the influx of racial and ethnic minorities would make property values plummet, or worse, the real estate agent would say, "You have a twelve-year-old daughter. What if she were raped? You'd have a mulatto grandchild." Fearful families then would make deals with agents to sell their houses for less than their value. One blockbuster, twenty years later, described what he was told to do:

> We were told you get the listings any way you can. It's pretty easy to do; I just scare the hell out of them. And that's what we did. We were not only making money, we were having fun doing what we were doing. We all liked selling real estate—if you want to call what we were doing selling real estate. And it got to a point that in order to have fun while we were working, we would try to outdo each other with the most outlandish threats that people would believe and chuckle at the end of the day. . . . I had fun at it. I'd go down the street with a [black] buyer and ask, Which house do you want? He'd pick one, and I'd ring the door bell and say, these people want to buy your house. If the lady said no, I'd say the reason they're so interested is that their cousins, aunts, mother, whatever, it's a family of twelve, are moving in across the street, and they want to be near them. Most of the time, that worked. If that didn't work, you'd say their kid just got out of jail for housebreaking, or rape or something that would work.

Blockbusting employs the neighborhood version of the domino theory. Neighbors start to hear that families down the street moved in the middle of the night and before you know it, large numbers of white families become susceptible to the offers of real estate brokers. In some cases blockbusters resorted to ex-treme measures. "There were instances of housebreaks that were arranged only to scare people out. That was the worst. . . . I don't think anybody to this day is aware that anybody arranged this. Nobody was ever arrested for it, convicted of it, or anything else.[39]

Before 1968 brokers and speculators benefited by a game called multiple mortgages. As New York Secretary of State John Lomenzo testified before the Senate Judiciary Committee, "Let's say the market value of the house was $15,000. The speculator would offer to buy it for $10,000, all cash with the homeowners readily accepting as they became panicked."[40] The next step is to offer it at double the price or more to a minority family with the incentive of an automatic mortgage qualification with no money down. The plan is backed by a complex scheme of buying triple money mortgages on the purchased house and selling them to banks and insurance agencies at discounts. The broker then could make a profit of nearly 90 percent. The major flaw is that the high mortgages car-ried by the minority family are usually far in excess of the worth of the property, making default of payment a constant worry.

Yvonne Simmons, one of the few black real estate agents on Long Island, ex-plained how this happened in Roosevelt:

The houses were less out here. Real estate agents would steer black people to cer-tain areas and the white people got nervous as they do sometimes. The real estate agents wanted to make money and this was the way to do it; to steer people to cer-tain areas and create fear in white home owners. It's all about money. For people that were prejudiced, this was like pushing their buttons. This was great for the people doing the steering. There are myths that when blacks move into an area, the property values go downhill.

These prejudices are precisely what blockbusters count on. Simmons went on:

Frightened people would sell cheap, they would try to get the most they could, but their overriding desire is to leave. On the other hand, blacks wanted better living conditions than they had in the city. They wanted their kids to go to better schools. So the brokers would sell to blacks at inflated prices, really upping the price. After a while some families who couldn't really afford it would get into financial trouble and lose their houses. But the brokers were long gone.[41]

Another profitable blockbusting tactic real estate agents use is moving welfare families to a neighborhood. These families, residents are told, have no stake in the preservation and upkeep of their homes or community, and property values will plunge. Fast money is made this way. In Roosevelt, for instance, most of the houses originally were one-family dwellings. Landlords and real estate speculators illegally subdivided single-family houses. Then each subdivision was offered to the county's welfare department which ignored the law and tripled the rent. Willie Pyatt, father of eight, told a *New York Times* reporter that he had had difficulties finding an apartment for his family in communities other than Roosevelt. Mr. Pyatt said that the welfare department had put him in a subdivided house, paying $200 for five bottom rooms. In all, the welfare department was paying $3,600 a month to an absentee landlord on behalf of the house's eighteen occupants. Pyatt said that "The Welfare Department is spreading the cancer by putting four or five families in a one family house and paying exorbitant rents for them."[42]

Yvonne Simmons confirms Pyatt's observation and blames the Nassau County welfare department for placing large numbers of welfare families in Roosevelt.

It's the fault of people in power. The county is in charge of the welfare system. If you have welfare families it would seem that you could divide them equitably, so that there wouldn't be a whole influx of them in one area. So many landed in Roosevelt. Of course when people don't own their own homes they tend not to take care of them as well as someone who can afford to take care of them. If you get your welfare check and you have a certain amount of money for A, B, C, and D, when it comes to getting some grass seed for the lawn, they're not going to think about that; they just think about survival.[43]

In addition to blockbusting, racial steering helped ensure ongoing segregation. Real estate brokers and agents designated certain communities as either white or black. No matter what community a family desired to live in, they would be taken to communities brokers and agents deemed racially appropriate. To attract particular constituencies, real estate agents advertised in papers such as the *Amsterdam News* in New York City and in southern papers read by blacks. Billboards on major roads leading out of southern cities showed black families living in attractive suburban houses in Roosevelt.[44] Similarly, whites were shown houses in white communities, even if they asked about other towns. Ads in newspapers and magazines read mainly by whites displayed images of white suburban home owners.

Alvin Dorfman, a lawyer with a long history of civil rights work in Freeport, and his wife, Shelly, a community activist, moved to Freeport from Brooklyn in 1963. They wanted to buy a house in an integrated neighborhood, but "the real estate agent wouldn't show us houses in black areas. When we pressed them, they showed us poor houses in Roosevelt and a few that were much too expensive. Then they showed us good houses in Freeport, near the Baldwin school district, an all-white neighborhood."[45]

In contrast, Ivan and Cynthia Ashby, who moved to Brooklyn from Barbados, wanted to move to Long Island when they had a child. The decision was tough for Cynthia; she didn't want to leave her family and friends. In 1977 the Ashbys went to a real estate agent because they were interested in buying a house in Baldwin on Long Island. "The real estate agent showed little interest in us and what we wanted because we were black. The neighborhood was all white and the house was expensive, but we had good credit to get a mortgage. We did show a great deal of interest in the house, but the agent sold that house to someone else. We still pass by the house every once in a while and see what could have been." Eventually the Ashbys bought a house in Freeport, which Cynthia was excited about, but Ivan "was so deeply concerned about the mortgage payments that he lost a great deal of weight."[46]

Louise Simpson, who worked at the Federal Reserve Board, and her husband, who worked for the post office, had to move from their Brooklyn project because they were earning too much according to housing authority guidelines. She recalls:

> We had to move. I really wanted to live near the city but since there were no fair housing ordinances in 1960, we didn't find any houses close to the city. We were steered to northeastern Freeport, really a part of Roosevelt. We were going to move to Lakeview, which was also being developed, but I felt the realtor pulled a deal and we ended up here. I'm sure I could not have purchased a house except in northeast Freeport.[47]

Ramona Crooks, who was head of the Freeport antiblockbusting real estate agency, explains,

> There were brokers in Massapequa, brokers in Seaford, brokers in Merrick [nearby nonintegrated towns], and when a black person went to them, they weren't going to show them a house in Seaford or Merrick. Most black people I interviewed wanted to live in an integrated neighborhood, but if you and your wife were black, if you went to a broker in Massapequa, you'd end up buying a house in Roosevelt or Freeport.[48]

Racial steering was so successful that it exists as a real estate tactic to this day.

Racial steering and blockbusting shattered Roosevelt. Local residents almost uniformly describe the transformation of their town as an instant event, quick as a prairie fire. Blockbusting in fact takes considerable time. In Roosevelt it took at least fifteen years. In 1957 the population of Roosevelt was 80 percent white and 20 percent black. In 1967 it was 60 percent white and 40 percent black. By 1980 it was 80 percent black.[49]

Blockbusting, however, did not occur without a struggle. The Roosevelt Community Relations Council, organized by Catholic, Jewish, Protestant, and other community leaders, worked hard to counteract fear and intimidation. Initiatives came from religious leaders, as Roosevelt was an unincorporated village in the town of Hempstead and had no political structure of its own.[50] In Hempstead, political life was dominated by a Republican machine, unresponsive to integration and essentially racist. The council sent out the following call to Roosevelt residents in 1963:

> For some time, a group of community leaders, both white and Negro, and the clergymen representing the churches of our community, have been meeting to discuss the real estate situation in Roosevelt. We are aware that certain real estate dealers have been using Roosevelt to effect the "fast sell" of homes. They have been doing this by cards left under doors, by phone calls, and by other more dramatic means of pressure, commonly referred to as blockbusting.
>
> The "Block Buster" is a dealer in real estate who gets people scared about property values by promoting rumors of invasion by minority groups such as Negroes. He buys their property for a song and resells for a large profit. He tries to panic a great number of families into listing their homes. His tools are ignorance, fear, falsehoods and rumors.[51]

The council advised residents to stand firm, resist the real estate brokers' high pressure and bring them to the attention of the council. If selling is necessary, residents were told, be sure to be represented by someone who knows your interests. If family homes are used by more than one family in your area, bring it to the attention of your clergyman. The council reiterated that "both the white and Negro populace are interested in keeping our town inhabited by God-fearing, law-abiding and loyal Americans."[52]

By 1967 another group, the United Civic Organization (UCO), composed of twenty civic, fraternal, and church groups, also was working to discourage blockbusting and maintain the 60 percent to 40 percent race ratio. One UCO member, Arthur Choice, who ran a successful local fuel oil business, summed up the feelings of many black residents: "There's one thing I don't understand. The view that just because Negroes are moving in, the town will turn into a ghetto. This is insulting to the Negro."[53] UCO's program called for federal intervention in the form of money to maintain racial balance and an end to blockbusting in all its forms—including the collusion between the Nassau County Department of Welfare and greedy absentee landlords who were placing welfare families in houses recently abandoned by whites. But Morton Decker, UCO's president, was doubtful about his organization's power to stop white flight. "How do you get through to white people who have stereotyped images and have never really known a Negro socially?"[54]

In spite of these community actions, by 1980 Roosevelt was 80 percent black, economically depressed, educationally deprived, and widely regarded as a ghetto—though not all Roosevelt home owners agree. Community organizations and churches have active memberships. Ruth Grefe, one of the remaining white residents, finds Roosevelt to be a hospitable community. With her husband, Grefe built her own house in Roosevelt in the 1940s. The Grefes raised a family and were pillars of their church and community. In the 1960s the Grefes did not succumb to the blockbusting scare; they stayed in Roosevelt, as they had permanent roots there—Ruth's family was one of the founders. Even after her husband died Roosevelt remained her town. Her neighbors look in on her and help her out, and she has many friends. She is still active in her church, where she is one of three white members. She describes Roosevelt not as a ghetto but as "a big family where everyone cares for everyone else."[55]

America's foremost community organizer, Saul Alinsky, once caustically observed that "integration is the time between when the first black family moves in and the last white family moves out."[56] This still rings true in many cases, and suburban segregation confirms the pattern. Only the tactics change, and most of Long Island—as well as the nation's suburbs—remain segregated, regardless of attempts to reverse the course. Sometimes, however, communities learn from the failures of others and successfully beat back the blockbusters, creating integrated communities. Freeport is one such town.

Chapter Fourteen

The Battle for Integration

Freeport managed to combat most of the blockbusting and white flight that plagued nearby Roosevelt. Many Freeport residents refused to sell their homes, and the town ended up subsidizing its own real estate bureau, outwitting the real estate brokers. Freeport did have serious battles over residential and school integration, but here African-American and white families—parents and home owners—forged an alliance to create an integrated, cosmopolitan, and multicultural suburban community, one of the very few in the nation. This did not happen by chance; nor did it happen without a great deal of strife. It was the product of the civil rights movement and the conflicts it stirred up in local residents: black and white, young and old, student and parent, liberal and conservative.

Before 1960 most of the neighborhoods of Freeport (south, southwest, northeast) were predominantly white and defined by class. Most African Americans lived in the center of town in low-income projects and apartments. In the early 1960s black middle-class families began to move into Freeport in greater numbers, although still in a segregated pattern. Residents referred to it as an old-fashioned dixie cup (vanilla and chocolate ice cream cut down the middle), with blacks on one side, whites on the other. Residential segregation affected school life. As residents recall, "In the early days, blacks would walk in one door to get the [school] buses to the northeast, the whites would use the other to go south."[1] Blockbusting began in Freeport around the same time unscrupulous brokers brought in families on welfare, promoted panic selling, and threatened neighborhood decline.

In 1964 the North East Civic Association responded to this threat by collect-

ing signatures and petitions from home owners stating their refusal to be so-
licited by real estate agents. More than 240 home owners signed the petition.
These signatures were sent to the New York secretary of state, who said, "We
will instruct realtors in the Freeport area not to solicit homeowners who listed
their names."[2] He then issued cease and desist orders to real estate brokers based
on these petitions. Four licenses were revoked. Although somewhat successful,
this campaign did not effectively stem the tide of blockbusting.

Freeport's elementary schools were, however, successfully integrated in 1964
without incident under the same plan that had caused the upheaval in Roosevelt.
By 1968 about 4,000 black families lived in Freeport, half of whom were above
the poverty level; some began to seek homes in traditionally white neighborhoods. *Newsday* described Freeport then as a community that was "neither a
ghetto nor snow white."[3] But under this peaceful facade racism was alive and
well. As Louise Simpson points out,

> It was a whole kind of condescending attitude associated with people in Benning-
> ton Park because a lot of these people had migrated to Freeport as domestics. So
> that condescending attitude of this is your status, that is your mentality and your
> daughter is going to grow up to be the same thing as you—was there. These were
> the blacks they had contact with, they did not have contact with black people who
> thought of themselves as equals.[4]

By 1968 the population of Freeport was more integrated than it had been, but
segregated practices persisted; sometimes "blacks were forced to sit in the back
of buses on the way to school."[5] Black students often were considered by their
white teachers as troublemakers and academically inferior. Tracking and discipline were prevalent in both public and parochial schools.

In Freeport's public schools these policies could be challenged, and the newly
arrived black middle class felt that retrograde racist customs could be changed.
Black parents and their children, who saw televised images of southern civil
rights confrontations, were intent on addressing the same grievances in their
own community. The public high school, which was 22 percent African Ameri-

can, became the focus of racial tensions in the community. Small incidents turned into big issues.

The battle lines were drawn. Black parents and some white liberals felt the need to confront racial injustice; some were embarrassed that they had not acted sooner. Some students, influenced by the nationwide militant college student movement, called for immediate action. Groups such as the SNCC (Student Non-Violent Coordinating Committee) and SDS (Students for a Democratic Society) demanded radical changes in education, particularly the end of segregated school practices in both the North and South. White conservatives felt that black students who took outspoken stands on the school system were not being punished severely enough.

Between December 1968 and April 1969 Freeport High School became the site of sit-ins, walkouts, and confrontations with the faculty and principal. As the town became polarized, some school officials tried to defuse tensions by listening to grievances and trying to bring black and white students together. In December 1968 black high school students demanded an end to the segregated bus system; that the school teach African-American history to all students; that the school hire black teachers, guidance counselors, and administrators; and that January 15 be celebrated as Martin Luther King, Jr., Day and made a legal holiday.[6] Marquita James, one of the few black teachers who taught social studies and race relations, recalls,

> By April, the black students put real pressure on the principal to desegregate the
> school buses and other things. The principal said that he wasn't strong enough to
> make a change and that the Klan members on the school board didn't even want
> to make it an issue. Students were having meetings in their houses and a plan was
> hatched to confront the principal . . . I came into the cafeteria and the principal,
> who was six feet, was standing on a table, his head bowed and students surround-
> ing him firing questions. After this incident the principal threatened to resign un-
> less the school bus changed. The vote on the school board was very narrow, the
> buses were desegregated by one vote. After the results of the vote were an-
> nounced, the black students stood in front of the building with clenched fists for

victory. A backlash followed: fights broke out, the mass media had a field day and all hell broke loose.[7]

The next day white students met with the principal to protest the way authorities had handled the cafeteria sit-in. "The Freeport Riots," as the press called them and local residents remember them, began on the evening of April 24, 1969. What happened would be considered minor in the city, but in a suburban context these were major confrontations.

On April 24 the student council called a meeting at the Village Recreation Center to try to resolve tensions between white and black students. Ironically, this meeting only exacerbated the problem. It revealed three clear constituencies: militant black students, white racist students, and white and black students who supported black demands but were eager to heal wounds and make peace. People got angry; groups of black and white students began to walk out. Outside the meeting "the action was confused and fast." Things turned violent. Two black youths were stabbed and one wounded by white students, and the white racist student leader was attacked by a group of black students and hospitalized.[8]

Town officials debated closing the school, but decided with some trepidation to keep it open and send police officers. Again violence broke out. Tables and chairs were thrown, windows were broken, police were wounded, and the American flag was torn down. Outside the school, cars were damaged and passersby attacked, but the only arrests were two black students charged with disorderly conduct.

In Roosevelt 200 black students gathered to discuss what had happened in Freeport. The group took to the streets and ran through the small business district breaking windows. Four whites were injured. The press invoked stereotypes in typically melodramatic fashion, with such headlines as "200 Youth in Racial Rampage" and "4 Hurt as Negro Youths Roam."[9]

Both black and white parents in Freeport were afraid to send their children to school the next day. School and village officials responded by lining the corridors and the outside of the school with more than sixty Nassau County and local police. Still, about 50 percent of the student body stayed away entirely. Black parents worried about whether the students needed protection *from* the police. As one parent put it, "This is like Selma and Detroit and Montgomery. Isn't this a mess? I know they're not here to protect my brother."[10]

The violence in Freeport was not an isolated event. In 1969 students throughout the country were demanding, demonstrating, and confronting power, from San Francisco State to Columbia University, often resulting in violence, police intervention, and arrests. As Dan Mandel, a local lawyer and activist, explained at the time,

> The core of this black upheaval isn't in the schools. It is more vocal there because youth often react with less restraint in many instances than adults. The problem is the economic inequality which forces a poor black child to go to school knowing he can't achieve the same material things as his white classmate. This community has not anticipated the needs of minority groups or tried to better the situation.[11]

In addition, black middle-class parents who moved to Freeport hoped that suburban schools would offer their children a better education in a safe environment. They were bitterly disappointed by the segregated buses, tracking (putting minority students in nonacademic classes), and unequal disciplinary practices but did not see any other more suitable place. As one Freeport resident said, "my parents moved to Queens when the Harlem schools got bad, then we moved to Freeport when Queens got bad. We bought a house and thought that we had bought some peace and quiet. Now it's bad here, but there is nowhere else to go. Now we need to stay and make this place live up to its promise."[12]

Disturbed by violence, threat of bodily injury, and fear that their children would be suspended, black parents began to organize. Louise Simpson's daughter attended Freeport High School and was active in the protests:

> My daughter told me that there were serious things happening in school because of the black demands and that she might be suspended. Over the weekend I met with some black parents who said they would be at the school on Monday. That Monday, I took off work and went down to the school to be there in case anything happened. I saw a lot of parents I did not know. They were new home owners who had moved to Freeport and were concerned about their children. What impressed

me the most was that there was a car full of black men sitting there to protect the children. It was the first time I had seen black men take off work to do something like this. And we really needed them.

We were there for several days, the white boys would come out with their chains and belts and so forth. I remember going to a school board meeting during the week and the black parents sat down in front to make their demands about what was going to happen to their children. These white youngsters, about two hundred of them, marched around to show their power. Talk about intimidation. I had my daughter with me and I was intimidated—even the police seemed scared.[13]

Chris Sprowal, a longtime labor organizer and community activist, was one of these concerned new home owners. Before moving to Freeport he had been involved in the Congress of Racial Equality (CORE) in both North and South and was an organizer for District 1199 (Health and Hospital Workers Union). He and his family moved to Freeport when he felt he needed a break from the intense activity, something he thought the suburbs would offer. He quickly realized he was wrong. Charismatic and skilled in grassroots organizing, Chris became a leader in the community and helped to form the Black Coalition, an organization of black parents who worked for racial justice. He was one of the men Simpson described meeting that Monday morning. Sprowal argued that his involvement in the school struggle happened

> because the black kids said that no one was supporting them in their demands and that they were being suspended at higher rates than white students. They had to riot to get basic demands. They said their parents didn't support them and nor did any community group. That's why when a group of twenty black men showed up at the school, the kids cheered and were proud of us for taking off work and staying all day.[14]

The situation was explosive. Both parents and children were deeply involved. Julius Pearse, the first black policeman hired by the Freeport Police Department, remembers the atmosphere as tense. Like Sprowal, he felt that the "black kids had real gripes, but no one was listening. They acted to make people listen." This was a difficult time for him; he often was accused of being an Uncle Tom. *Newsday* noted, "Julius Pearse was expected to go to Freeport High School in a dual capacity—as one of the policemen on guard against disruption and as a Community Relations officer quietly trying to bring black and white students together."[15] Yet his unique position also gave him certain advantages. Pearse had access to community organizations as well as the white establishment and the police. He recollects:

> I met with community groups to tell them I would protect them, but I couldn't tol-
> erate broken windows. But windows were broken. I then told the local leaders to
> talk to the kids. I told them this because I knew my side would call in the National
> Guard and the state police. I had to pacify the militants under the law. There was
> organization and agitation on both sides. There were white agitators as well.[16]

Whites too began organizing. These parents considered the school a harmful and unsafe environment for their children and called for law and order in frankly racialized terms. Integration was a menace, they argued. One white parent told a reporter, "You see it at Cornell and you see it at Freeport High School. Liberalism didn't make this country great and it's not going to help us now. We have to crack down on every law violated–hard."[17]

Jomer Rand, one parent whose daughter complained about unsafe school conditions, became a leader overnight and the most notorious white conservative in town. He lived on the south side of Freeport in a white working-class neighborhood not yet integrated, and he had no contact with black people. He had been a professional wrestler and teamster. He was known to be aggressive and angry. Rand recalled being a "couch potato" who before the demonstrations spent his considerable leisure time watching "the boob tube" and tuning out. "From 1952 to 1969, I was the average tax paying, truck driver, functioning alcoholic." This routine abruptly ended the night of the "riot."

> This friend of mine, Gus, who was an electrician, his daughter was beat up. I hap-
> pened to run into him and he said: We're going to a meeting tonight. I said what
> kind of meeting. And he said there's trouble and I said, yeah, I heard it over the ra-

dio. And he was livid . . . this man. He said: "I'm gonna get a shotgun and I'm gonna shoot some niggers." I said, "Gus, let me calm you down," so I went to the meeting and I became a community leader by default.[18]

Putting his union experience to work, Rand organized an inchoate group of fifty white parents. Although many had never heard of picket lines, he got them to picket the high school and junior high on that same Monday. Rand and his group showed up bright and early with placards that read, "No School Until It's Safe," "How About *Our* Civil Rights?" and "Safe Johns for Our Janes."[19] When the press approached the group, Rand immediately assumed the role of spokesperson.

The Concerned Parents of Freeport (CPF), as the group called itself, decided to hold a meeting at the Sons of Italy Hall. Between 400 and 600 people packed the hall. Black parents who tried to attend were barred from entry. Rand said it was "because we don't know any blacks and they're the ones who are beating up our kids, let's get to know ourselves before we invite any blacks." While the crowd refused to listen to Mayor Robert Sweeney or the president and vice-president of the school board, they did listen to Rand, who exclaimed, "We feel our children are like a bunch of white sheep that have been attacked by black wolves while the shepherd stands around."[20]

Speaker after speaker, voices shaking with emotion, criticized the mayor and school board officials for "handcuffing the cops and going easy on the Negroes." Rand drew wild applause when he called for overt police intervention: "If you want to take the handcuffs off our police just tell the mayor and the school officials." He then brought the crowd to its feet by declaring, "If some of the black people have decided to declare war on white people, they should know that war works two ways . . . . I'd rather have my kids out of school with heads empty of knowledge instead of in school with heads full of welts." CPF demanded the suspension of any student who left school without permission, carried a weapon, or participated in an unauthorized meeting during school hours. They wanted the arrest of any student found in the halls without permission, that the halls be patrolled during school hours, and public review of demands made by black students. They also demanded that school officials grant these conditions or re-sign.[21]

Sixty black students were expelled or suspended soon after their participation in demonstrations. The Concerned Parents of Freeport thought they had been successful because the school board conceded to all their demands, but they un-derestimated the power of the white liberal alliance with civil rights and black power organizations. One black parent on behalf of her daughter got a court in-junction to block the suspensions. In court papers she charged the school board with "complete capitulation to white racist parents," claimed that the hearings were being held in "an atmosphere of hysteria," and charged that top-ranking school board members attended a "white extremist meeting where blacks were systematically excluded."[22]

The parent also charged that no white students were suspended, even though they had been involved in unlawful activities. One board member admitted that none of the students who were suspended or expelled were white, but added that "there is absolutely no racial motive behind our actions." After much pressure and legal maneuvering, the suspensions and expulsions ultimately were dropped, although some students were taken out of the day session and sent to night school.[23]

In the aftermath some Freeport residents organized a group called the Hu-man Relations Commission, whose purpose was to find a meeting ground be-tween black and white students in the high school. The commission hired Leroy Ramsey, an expert in race relations, who coordinated a six-week summer retreat where black and white students and teachers were paid to study the problems of the community and seek solutions. Another school-sponsored group sought ways "to open communication among people of different ethnic and racial back-grounds in an effort to redefine a sense of common purpose among the citizens of Freeport."[24] Out of these meetings the town decided to build a recreation center, so that youngsters would have an outlet for their energy.

In the meantime the CPF and their leader, Jomer Rand, did not stop at school issues. Next they went after Julie Pearse, who had given a talk to a local community group during which he referred to the members of CPF as "the sons

and daughters of the KKK." He also counseled his audience to overlook CPF because there were many white people in Freeport who believed in equality. Rand
insisted that Pearse had called Freeport a KKK town and demanded that the
mayor conduct a hearing to fire him. At the hearing, which was open and widely
attended by white and black activists, Pearse told Rand in front of the police
chief that he was "going to give in his badge, take him down the stairs and kick
his butt." No violence occurred as a result of this threat, and the mayor dropped
Rand's charges against Pearse.[25]

The Freeport community, brought together by strife, appeared to be coming apart at
the seams. This unstable and sometimes violent time—not exactly the suburban
dream—created the perfect climate for blockbusting. In 1970 blockbusters descended on Freeport, flush with victory from Roosevelt and ready to begin their
campaign of scare and sell. Some white families moved out to less turbulent
Long Island enclaves, and black middle-class and poor families started to move
in to areas where previously there had been few African Americans. Local residents feared their town would be stigmatized by rebellion and might go the way
of Roosevelt.

Such fears were fueled by the media's depiction of Freeport as a town doomed
to become a ghetto. *Newsday* ran an article entitled "Freeport: A Village Where
the Races Go Their Separate Ways." Even Mayor Sweeney, a Republican, objected to the biased coverage and wrote an angry letter to *Newsday*.

> *Newsday* seems determined to present the most negative, most distorted view
> possible of what is really a fine community.... The article is headlined
> "Freeport—A Village Where the Races Go Their Separate Ways," and the impli-
> cation is clear that Freeport is somehow unique in the nation and the world when
> it comes to problems between the races. If Freeport is indeed unique, it is the fact
> that we have made greater efforts and greater progress in human relations than
> have most other communities throughout the United States.
>
> This article could have been written from a positive standpoint—and it
> should have been so written—if you had any interest in drawing a true picture of

Freeport. Instead, your reporters obviously were so intent upon their own precon-
ceived ideas that they produced a conglomeration of inaccuracies.

   If your reporter wanted a true picture of race relations in the area, he could
easily have determined that organizations such as Civic Leagues and Block Associations are comprised of black and white residents working together continually
for a better community.[26]

Residents routinely complained about *Newsday*'s depiction of their community. Freeport dweller Kathleen Glass wrote a letter to the newspaper stating,

   I vehemently protest the slanted conclusions and racist implications reported.
   Suburban problems germane to most Long Island communities are depicted as
   cause and effect results of black migration to heretofore unblemished white neighborhoods. . . . No, I am not the Mayor of Freeport, but rather a wholly satisfied
   resident, living on a lovely and long time integrated block, only asking that
   Freeport be given the positive media attention it deserves.[27]

In spite of *Newsday*'s depiction of Freeport as a new ghetto, the town became
increasingly integrated. A black resident, comparing Roosevelt to Freeport, explains the reasons why whites would not abandon the community: "Freeport will
never turn all black because Freeport has resources that Roosevelt does not
have—a waterfront and mansions. No one is going to give up something you can
make an economic entity. Freeport has too much to offer to give it to blacks, to
afford it to be a total black community."[28]

Freeport would remain integrated, because unlike many other towns on Long
Island it was an incorporated village with its own government, police and fire department. Residents therefore had a greater stake; Freeport encouraged civic associations—many of which had existed since the 1920s—as well as independent
political parties loosely affiliated but somewhat independent of the dominant
Nassau County Republican Party. During the 1960s Freeport was governed by
the Village Party, a nominally Republican Party that included a range of perspec-
tives from left-wing Democrats to the mayor, who described himself as neocon-
servative. Former mayor Robert Sweeney recalls, "The Village Party was a

strong coalition. We had many arguments because it was a diverse group, but we were all interested in what was good for Freeport. So it worked out."[29] Dan Mandel, a lawyer and the Democrat on the mayor's council, declared, "The thing that always used to amaze me about Freeport was that we would go to meetings and yell and shout. But after the meeting was over, we would shake hands and talk. This made it possible to function and accomplish things without becoming embittered and drawing lines that no one would step across."[30] Alvin Dorfman, a left-wing Democrat, speaking of the Village Party caustically argued that "there are liberal, active, cultural families here that are dedicated to their community. People here are committed to Freeport and feel that they have more control, because unlike Hempstead, you can really badger the Mayor."[31]

Even these political outlets could not prevent an emotional struggle. Blockbusting took advantage of fears and panic caused by the so-called Freeport Riot; but as blockbusters advanced, many civic associations in all parts of town proposed antiblockbusting measures to stem the tide of fear. Local civic associations offered guidelines to discourage blockbusting similar to those proposed in Roosevelt by the United Civic Organization.

In March 1971 a black family moved into an all-white block where Gina Pellegrino and her family lived. Gina reported, "Just a few days after the block was integrated, we were deluged with phone calls asking, 'Do you want to sell?' There were postcards saying: 'Is your house for sale?' I went away for a weekend and when I got back quite a number of people were getting ready to move." To combat the onslaught, Pellegrino and other area housewives organized the North Long Beach Block Association to try to prevent panic selling by their neighbors. "We give confidence to each other. I won't move, you don't." When asked by *Newsday*, why she was doing this, Pelligrino explained that she and her neighbors "favored living in an integrated area, but not an all black neighborhood."[32]

These women and thousands of Freeport residents signed cease and desist orders and sent them to the office of the New York Secretary of State. Responding to the deluge of petitions, Secretary of State John Lomenzo ordered real estate brokers to stop these nefarious practices or face fines and loss of their licenses. One resident told *Newsday*, "We want Freeport integrated. We stress that. It should be a self-sustaining community. We don't need panic."[33] In a further effort, For Sale signs—an intimidating symbol of the blockbusting mania—were banned. This was the only ban of its kind on Long Island.[34]

Homefinders, a village-subsidized real estate bureau, grew out of this campaign. Its purpose was to make sure the community was racially balanced. The bureau eliminated the real estate broker's fee and allowed direct contact between buyer and seller. Volunteers introduced home owners to prospective buyers, showed houses and conducted tours of the neighborhood. Then privately buyers and sellers would arrive at the price. To find buyers, Homefinders advertised in the *New York Times, Long Island Catholic and Jewish Weekly,* the *Village Voice,* and *Metropolitan Home* and sent pamphlets to newly wed apartment dwellers on Long Island and colleges and corporations throughout the country.[35]

Operating out of city hall, Homefinders counteracted the negative publicity about Freeport by presenting the town in a positive light. It highlighted Freeport's physical assets, its waterfront, elegant mansions and old houses, while emphasizing the social benefits of living in Long Island's only integrated community. Many families found their dream houses through Homefinders. The four members of the McTighe family, cramped into a tiny apartment on Long Island, fantasized about owning a home but never thought they could afford one. "We once went to a broker in Massapequa but they were pushy and put a lot of pressure on us to buy, and besides, the fee pushed the price up and made it impossible for us to afford anything," said Jack McTighe, a salesman for Pan American airlines. Luckily he received a pamphlet from Homefinders offering to help him find a house in Freeport. There would be no pressure and fee, and the houses were available in a price range his family could afford.

The apartment building the McTighes lived in for ten years was occupied by white people. His new house was on Connecticut Avenue, an integrated block. "We didn't know who lived on the block and we didn't care," Agnes McTighe said. "We have black neighbors right across the street now. It doesn't bother us."[36]

Word of mouth also helped. Barbara Patton, who became the first minority representative from a suburban district to the New York State Assembly, moved to Freeport from Brooklyn after she divorced. Her children were in Catholic school in the city, where she was paying more than she could afford for tuition.

I decided that if I was going to raise my children by myself, I wanted to do it in suburbia. Like everyone else, I wanted to make the leap to Long Island. I was fortunate in that I was an only child and my parents bought me a house. When I was deciding where to move, I had white friends in Baldwin and I told them, "Now, look, I don't want to move in and then have a cross burned on my lawn." They said to me that I could probably move to Baldwin, but as a Jewish family, they didn't feel comfortable on their block, so as a black family I wouldn't feel okay here. They said there is a community, next door, Freeport, and it's integrated with neighborhoods with beautiful houses. So, I bought a four-bedroom Tudor house where an integrated public school was right around the corner.[37]

By the 1970s older white middle-class neighborhoods in Freeport were more integrated, and another big blockbusting effort would have tipped the balance. Now the challenge was to find white home owners who would want to live in integrated neighborhoods. As Ramona Crooks, the head of Homefinders explained,

If you want to keep this village so that people won't have to say, "Well, we want to leave Freeport because there are too many blacks or too many anythings," the only way you can do that is to keep everybody coming in. If there are too many blacks, then there have to be whites coming in, too. It's as simple as that. The more racist whites leave, but they are replaced with more liberal white people who want to live in an integrated cosmopolitan community.[38]

Although this strategy worked for the most part, it met with some criticism. Real estate brokers felt that Homefinders restricted their right to operate in a free market. Harry Berman of Berman Real estate said, "We as brokers are like merchants in the village. Why should we have competition from the village itself? This is unfair competition, especially since we have to show to blacks and whites. If a person knows he can get a house without a broker's commission, he'll tend to go to them."[39] Some black activists meanwhile accused Homefinders of subsidizing white families by allowing them to buy houses below market value to balance a neighborhood. Black families in need of housing often were on their own, paying more than market value. The Freeport Economic Opportunities Commission director, Jose Rendon, said, "I don't see them putting ads in the minority oriented *Amsterdam News* or *Jet Magazine.*"[40]

Despite such criticism, a powerful alliance of Homefinders, civic associations, local political parties, and city hall succeeded in promoting Freeport as one of the few communities on Long Island where integration worked. Those who didn't want to live in an interracial environment left, those who did stayed. As one white resident said, "Freeport has become a little UN."[41]

Former Mayor Dorothy Storm acknowledged,

> We in Freeport work hard to maintain a stable, healthy integrated Village, but, we have always recognized that there are outside forces working against us by steering away those who may have wished to buy a home here, and steering others to us who were made to feel they had no other option. However, the people of Freeport, all of us together, fight back. We believe everyone has the right to choose whether or not they wish to live in Freeport. They must have the same right in every community in this county, on Long Island and in the nation. It is indeed the law of the land.[42]

Homefinders continues to operate at the beginning of the twenty-first century. It is one of the few programs of its kind in the nation.[43] While it may have encouraged some unfair pactices, it has served a beneficial purpose in defeating blockbusting and actively encouraging integration.

The parent organizations that clashed with each other during the riots—the Concerned Parents of Freeport and the Black Coalition—also began a process of reconciliation in 1971. Jomer Rand explained what changed his attitude: "There is a renaissance in Freeport. At first, every black face was an enemy, but the scars are being healed. We found that the problem we had in Freeport was not a black problem but a community problem." Chris Sprowal was less ecstatic, but also saw progress. "There has been a lot of hassle and there still is, but for the most part there has been a conscientious effort on the part of the school administration to sit down with the community and make the system work better. The lines of communication are open." In 1971 both groups supported a Black Awareness Day at the Freeport high school. At first the school board resisted, but the Black Coalition, CPF, and liberals joined together "to win an okay."[44]

How could the leader of the white conservative CPF and the leader of the militant Black Coalition become political allies? Both were notorious figures in the community as well as antagonists. Both devoted a majority of their time and energy to community activities. Both were street smart, tough working-class guys, large in stature and in voice. As a kid, Sprowal spent time in reform school and later did a stint in jail, where he kicked his drug habit cold turkey. He walked out of jail and into CORE. Rand was brought up in a Jewish home in an Italian neighborhood. After his father died his mother remarried an Italian man, a professional wrestler. He trained Jomer, who became a professional tag-team wrestler with his stepfather. He also had a job with the Pinkerton Detective Agency and was an active teamster.

Although Sprowal arrived in Freeport with a long history of civil rights activism behind him, Rand woke up to the world of civil rights in 1969 during the local riots. During the disruptions, Jomer had a significant encounter with Chris:

> When I met Chris at the school, he frightened me with his appearance. He was
> wearing a dashiki, had woolly hair and blue eyes. And he was talking about what
> we're going to do to this community, man, and he was looking at me eyeball to
> eyeball. It was outside the school and he and I were alone and I remember, I
> looked into his beautiful blue eyes and said: Chris, you got kids in this school and
> I got kids in this school. And I said if my kids got to get hurt, I know where you
> live and you know where I live. Do I have to be any clearer? The fright I got from
> the riot, I turned that first fright into righteous anger and saw Chris as a potential
> threat to agitate the children. . . . But, later, I found out that Chris was much more
> than the agitator I created out of my fright.[45]

After that encounter "strange things" began to happen to Rand. "I started to ask questions. I started to go to the library. I wanted to find out what made the children erupt like that. I hated to read, but I read Malcolm X and that's when I

started to understand how a black man whose life was like mine would think."
Even though Rand continued his leadership of CPF, doubts plagued him. One
day while driving his truck to Northport, Rand had a vision:

> As the sun was coming up, all of a sudden, the sun hit me in my eyes. I put on my
> sunglasses, but the sun was glaring right through the glasses. As I'm driving, I
> hear this voice in my mind . . . and it's telling me that everything I'm doing in
> Freeport, not only with my activities but the way I'm doing it . . . this voice is say-
> ing . . . I don't like it. And I said if that's you, God, you better help me because I
> can't help it. You have to help me. And I started to cry and cry. At that point, my
> life changed.

One result of this spiritual conversion was that he and Chris started to get together—Jomer having made overtures. He also joined a black Pentecostal
church. Afraid to go alone, he asked Chris to accompany him.

> I said, "Chris, will you come with me to this church." He said "Man, I'm not into
> that religion shit." I said: "I know Chris, but I want to go to this church and it's all
> black. I'm afraid to go by myself." He says, "Okay, you owe me one." So Chris es-
> corted me down and he sat with me. He says, "Next time you're on your own." So
> I went and I was the only white person there. After six weeks, I asked Pastor Mc-
> Carty, "Should I be here? You know my activities in Freeport." And she said,
> "Brother Rand, the moment you walked through that door, Sister Dees who has
> the spirit of the sermon, discerned that you should be with us." And for the next
> three and a half years, I was a member of that congregation.

Jomer equates his spiritual awakening to Malcolm's experience at Mecca. "I
saw the way God transformed Malcolm at Mecca. I could relate to that. Freeport
was my Mecca."[46]

During the 1960s and 1970s many people, like Rand, threw over old beliefs
and fears, pulled by the power of the civil rights movement. While Jomer used
religious language to explain his transformation, he was expressing what it meant
to wake up to a movement whose aspirations deeply affected him. He acknowl-

edged having been a racist through lack of knowledge and encounter with people whom he had conventionally thought of as a "threat." Real confrontation—not those in his mind—led him to Sprowal, to Malcolm X, and a reexamination of his attitudes. Rand's conversion deeply affected his politics and he made a decision to fight for "the rights and desires of those who never had a voice." In 1973, Rand became Chris's campaign manager when Sprowal ran as the first black candidate for Village Trustee.

Sprowal, too, changed his attitude toward Rand and his organization. He saw that working-class white and black people had more in common with each other than with the middle class. As he stated publicly in the *Long Island Kernel* during his campaign, "I'm going to actively support the people who used to be referred to as 'white racists.' We find they aren't racists. They are people concerned about their jobs, about taxes, about quality education. So are we. Freeport blacks have a hell of a lot more in common with that blue collar worker in South Freeport than with the liberal in the Northwest with a $100,000 home."[47]

This new working-class alliance threatened the Republican Party, which had been actively courting Rand and grooming him for political office. Politicians such as Nassau County Executive Ralph Caso, Republican Party leader and State Assemblyman Joseph Margiotta, Nassau County Congressman Norman Lent, and Nassau County Supervisor Francis Purcell advised Rand in many meetings not to "get involved with the black community, don't get involved with Chris, don't get involved with the EOC [Equal Opportunity Commission]."[48] Rand did not heed their advice and remained active in the EOC, welfare rights, and civil rights.

That these two men, representing such divergent viewpoints so often polarized in other communities, could bridge their differences and form a working multiracial coalition represented a significant breakthrough, not only for them but for the whole town of Freeport. The initiatives following the rebellion made Freeport into a different place. As one resident put it, "The tolerance level was established. We found methods to live together."[49] Freeport became a place where housing was racially integrated in both middle- and working-class neighborhoods, where quality integrated schools became the norm, and where cultural life—from the library to the local arts center and orchestra to the new

Recreation Center to ethnic festivals and the lively seaport—make Freeport more cosmopolitan and multicultural than most suburbs in the United States.

As Julie Pearse recalls, "It is now impossible to tell a black neighborhood from a white one." Called to the scene of a late-night crime in the northwest section of Freeport with his white partner, Claude, Officer Pearse suggested that his partner enter this affluent home, "as I didn't want a hard time. Claude knocked, a black man answered. This showed how my own prejudices got in the way. This guy was an executive. In the northwest now, you can't tell from the outside if it's a white or a black family."[50]

Chapter Fifteen

Old Towns, New Families

These days the houses Levitt built for mom, dad, and the kids sometimes accommodate three generations or single-parent families with boarders. More than a quarter of these houses now are occupied by single-parent families or mother-daughter combos.[1] Suburbs have become their own point of origin, spawning generations of families who live and work near each other and view the city as tourists would. In a poll conducted in the 1980s, 71 percent of Long Islanders disagreed with the statement, "Long Island is merely a bedroom community of New York City," while only 16 percent agreed.[2]

In the present period the extended family often fills in for a broader community of neighbors and friends. Roberta Coward, a Freeport mother of four, summed it up this way:

> I socialize mainly with my seven sisters and brothers. My brother lives up the
> street. Everybody lives in Roosevelt or Freeport. My thirty nieces and nephews
> are all here. We all had children at the same time. If one had a child, we all had a
> child. My youngest, Nikki, is eight and the only one I had by myself. They all
> said, "Go ahead fool. We're not following you this time."

Karen Roberts, Roberta's twenty-five-year-old daughter, makes the same point from a different perspective. "We all hung out together in one family, all the older boys were like brothers. Most of them are still living at home. In our family they don't leave their mommies easily."[3]

Suburban life has been flexible enough to adjust to changes in people's lives, but sometimes new family patterns collide with the limitations of the suburbs. For instance, most women today work; according to the 1990 census women comprised 45 percent of the labor force on Long Island.[4] Many simply do not have time for making cooperative child care arrangements, maintaining community services, or even offering the traditional ride to the station. Changes at the train station are symbolic of this transformation. Formerly, "The wife would drive the husband to the station in the DeSoto station wagon and kiss him goodbye. . . . But the emergence of two-career couples during the last two decades has created a demand for one and often two spaces at the station where once none had been needed. . . . Parking is one of the most serious problems we have," said Dan Brucker, a spokesman for Metro North railroad.[5]

Furthermore, there aren't enough day care and after-school programs to meet the needs of parents' work lives. Time lost in commuting makes scheduling difficult. Public transportation is almost nonexistent, so children must be chauffeured. Women no longer may be depended on to provide key services, shopping, driving, and organizing community and domestic life. Indeed, the problems many Americans face today are largely the result of changed economic conditions; many prefer not to acknowledge that the culture that produced the traditional nuclear family no longer exists.[6]

As Nancy Arroyo, a divorced working mother who lives with her family in Levittown, explains:

> There's a real problem here for working mothers. PTA and teacher meetings are always in the afternoon. They closed up this school rather than rent it to social services and use it for a day care center. After-school activities have mainly boy things, basketball and sports. What if you have a girl and she isn't athletic? What if it rains and there's no sports that day? The high school principal at my brother's graduation even had the nerve to say that Levittown should remain with its traditional background and mothers should stay home with their children.[7]

Given this situation, extended families often stretch themselves to provide a support network. Parents work overtime in the evening to take time during the day to attend school meetings. Arroyo's family schedules their summer vaca-

tions on a staggered two-week basis so that everyone can take turns watching
Nancy's daughter. Other families struggle to arrange their work schedules to
meet the daily needs of children. Even couples who remain married face problems juggling work and family. As Barbara Ware observes:

> I need to have a lot of connecting devices which allow me to work. I have to func-
> tion as if I'm a single parent because my husband doesn't participate. My children
> have had the same baby-sitter since they were six months old. The microwave was
> the best thing that ever happened to the working women. I can leave them home-
> cooked, nutritious meals with no worry about them using the stove.[8]

The suburban ideal of the 1950s was a stable community based on long-term
home ownership. Yet people's lives have proved to be more complicated and
variable than the lives of billboard suburbanites who smiled in Levitt's ads.
Consider this description by Roberta Stim, a member of the pioneer Levittown
generation:

> In the old days we prided ourselves on being good neighbors. About fifteen years
> ago, my next door neighbors sold their house and moved to Florida. A landlord
> bought the house and I went over to introduce myself to four guys who moved in.
> I brought them a cake and invited them to my house to meet the neighbors. Then
> they moved out and another group of guys moved in and I went over with my cake
> and invited them to my house. Then they moved out and two couples moved in. I
> was a bit taken aback when I went over with my cake and found out that they were
> Jews for Jesus, but still I invited them over. A year or so later somebody else
> moved in and I'm not sure I even went over to introduce myself. Right now the
> house is occupied by someone I have never met.[9]

By the 1970s traditional family patterns established in the 1950s took on dramatic
new directions and reversals. The women's liberation movement challenged the
ideal of the middle-class housewife. Women started to enter the full-time labor

force in large numbers. By the late 1970s the declining economy and soaring inflation made a second income necessary in most cases. Women were responsible for three-quarters of the growth of the labor force between 1980 and 1990—although still overrepresented in lower-paying fields such as elementary education, clerical work, and social work.[10] Moreover, married women with children entered the paid labor force.

These changes can be seen in the experiences of a group of African-American Long Island women. In the early seventies these women lived in ways similar to those of Levittown women in the 1950s. Many had small children and were not part of the paid labor force. Contrary to the belief that black women have always worked, some were firmly ensconced in the suburban middle-class milieu of homemaking. Clara Gillens, who grew up in a Harlem project, explains:

> I came out from New York City, first to go to the Upward Bound Program at Hofstra College. I got married and bought a house in Roosevelt. None of my friends got out of the projects.
>
> I was fortunate. I use that term because everyone uses that term. I was able to live the typical suburban type of life, a house, a dog, two kids, a pool in the backyard. I didn't have to work. I had a husband who preferred to have a wife at home. . . . My son would go outside in his white sailor suit, with white ankle socks and the little white shoes to play. My friends would say to me, "He can't play like that." He'd be sitting there and all the other kids would be running around playing and he was sitting on the step because he couldn't get dirty. I was perfect, good at it. The floors shined, the countertops sparkled. My biggest concern was what was for dinner and getting all my women friends out of the house before my husband came home.[11]

One of Gillens's neighbors, Barbara Ware, painted this picture of herself:

> I'm a Roosevelt born and bred baby, my husband and I met in high school. I was a cheerleader, he was the football player, my knight in shining armor who became the fire chief, and we were the pillar of the community citizens. I had a little daughter. We bought a house in Roosevelt. I was Susie Homemaker. Believe me, I baked bread, I cooked and prepared every meal. I mean I took menu orders for

breakfast, pancakes for one, french toast for another, and scrambled eggs and on down the line. I was everything that the TV and media told you that you should be if you were "a good housekeeper."

Other women friends urged Barbara to break out, but she didn't listen. Traditional middle-class expectations were hard to leave behind:

I believed all these women who were telling me to go out and work and make it your own way were wrong because society and the TV and my own middle-class family told me that's the way it was done. I had no imagery to follow except what was on TV and in magazines. I got a recipe file with cards, that's how I learned to bake bread and all those things you were supposed to do.[12]

In the early 1970s some suburban black women embraced the feminine mystique with gusto, at least for a while. Others stayed home but felt bored and constrained. Roberta Coward said:

I never liked staying home. If I had continued staying home, my children would have been in Creedmore [hospital for the mentally ill] or drug addicts or something. It didn't work. I was hyper. I'd scrub the floor five times a day, clean the house, scrub the walls; I was going crazy. I had to go to work. My husband didn't like my going to work at all. After I had my last kid I added an extension to my house and went into such debt; but this was just an excuse to get me back to work. I got better after I worked.[13]

Like their white counterparts in Levittown, these women developed a tightly knit community centered around their small children and, increasingly, their own dissatisfaction and boredom. As Gillens puts it:

There was a whole group of us. We did a round robin at each other's house during the day. Barbara and I were tight and we had another buddy and we did the home party thing for a while, selling jewelry, Tupperware, Avon products. Then we got bored with that and all enrolled in a class and took up typing. We'd decided to become executive secretaries. At that point I decided I wasn't getting any younger. "What am I doing here?" I asked. I decided once and for all I'm going back to work.[14]

Barbara Ware shared Clara's feelings:

I was just bored. I sold things. Finally I put my daughter in nursery school because that was what you were supposed to do. I had nothing to do. Literally, how can you clean your house and watch stories all day? I was brainwashed as a housewife. You had to be home, there were all these regulations and stipulations. Then after my son, Junior, was six months old, I decided I'd driven myself crazy and I was going to work.

Ware felt that she was well prepared for work, though she had no idea what to look for. She went to the Community Economic Training Agency (CETA), a government-sponsored training program administered by the South Nassau County chapter of the National Organization for Women (NOW). She told them: "I don't know what I have to offer people, but I've run a house. I know how to budget, I think good, and whatever you give me to do I'd be good at."[15]

At CETA Barbara met Pat Sullivan, her future business partner, an Italian mother of three who had grown up in Levittown. As an adolescent Sullivan had been advised by her mother to go to nursing school. Pat explains her mother's logic:

My mother said you should get an education for a rainy day. In my marriage this nursing came in handy. I worked when my husband allowed me to, when we needed a second salary to get a loan or add an extension on to the house. Then I wanted a full-time job. My husband had a fit. The skies opened up, it poured. This was one of the final steps leading to my divorce. Funny, nursing was always a decent salary as a second salary, but when I became a single parent it wasn't enough. I didn't stay with nursing. I went to NOW to get some new skills.[16]

Women went to NOW not only for career counseling but to find companionship as well as strength and sustenance. In the early 1970s NOW acted as a bridge between the domestic sphere and the wider world of employment and independence. Pat Sullivan reported:

> When I was going through rough times in my divorce some friends brought me to NOW. At NOW they said all these things I had been saying all along, only nobody listened to me. My neighbors thought I was cute and crazy because I had these radical ideas about sex, like demand orgasm, like don't let him get away with it. In my neighborhood everyone liked me. I was very popular, but I was different. I thought things were unfair in my marriage but my neighbors told me, "Stop talking feminism. You made your bed, you sleep in it. You have a cross to bear." At NOW I was not different, I could talk and people listened and even agreed with me.[17]

Barbara Ware, although she had gone to NOW for a job, quickly developed awareness about a range of issues. Her new political sensibility caused problems in her family and community:

> The only thing before this I knew about NOW in my black community was bra burning and white middle class. When I came home and said I was working for NOW, and talking pro-choice and women doing men's jobs, my family creamed me, the community started to cream me and it put me in a very delicate situation.[18]

Despite this pressure, Ware and Sullivan got jobs at CETA training women to do nontraditional work, particularly in construction. After the CETA grant ran out they continued working on their own and started Job Opportunities for Women (JOW), a growing and prosperous business that receives state and local contracts for carpentry, plumbing, electrical work, and energy-saving weatherizing. They attribute their business success to their rigorous training as homemakers. As Barbara puts it:

> We have never lost money on any job. I attribute everything we achieve to good management that comes from our both having been housewives, period. Homemakers really bring a lot of skills into the workforce. You are the ultimate manager,

you manage finances, banking, time. I mean you do all that. For women who say, "I can't lift things," when I'm lifting a forty-pound toddler, laundry, groceries, and putting the key into the door and without dropping anything, you're lifting a hundred pounds. We're clear thinkers because we have to be. We can get Johnny from the baseball field, Sally from the dance lessons—I mean the coordination capabilities of women are incredible.

Ware credited JOW's achievements in part to the support of women who helped JOW overcome the bias of the male construction industry. "The secretaries on all the jobs really plug for us. When a boss tells them to 'call back, I'm busy,' the secretary says, 'Oh I think you should take this call. It's important.' Sisterhood has stood us in good stead."[19]

NOW also had an impact on Clara Gillens. As was the case with Sullivan, joining the workforce led Clara to her divorce:

I think my working and becoming more receptive to the world around me really contributed to the breaking up of my marriage. I was exposed to things I had no idea about before. Once you are exposed to things, there is no going back. You can't be the same kind of person. My husband put a lot of pressure on me to continue doing the things he wanted me to do, and it was totally impossible. When I got divorced, I took a good look at my life and my divorce led me to feminism. NOW also had a lot to do with helping me get rid of a lot of my inhibitions.

Gillens got a job first in banking, then in accounting. In 1983 she and a partner began her own financial consulting business, mainly for nonprofit organizations. Clara attributes her success to a good support network and friends:

We all go back to the diaper days when we raised our children together and hung out in the backyard by the pool. We all sat around and did nothing together. We sold jewelry together. We went through NOW together, and now we all own our own businesses. Some people think you can't own your own business and have a social conscience. But that's just untrue. We all have both. It comes out of our experience as women.[20]

During the 1970s, the women's liberation movement was changing the lives of the female pioneer settlers in Levittown. Their children were now grown, inflation was making a dent in their husband's paychecks and community work no longer felt fulfilling. Many women were going back to college, into the work force and into the women's liberation movement. Helga Baum, a pioneer of Levittown, remembers:

We all went through the women's movement. I was active initially in 1969. I joined a consciousness-raising group because we could now have time for ourselves. We could actualize ourselves. We felt a freedom. We had freedom for the first time to do the things we wanted and needed to do for ourselves.[21]

Work was freedom for these Levittown settlers. They too found that their suburban experience prepared them for the world of work. These women became social workers, job counselors, and teachers.[22]

Some suburban women went to work because they no longer felt needed at home. Rose Cimino of Levittown said she had been a contented mother "whose dream was to be a housewife and watch my children grow and mold them." When her children reached adolescence, however, she felt that "my two children didn't need or want me anymore. I felt I should be there for them, but they didn't feel it. They were pushing me aside." Her daughter urged her to take a job and she resigned herself to working. She got a job at Grumman, one of Long Island's largest defense contractors, and it proved to be a good experience. She discovered that work helped her develop a new sense of self: "It was very good for my self-confidence, I felt like a person, not just aperson who cooks and cleans and takes care of the house. I got dressed up. I was a lady. I was needed in another capacity now. I made lots of good friends at work."[23]

Grumman was segregated by gender: most men worked in the aerospace division, most women in data systems. Cimino became a secretary in the personnel department of the data systems division, where she formed close friendships with Dorothy Bass and Donna Gagliano, among others. Her work group was racially integrated and became a new kind of community, despite differences in racial and social backgrounds.

Dorothy Bass, a black divorced mother of three, had always worked and described herself as "not too domesticated." She started at Grumman as a shift keypunch operator and worked herself up to a secretary. She described her work group:

> We were a department of fourteen. We were very personal, very close. We became on-the-job and off-the-job friends. We shared problems at work, but also family matters, children, and when anyone had a need we were all there for support. We've known each other more than twelve years. We were inspirations for each other.[24]

Divorced women in particular turned to each other. Despite the liberation movement, women without husbands felt alienated and ostracized. When Donna Gagliano was in the process of divorce, for example, Dorothy was the only divorced woman she knew and was a model for her:

> She made it and she's not a bad person. She works, she raised three kids, and even owns her own house. When she was getting divorced, she went to school to maintain her sanity and graduated from New York Tech. She also told me things she had been reading, articles about women which said you're a person too, not just an appendage; you're important, too.

Part of what caused tension between Donna and her husband was his effort to achieve middle-class social recognition by "keeping up with the Joneses." He thought this would provide him the social prestige he was denied on his job as a baker. For Donna, his consumerist competitiveness exacerbated the growing differences between them:

> My husband always had the best no matter what it was. There could be nothing better than what he bought. It drove me up the wall. He kept up with the Joneses.
>
> We were very friendly with our neighbors and the neighbors bought a boat. So he decided he had to buy a boat. So we ended up buying a boat, and it was basi-

cally the same kind of boat, except my neighbor had the cadillac of boats and we
didn't and that bothered him.

My neighbor went out and bought a bigger engine. Now, this really bothered
my husband, so he had to buy a bigger engine. We argued for days over this stupid
engine and the only thing he said is, "If Carl and I were on the water racing he
would definitely beat me." This was the last straw.[25]

After she divorced in 1978, Donna was forced to move back home because
she couldn't afford her own apartment. Divorce sometimes means that
women—often with their children—move in with parents. Homes built for a
mother, father, and young children then must adapt to several adults, each with
their own cars and separate routines. These multiple family situations cause conflicts, especially between mothers and daughters. As Donna pointed out: "Your
mother is always your mother. As much as I do and come and go as I please, it's
always 'put your coat on, you're going to get a cold, you're working so hard.'
You're like a little kid again."[26]

Karen Roberts, twenty-five, lives with her mother, Roberta Coward, in
Freeport and has a three-year-old son. Although she went to college, joined the
military, and got married, when she divorced she had no alternative except to return home:

After I got divorced I had too many expenses, rent, day care, car payments, all
that stuff. It was easier to come to mom and pay $25 a month rent. There's only a
certain amount of money you can make on a job. If it was up to my father, we'd
never leave home, we'd just put extensions on the house. He's West Indian and
believes children should never leave home.[27]

Although Karen said that she "appreciated it more coming back home because you're not at the age when you're fighting all the time," her mother,
Roberta, saw it differently:

When I come home from work I can't stand seeing piles all over the place. I mean
you could shove everything in a closet, just don't let me see it. Karen's a let-me-

see-everything type kid and we fight about this all the time. Karen's lucky that I'm a stay-at-home mother and she's a go-out-at-night kid because this provides her with baby-sitting.[28]

Karen said her mother "is one of these people who sees dirt everywhere. I'm not. When I have my own house, then I'll be neat. Back home, I revert to being a child."[29]

Suburban households are changing in other ways as well. Although illegal in most communities, more and more residents are partitioning their houses and renting out rooms. Long Island real estate agent John Juliano articulated his understanding of this new phenomenon:

Sure, it's illegal. What it is about is that people can't afford to keep their house, the taxes are high, the utilities are high, the payments are high. And they rent a furnished room here and there and add a kitchen. I mean let's face it, not everyone can afford twelve hundred dollars a month mortgage. It works out for both parties. The kids got to live somewhere, their fathers and mothers live here, they want to stay close by without staying in their [parents'] house. So they rent. The six to seven hundred dollars helps the person that lives in the house and it helps the kids stay locally. I can't rent these because I'd lose my license. The law should be changed. So many people do it and making it legal would protect owner and tenant.[30]

What would advocates of suburban single-family home ownership say about the growing population of renters in their midst? Many divorced and widowed people can't maintain their mortgage and rising tax payments without taking in boarders.[31] Dorothy Bass explained her need to take in a boarder:

When I got divorced I used the money from my divorce settlement to buy a house. I was lucky. For two years I had a good roomer. It's against the law, but as long as you don't cause problems, it's okay. If anything happens, your insurance is void. I partitioned the house and made a separate entrance. I wanted a single guy. They tend to be out a lot and they don't cook. I was here alone with my son and if the neighbors don't see a male there might be problems. I needed him for protection. It helped a lot. We never saw him and he paid his rent on time.[32]

The home built for the nuclear family now houses grown children as well as nonrelated adults. Sometimes boarding solved family problems. As Rose Cimino said:

I was very surprised when my daughters decided to leave my home and go out on their own. In the old Italian family, no one leaves the house until they get married. I was very, very hurt when one of them told me she would like to get her own apartment. I said, "why would you want to do a thing like that? You have everything you need right here." She said, "Well, I'd like to learn how to be independent and live on my own. I don't want to go right from my house to being a married person." I said, "You can be an independent person right here. You can pay your own car insurance," but neither one of them bought it.[33]

The solution to this crisis was that the daughters moved in to their parents' house in Levittown, inhabited by Rose's grandmother. They partitioned the house into two separate apartments with a common kitchen. The daughters pay rent to their mother and provide companionship to their grandmother.

Moving back home, boarding, and modified living arrangements varied the landscape of suburban life. A 1987 *New York Times* article reported, "The proportion of young people living at home was higher in 1985 than in the last three censuses."[34] The cost of a private house today is astronomical, with hardly any for sale at a reasonable price. In 1990 Levittown houses sold for more than $300,000. Even fewer houses are available for rent, except for illegal rentals; and those tha are available have inflated rents. According to the *New York Times*, real estate brokers report that "the 500 to 700 families a year buying homes in Levittown now include, almost without exception, at least two wage earners. . . . Many buyers are on their second marriage. Others, single parents, relatives and unmarried couples, reflect the changing times and multiplying variations on the nuclear family."[35]

*   *   *

The growing number of gay and lesbian couples and single people living on Long Island also changed the demographics of suburban households. Gay and lesbian couples exchange a more open lifestyle and urban community engagement for a less visible suburban existence "muted by half truths meant to protect double lives."[36] Sandra, forty-three, and Kathy, twenty-seven, blend in to their Malverne Long Island community, living in their white shingle ranch with their three children, a cat, guinea pigs, and a carefully tended backyard and pool. On the surface they are typical suburbanites who have lived and worked in Long Island all their lives. With divorce prevalent, two people of the same sex living in one house doesn't necessarily raise eyebrows anymore. Sandra and Kathy don't go out of their way to advertise their relationship. When interviewed by a *New York Times* reporter, they requested that their real names not be used. "Thus far, the neighbors haven't reacted. While Sandra argued, 'We don't care what people think; we're not really in the closet,' Kathy said, "People don't want to see. They don't want to know. They would prefer to think there aren't any of us here.'"[37]

Although there are a few bars, organizations, and publications that are openly homosexual, most gays and lesbians socialize in insular groups. Occasionally bias incidents provoke people to break their silence and protest, but most fear homophobic reaction and cannot count on community protection.

Lenore David summed it up. "I had been pestering my partner Sally to move to the suburbs since the 1970s, but she was scared and said if I moved I'd move alone. Well, the years went by and we began to hear of other couples who lived closed but relatively normal lives in Long Island. Finally Sally agreed and now she claims she wouldn't be caught dead living anywhere else."[38] Life in the suburbs has become more cosmopolitan, the majority of women work outside the home, families take in boarders and roommates, older children live with parents, gays and lesbians live in peace—albeit somewhat uneasily—and all contribute to a more diversified culture. Or, as Sally explained, "suburbia just isn't the sticks anymore."[39]

Part Six

Critical Junctions

Chapter Sixteen

Utopia Revisited

By the 1980s a sea change had transformed the suburbs into a metropolis—a "technoburb," as historian Robert Fishman called new, economically viable decentralized city.[1] Suburbia's highways and byways contain shopping malls, high-tech industrial parks, office complexes, and schools, and residents look to their immediate surroundings for jobs and all other needs. It is the beginning of postsuburban Long Island, where people not only live but work and play. Like other suburbanites around the country, Long Islanders had come to see their communities as independent entities. While such changes were a boon to people employed in information-age and service industries, new issues arose, problems more often associated with urban life: traffic, congestion, unemployment (especially in the aerospace industries), crime, overcrowding, and a growing sense of anomie linked to the loss of community.

While Fishman argues, "with the rise of the technoburb, the history of suburbia ends," his claim is only partly true. Although suburbs have continued to shift and change, they were never intended to function as cities. Suburbs have an old infrastructure, not designed to meet difficulties brought on by expansion, changing demographics, and economic transformation. Lacking mass transit, for instance, the technoburb has created a maze; suburb-to-suburb commutes have quadrupled since 1960, now accounting for 44 percent of all commuting within the United States. Every morning and evening—and increasingly in the middle of the day—an overloaded network of local roads and highways are clogged with traffic as commuters, shoppers, truckers, and other drivers try to crisscross a landscape of diverse neighborhoods, shopping centers, and office parks. *New York Times* reporter Andrew Revkin starkly makes this point: "In essence suburban sprawl has created something that might be called suburban crawl, a chronic, creeping congestion."[2]

Malls are a significant indicator of this cultural and economic transformation. According to historian and editor Roger Wunderlich, Roosevelt Field exemplifies the transition from city-oriented Long Island to a locally centered lifestyle. The mall developed a dynamic of its own, a place of action and distraction, a kind of safe mini city. As author William Kowinski points out, "Soon the Roosevelt Field mall became not just a place to pick up a few things between trips to the city, but an alternative to the city itself . . . Roosevelt Field brought a little more bigness and speed, and a bigger mix of people."[3] Yet malls are different from city streets; they are controlled commercial environments that have trouble absorbing new functions and new people. Designed originally for young parents with children in tow, malls are in fact the central gathering place—the source of consumption, amusement, and recreation—for people whom the original suburban designers did not even consider: teenagers, single and divorced single parents, and the elderly.

Indeed, by default the mall has become downtown, the public space once occupied by Main Street, the Town Hall, or bustling retail city streets. Yet despite their convenience and glitzy appeal, malls have proven themselves a public space only in the most limited sense. Just as private housing mimicks the common spaces of public housing but ultimately discourages any communal activity that threatens their commercial success—such as pro-integration activism—so malls play the role of town center only so far as profits are concerned.

In the 1980s malls began to provide suburban residents with public libraries, medical centers, churches, exercise clubs, coffee shops for senior citizens, day care for shoppers, voter registration, car dealerships—in short, all the comforts of commercial and civic life, part small town, part big top. Although malls have become the new town square, people do not have the same civil rights in a mall that they do in the village square or city block. In 1976, for instance, the U.S. Supreme Court ruled that since malls are privately owned, individuals do not have the same free speech guarantees under the Constitution that apply in other public places. Thurgood Marshall dissented, arguing that the mall was a public square where civil rights had to be enforced. Columnist Frank Rich elaborated on Marshall's argument in the *New York Times*: "Malls have had less serious scrutiny than any other populated environment—in part because their owners invoke legal precedents that have found malls to be private enclaves, not the un-designated townships they've become."[4]

Numerous cases have confirmed that malls are considered private property and therefore not covered under federal or state antidiscrimination legislation. Unlike the city, many malls ban pamphleteering and other political activity. Even browsing or comparison shopping can be construed as unlawful activity. In 1996 Ronald Kahlow, a software engineer, was comparison shopping for a televi-sion set in the Best Buy Mall in western Virginia and punching prices into his laptop computer. A guard asked him to stop. He refused and was arrested for trespassing. He returned the next day with pen and paper and was again charged with trespassing and handcuffed. Although Kahlow eventually was found not guilty, this case demonstrates that even the basic rights of citizens do not hold in these commercial private spaces.[5]

A 1997 case in Buffalo, New York, demonstrates this in starkly racial terms. A mall's management allowed buses from the suburbs onto its property, but not those that came from nearby, predominantly black, neighborhoods.[6] One African-American teenager, forced to cross a seven-lane highway to get to his mall job, was hit by a car and killed. Malls are as public as the Woolworth's lunch counter integrated by black students in the 1960s, yet the government does not require them to provide equal access—a clear violation of civil rights.

Malls not only regulate access and activity, they also control behavior. As adults became financially strapped in the 1970s, malls began to court the youth market. Specialty chains, such as The Limited, began to target young women in particular, even offering them their own credit cards with easy terms.[7] This new marketing device was so successful that hundreds of teenagers started coming to malls after school. This was in part because suburbia offers so few gathering spots; but even though malls want adolescents lining up at cash registers, they fear them socializing in the malls' open spaces.

Teenage socializing became a perplexing dilemma for mall managers who re-lied on the image of order and security to maintain their older clientele. A New Haven mall owner declared, "The kids are our main market; the only way we can survive is to cater to them, not to restrict their access. You don't want hundreds of kids loitering around, but also you don't want to chase away your main customer base either."[8] Outright plans to restrict teenagers were not feasible. In order to keep the kids as customers, elaborate surveillance and security systems had to be developed.

Mall owners had to change their strategy from low-key to high-tech, high-maintenance. As *Chain Store Age,* a magazine for mall executives, put it, "In a business that is as dependent as film or theatre on appearances, the illusion of safety is as vital or more so, than its reality."[9] Equipped with state-of-the art surveillance, malls such as Roosevelt Field now have systems that can illuminate parking lots like a baseball field and video cameras that can zoom in on license plates in the lots' remotest areas. In order to protect the image of safety, clearly marked security patrol both the parking lots and the mall's inner court. In Roosevelt Field mall security guards wear broad-brimmed hats like sheriffs and ride around ostentatiously in golf carts.

This lack of public turf for teenagers in suburbia spotlights another problem. For adolescents, the mall became the place—sometimes the only place—where they could be independent from home and school; and unlike parents and younger children, teens inhabit separate spaces, separate worlds. This became most noticeable in the 1960s urban drug culture, which by the 1970s had spread to the suburbs and continues into the present.

Betsy Israel's autobiography *Grown-Up Fast,* set in Massapequa, Long Island, highlighted the new adolescent scene:

> By late 1972 marijuana had settled in on Long Island like McDonalds: it was fast,
> it was easy, it was everywhere. . . . The pot community at Tremor High—on any
> given day, some 60 percent of the 3,500 member student body gathered in a
> wooded marsh area. . . . At 8:10 each morning a mushroom cloud of dope as-
> cended through its mossy trees . . . that throughout the day attracted a platoon of
> green army-coated boys and followed by girls in corduroy bell bottoms, girls with
> string shag hair cuts.[10]

If in the 1970s marijuana was seen as a sign of rebellion, by the 1990s alienation, drugs, and mall culture fused together. As Mark Hunter, played by Christian Slater in the movie *Pump Up the Volume*, laments:

> I just arrived in this stupid suburb and all I can do is drive out to the same stupid mall, and play some video games and maybe if I'm lucky smoke a joint. There's nothing to do any more. All the great themes have been used up and turned into theme parks. Everything decent's been done. I'm tired of living in this exhausted decade, with nothing to live for, nothing to cop to.[11]

Levittowner Lilia Paige had said, "Our children are our products. After all, we moved to suburbia so they could taste the good life. We never expected that they would turn against us and become hippies."[12] Had something gone awry in suburban America? What happened to "the good life"? The era of Vietnam and its aftermath witnessed a dismantling of the basic assumptions that had fueled post–World War II patriotism and prosperity. With young men returning from Vietnam in body bags or suffering from post-traumatic stress syndrome, and with the country torn by conflict over whether the American dream was fairy tale or nightmare, confidence in suburbia as the safe haven began to ebb. As the Vietnam war fades from memory, so too does the suburban dream.

Long Island—which had championed a new and better way to live in postwar America—now struggles with problems that were never expected to reach its doorstep. In the 1990s Long Island has become "a bellwether for the nation's older suburbs trying to adapt to an uncertain and threatening future."[13] In 1997 Long Island had the highest rate of AIDS of any suburban area in the nation. Ironically, homelessness, although less visible than in densely populated cities, is widespread. Forty thousand people were homeless in 1992 in a world where home ownership is a primary social value. In the same year, suburban robberies—from gas station holdups to purse snatching to armed theft of luxury cars—were on the rise, in some cases at record levels.[14] Although the crime rate has since dropped, residents still live with insecurity and fear. Infrastructure—

roads, bridges, water, and public buildings—is in a state of decay. The rising cost
of taxes, housing, and utilities has caused more foreclosures on Long Island than
in the 1930s, and there is little affordable housing.

Despite heightened security, crime even appears in malls. Newspaper, radio,
and television news highlight incidents of mall crime—car thefts, robberies, and
kidnaping—and shoppers have come to see the mall as an unsafe environment.
Particularly hair-raising was the 1994 stabbing of a college student killed in a
brawl on the floor of a Victoria's Secret store in the Green Acres Mall in Valley
Stream, Long Island. After this incident the mall installed rooftop surveillance,
perimeter patrols, and an electronic camera that can zoom in on a slice of pizza.

Based on actual incidents, such stories are embellished by the mall rumor
mill. According to mall officialdom, many reported crimes are fiction, scuttle-
butt, and coverup. In suburban Maryland, for example, police chief Ron Delany
said that his department had "received calls from citizens who were worried
about rumors of men hiding underneath cars and slashing women's ankles.
There were also inquiries about a false report of a man dressed as an elderly
woman who was roaming a mall with a hatchet tucked inside his coat."[15]

Given this morass of real and fanciful, people now lock their doors, buy elaborate security systems for home and car, and say they are afraid to get to know
their neighbors. Nationally broadcast stories of Amy Fisher, the "suburban
Lolita" who stabbed her lover's wife, Mary Jo Buttafucco, or six-year-old Katie
Beers, who was imprisoned in a walled-in dungeon by her "concerned" stepfather, John Esposito, only serve to highlight that the once placid veneer of Long
Island and its safety boundaries can no longer be trusted.[16] Moreover, as Reverend Roger Tom from Freeport suggested to a New York Times reporter, "If
Amy Fisher were black and living in Harlem that story would have gotten no
more than first day reporting. But the fact that Amy and now Katie Beers are
white suburban kids makes them more comfortable and easier for others in the
nation's suburbs to relate to."[17]

Many older residents perceive that suburban life has changed fundamentally; almost
no one believes anymore that the suburbs promise a secure, affordable good life.

At fifty, Agnes Geraghty, who moved from Queens to Floral Park with her three kids in 1972, observes:

I don't have the peace of mind I once did. Last year our house was robbed while we were home. This scares me. Every day I hear similar stories from people who live nearby. I see how expensive it is now to buy a home, especially on Long Island. I worry about my kids and what they are going to be facing in a few years. We came here for a better life for our kids and I wonder where they are going to go for a better life for themselves. I have friends whose kids just got married and moved to Queens. I have to wonder: Is this a step backwards? What about their suburbia?[18]

Given the problems suburbs always faced, this may seem nostalgic, yet many residents continue to see the older suburbs as a place where houses were once inexpensive and neighborhoods secure, and worry that overdevelopment, inflated real estate, and congestion is destroying their dream. These fears are compounded by a deep-rooted insecurity fueled by layoffs, crime, and a decline in community cooperation. Parents worry that the suburbia of yore may not be realizable for the next generation.

Children also worry about their parents' future. As Linda Brown, age twenty, who lives in Massapequa (which she refers to as Matzo-Pizza, a reference to the large Jewish and Italian population), said:

My parents' years in suburbia have been filled with a great number of changes. They moved into a small town which is now built up with office buildings, fast-food restaurants, shopping malls, increased traffic, a higher crime rate, and less community unity. As they near retirement they wonder, as many do, if their dream of suburbia on Long Island can continue. The place that once seemed like paradise is now almost pushing them out. The taxes are high and they do not know if they can live as comfortably after retirement. To maintain their lifestyle they may have to move out of state.[19]

Although economic decline dampens the prospects for middle- and working-class families, Long Island still remains wealthy as a whole—which also is part of its problem. The median income measured in the 1990 census is among the highest in the country, at $60,619 in Nassau and $53,247 in Suffolk. However, most wealthy home owners do not support subsidized housing, low university tuition, after-school centers, public transportation, homeless shelters, AIDS centers, or more taxes to pay for these services.

Long Island has few governmental resources to deal with the onslaught of economic and social difficulties. Nassau County, with its population of 1.3 million, would rank sixth in the nation if it were a city—more people live there than in Atlanta, Boston, San Francisco or Washington.[20] Instead Nassau is a decentralized entity, composed of a confusing labyrinth of incorporated towns and unincorporated villages that have little ability to solve problems that transcend municipal borders. In the late 1940s, when Nassau's population soared, little was done to reform its outmoded structure, created intentionally by the robber barons. More than a century later, little has changed.

The decentralized, Republican political structure is highly influenced by wealthy home owners and is unresponsive to the needs of an increasingly diverse population. In a harkening back to the Gold Coast era, "When Canon USA wanted to move its North American headquarters from Lake Success to a larger plant near the horse farms of Brookville [in 1992] . . . home owners on the wealthy North Shore blocked the move even though it would have saved about 1,500 white collar jobs."[21]

People are starting to leave the suburbs. Between 1980 and 1990 the population of Long Island decreased for the first time, largely owing to departures by retirees and out-of-work or underemployed former military workers. By 1994 Grumman had downsized more than four-fifths of its workforce. After twenty-four years of working at Grumman, Kenneth Euring was laid off. In 1997 he worked at Home Depot for less than half of his former salary. Euring's wife then had to work two jobs, shop at food warehouses, and scrimp on gas. Worried about crime, Euring taught his two teenage daughters to shoot a pistol. He doesn't know the names of most of his neighbors, many of whom are renters. Euring's parents moved to Suffolk County in 1956 to take advantage of the quiet streets, good schools, friendly neighbors, and unlocked doors. Now his whole family desperately wants to move.

There are many like Kenneth Euring, who are out of work due to layoffs in the aerospace industry. As one laid-off Grumman worker said, "If you'd been there 20 years or more you got two weeks notice and a nice severance package. Otherwise it was fifteen minutes notice, pack up your stuff, sign these papers, nice knowing you." Grumman, like Lockheed and other huge military-driven aerospace industries, had presented themselves as family-friendly corporations based on worker loyalty and a promise of security. Grumman provided its workers with such diverse activities as bowling, C.B. radio, tap dancing clubs, dances, and picnics. Thus they used paternalism to discourage unions. This sense of family proved empty when jobs disappeared, leaving many workers reeling and bitter.[22]

If Grumman were truly family friendly, why didn't they retrain their workers to make new products? One downsized Grumman worker told author David Beers, the workers did not "understand why conversion was an impossibility for a company like Grumman. Why did Long Island's largest supplier of skilled jobs get gobbled up and emptied out? Why didn't Grumman ever think to build trains or buses? Airplanes, cut off the wings, cut off the tails, whuddaya got?"[23]

The downturn in regions like Long Island that lived on military contracts recalls the decline decades earlier of rust belt cities where people had relied on jobs in heavy industry.[24] The information-age, high-tech industries that replaced heavy industry cannot absorb these workers. With the promise of security gone, families like the Eurings can no longer expect life for their children to be better than it had been for them. As *New York Times* writer Herbert Muschamps, who recently dubbed postwar suburbs "first ring suburbs," observed,

> The transition from a [military] industrial to a service economy has undermined the security of the blue collar middle class. In short, the first ring is in a state of emergency similar to that suffered by the cities [that] suburbanites fled. . . . Thus far, the first ring's predicament has drawn scant official attention: it doesn't look as apocalyptic as inner city blight.[25]

But to those who live it, it feels similar.

*   *   *

Not only are the economic underpinnings slipping away and the culture is rapidly changing, but the very qualities that made Long Island desirable—the environment itself—is corroding and turning toxic. The dangers of nuclear power plants, such as Shoreham (now closed down), the polluted water seeping out of Brookhaven National Laboratories, and the chemical and medical waste dumped on Long Island beaches have been headline stories.

Some Long Island women are convinced that such toxins are making people sick. Long Island has one of the highest rates of breast cancer in the United States. A group of women from Long Island who survived breast cancer made national headlines when they expressed outrage that governmental studies had omitted the environment as a possible cause, instead blaming their affluent lifestyle and diet. The group, called One in Nine, pointed out that blaming the victim was not a cure and that the highest rates of cancer were in mixed-income communities. Marie Quinn, founder of One in Nine, declared, "Is water studied enough? . . . Electromagnetic fields, dishes that take in TV, and radio waves? How about homes that have been built on top of waste dumps that have been closed areas where there were factories years ago and dumped toxic materials? I don't think these things have been examined closely enough."[26] These women have met with both resistance and success. The possible link between the environment and breast cancer is now being studied by the National Institute of Environmental Health, the National Academy of Sciences, and the Centers for Disease Control. To date these studies are ambiguous and have yet to pinpoint the exact causes. Without adequate information, residents live in fear of drinking the water and eating local produce.[27] Levittown, now considered a cancer cluster, has become a center for residents' research. When prompted by the *New York Times* what came to mind when asked about the meaning of "home," the Levittown women replied in unison, "Safety," then "fell into a troubled silence."[28]

The suburbs had always promised prosperity, upward mobility, a healthy life in an unpolluted environment, safety and tranquility, and above all, the best place to bring up kids. Although this promise still fuels many dreams and infuses a nostalgic political rhetoric, the future is in doubt. Although most Americans today live in the suburbs, the elements of the covenant are elusive. What remains for many is a sense of quiet despair and faint hope. As Grace Grillo put it:

Suburbia as I once knew it sure has changed. Long Island has gotten so built up and so crowded with shopping centers, houses, and people. Because of all the cars, it takes forever to get to places. You still need a car to get around, though. Many of the older people have retired and moved away from the neighborhood and young people have moved in. It is not the same quaint neighborhood it used to be because so many of the young people have to work to meet the rising costs of living on Long Island. The grass and trees are still here, but I wonder how much longer they will last, because the building just keeps going on and on. All of the open spaces are now covered with cement. Long Island is getting to look more and more like the city. Oh well, I guess you can't stop progress. If that's what you call it?[29]

A representative of the younger generation, Ron Rosenbaum, sees the present lack of hope as a necessary counterpart to the overly hopeful promises of the past:

Long Island after all was supposed to be the future before the future. We always had a head start on the life cycle of suburban baby boom culture because we were the first born burbs of the baby boom; a burbland created almost all at once, very fast and virtually ex-nihilo right after the war. . . . Now there's an unmistakable sense of a lost future in Long Island, a peeling-vinyl, soiled-astro turf, diminished vision of the future that is one so much less than the one we were promised, the one we longed for. A sense of the aimless derangement that disillusion over a lost future produces.[30]

People continue to fight for Long Island's future. Residents reclaimed their environment by closing down the nuclear plant in Shoreham, protested Brookhaven National Laboratories for polluting the water, and organized to find out why Long Island's breast cancer rate is so high. Suburban sprawl has emerged as an important issue: women, for the most part, are fighting developers to preserve whatever open spaces are left. Long Island also is benefiting from a strong national economy and is a growing center for computer industries. Long Island today is more diverse racially and ethnically than ever before.

The coming of the technoburb and big city problems it brought severely di-

minished the postwar dream, yet people still yearn for affordable housing in a
quiet, safe community. Private enterprise will never solve these problems; out-
dated municipal structures turn a deaf ear. Updating the subrbuan dream to
meet these challenges requires visionaries such as those in the 1920s and 1930s,
who saw social problems as questions demanding democratic, utopian answers.
Reinventing suburbia for the working and middle classes remains a challenge for
the new millennium.

Chapter Seventeen

New Immigrants

Beginning in the 1980s many older white residents began leaving Long Island suburbs for more rural places or warmer climes. At the same time, a mosaic of immigrants, mainly from Central America but also from South America, the subcontinent of India, Asia, and the Middle East, were moving to Long Island. Japanese, Iranians, Koreans, Cubans, Haitians, and Vietnamese, as well as Indians, Pakistanis, Guatemalans, and Salvadorans, were part of a national trend in immigration. No one knows exactly how many new immigrants live on Long Island. Even the Immigration and Naturalization Service cannot estimate the number. Some experts point to the growth of the Salvadoran population as an indication of the extent of the surge: "In 1979 before civil war broke out in El Salvador, there were as few as 5,000 Salvadorans living on the island. Today according to immigrant groups and outreach workers, the number is well over 100,000."[1]

Unlike their turn-of-the-century predecessors, these immigrants were not of one class. They were wealthy, educated, middle class, working class, uneducated, and poor. Traditionally families moved to suburbs to escape metropolitan exigencies and acquire a private house, with a car in the garage and a yard on a quiet, uncluttered street where children can roam freely. For poor immigrants this is not the case; they live and work in situations that rival the worst turn-of-the-century sweatshops and tenements, exposed by muckrakers like Jacob Riis and Lewis Hines. Few muckrakers today expose the suburban underbelly. Omar Enriquez, organizer for the Workplace Project, suggested, "The problem is much bigger on Long Island than most people will admit. We have a dirty secret here."[2]

Generally poor and unacculturated, the new immigrants challenge the suburban image while their labor helps to preserve and enhance it.[3] "With unemployment at 2.8 percent in Nassau and 3.7 percent in Suffolk, experts and local officials say many of these [low-paying] jobs would not get done without immigrant labor."[4] Nonetheless, some older residents—especially those who live near the immigrants—just don't want them in their backyards. As Vincent Bullock, seventy-five, of Farmingdale, Long Island, said, "[The] long and short of it [is], they're knocking down my property values and I'll be damned if I'm paying a dime to help them do it."[5]

Part of the problem is that many suburbanites and public officials see the issue as cultural rather than economic. Older residents, white and black, complain about men hanging out in groups on suburban street corners, talking and listening to loud music until late at night; yet none of them bother to ask why these new residents are out on the street.

One of the factors that had always differentiated suburbs from cities is the absence of street culture. Front porches and stoops rarely were found. Street life for new suburban immigrants, however, is a result of cultural traditions and overcrowding. As one longtime Freeport resident explains, "Suburbia does not like the idea of people congregating fifteen to twenty of them on suburban street corners, sitting on top of their cars blaring their big radios."[6]

Long Island villages need to both familiarize immigrants with the tacit customs of the suburbs and get longtime residents to accept the different mores of their new neighbors. The village of Glen Cove issued a short flier explaining what is and is not considered acceptable: public drinking is against the law, but outdoor gatherings are not illegal, unless they block the street.[7]

Another striking difference is that most newer immigrants bypass the city and go directly from the airport to the suburbs, a pattern that had begun in the late 1950s, when the majority of suburban immigrants were Puerto Ricans. Cubans joined them in the 1960s and 1970s; in the 1980s Dominicans, Haitians, Jamaicans, Salvadorans, and others arrived from the Caribbean. Jennifer Gordon, organizer of the Workplace Project in Hempstead, makes the point that,

"Long Island has become a center for Central Americans in the New York Metropolitan area and is home to more of them than New York City or any other urban area."[8]

Advertisements promising cheap property, jobs in farms, greenhouses, nurs-
eries, factories, and domestic service brought many rural Central Americans to
the United States. Others, mainly from El Salvador and Guatemala, came because of political oppression and violent civil wars. Rural families tended to be
attracted to Suffolk, while those from cities came to work in the non-unionized
light industries of the South Shore of Nassau County, to towns such as Freeport,
Rockville Center, Westbury, Glen Cove, and Hempstead.[9]

By the late 1980s pressures began to mount over issues related to the new immigrant presence in schools, housing, jobs, and suburban culture. Long Island,
like other suburban areas, had little experience in dealing with newly arrived, diverse immigrant populations. Recession, budget cuts, a skyrocketing real estate
market, and anti-immigrant sentiment all conspired against integration into the
existing culture. Unlike large cities, suburbs have few local governmental agencies, social services, or homeless shelters to accommodate immigrants. Since
many are not eligible to vote, politicians have no motivation to help these groups.
Nonprofit advocacy organizations such as the Community Advocates in Nassau,
the Central American Refugee Center, and the Workplace Project in Hempstead—an impressive center that assists immigrants with legal problems, holds
classes in English and legal rights, and helps Hispanic residents in organizing labor co-ops—along with many churches have attempted, sometimes successfully,
to fill the void. Like other pioneers to suburbia, immigrants rely on each other,
their extended families, and informal networks.

Central American immigrants depend on an unconventional, illegal, and
mostly informal economy—so hidden and secret that "Salvadorans call it by the
Spanish phrase, *baja del agua* [underwater].. . . In this economic underwater of
Long Island there is nothing extraordinary about a suburban home doubling as a
dental office or a restaurant, or a makeshift pharmacy in a bodega."[10] Most immigrants have to make use of this underwater economy. Sara Mahler, anthropologist, describes why: "You cannot survive on Long Island with the wages they
are earning. In El Salvador, they hear they can make six dollars an hour and

translate the worth to their home country. When they get here, they are shocked by the cost of living." In Hempstead, Westbury, and Brentwood,

> a licensed dentist charges about $55 dollars for tooth extraction, in the underwater, the bill comes to $25 dollars. A Main Street restaurant asks $1.25 for Salvadoran pupusas [made of thick tortillas and meat] but underwater cooks charge 75 cents. You can get your laundry done for two dollars and pharmaceuticals for about a dollar a pill.[11]

Although such networks offer the advantages of familiarity, language, and costs, they have disadvantages, too. Consumers have no legal recourse if service is shoddy or deleterious. Sometimes you get what you pay for, sometimes you don't.

The only work available to recent immigrants, who speak little English and sometimes are undocumented, is badly paid and erratic, with long hours and poor conditions. Immigrants often work as day workers doing landscaping or construction for local contractors. Some have more regular jobs in light manufacturing, building, cleaning, maintenance, and restaurants, or work as cashiers, stockroom clerks, gas station attendants, and domestics. Most of these jobs place immigrants at a disadvantage, because "They often take place outside the realm of the law. Employers are rarely registered with the appropriate authorities; many of them neither comply with labor laws nor pay taxes to the government and often, they fail to participate in mandatory insurance programs such as workers compensation or disability."[12]

Maria Luisa Paz (who used a pseudonym because she feared giving her own name) was undocumented and worked in a commercial laundry with 300 other Central American workers. Their work consisted of disinfecting, washing, pressing, and folding mounds of hospital linen. Her job was to fold the sheets that came off the presses. The damp sheets were scalding hot and seldom was she given anything to protect her hands. After a recent Occupational Health and Safety Organization (OSHA) inspection, the company was forced to hand out a few pairs of thin uninsulated gloves.

In the room where Paz worked the temperature was often 100 degrees. After a few weeks Paz's gloves had holes burned in every finger and her fingers were covered with large, watery blisters. Her shirt was splattered with blood from frequent heat-related nosebleeds, and her arms and legs were flecked with white chemical stains. She was not alone. Other workers had been injured as well: one man lost half a finger, another was severely burned on the chest by chemical water that had boiled over, and a woman fainted on the job from heat and fumes. When Paz complained, the owners responded, "We didn't do anything wrong; those health problems are your fault." She then was asked to produce work authorization and was fired when she couldn't. Pax then contacted OSHA about filing a discrimination complaint, but was discouraged because the OSHA investigator told her he couldn't do much for illegals like her.[13]

Suburbia would like simply to ignore these new faces, but often they become all too visible. One way they obtain work is by lining up along major thoroughfares in the morning so that work trucks can fetch them. This creates a problem for local residents, who resent this unsightly practice and gripe to the police, who then try to enforce local ordinances against loitering. In Glen Cove one policeman warned a group of men who had strayed into the street, "It's against the law to hang out in the street in groups, that's from the Mayor himself. We'll have to give you an appearance ticket or jail at worst, if we see you hanging around." When this message had been translated into Spanish, the full meaning sank in. Francisco Martinez, a Hempstead resident from El Salvador, "raised his hand and spoke, 'One question! We don't have the right to buy a coffee? If we go to buy a coffee, they are going to think we are hanging around'."[14] After much ruckus Glen Cove resolved the visibility issue by creating an unobtrusive location for the shape-up (work truck pickup). There are at least five other similar shape-up stops scattered throughout Nassau and Suffolk counties.

In another Long Island town, Inwood, residents in 1994 attempted to remove workers from the corner where they were lined up waiting for employment. The residents complained that the workers were disrupting the neighborhood. Workers were videotaped, verbally harassed, and physically threatened by townspeople who eventually had the police blockade the street. With the help of the Workplace Project, the workers negotiated a settlement for a better place to wait. If towns see these gatherings as disruptive, organizers find them useful for making workers aware of their rights and helping them set new wage standards.[15]

Another hazard immigrant workers face is being cheated out of their wages by fly-by-night companies. Raoul Melendez (a pseudonym) waited on a street corner in the town of Franklin Square with sixty other Latino men at six in the morning. Melendez thought himself lucky to find a job with a landscape company that employed him at first for a few days, then for two weeks. He began to relax waiting for his first paycheck.

Unfortunately, his hand was badly cut by a lawn mower. His employer drove him to the hospital promising to return, but never did. Melendez was not paid for any of his work and was sorely in need of Worker's Compensation—but the company that hired him was not listed in the phone book and not registered with the Chamber of Commerce. Melendez was never paid.[16]

One of Raoul's friends at the Franklin Square street corner, Miguel Gueverra (also an assumed name) was not paid for nine days of work with another landscape company. He tried to confront the boss, who told him that the owner of the house didn't pay him and "when I don't get paid, you don't get paid." Gueverra, along with other workers and the Workplace Project, devised a strategy. They figured out where the landscape boss was working and went to the job site to confront him. Disturbed by the noise, the owner of the house came out and witnessed the confrontation. The home owner was horrified and the landscaper embarrassed by being caught. The boss agreed to pay the money because the home owner said to Gueverra, "If he doesn't pay you the rest like he promised, I won't be paying him what I promised either." The next week the debt was paid in full.[17]

In order to circumvent these irresponsible employment practices, the Workplace Project has set up a landscaping cooperative. The Cooperative Landscaping Innovation Project (CLIP) serves over fifty private clients and a church. Workers are responsible for both the administration of the business and the landscaping itself. Everyone votes on the issues and owns a part of everything. They make $12 an hour, far more than the going wage. As Jose Martinez, who fled the war in El Salvador, where he worked as an electrician, exclaimed, "The miracle is happening. After nine years as a day laborer, I have become my own boss."[18] Another sign of the Workplace Project's success is the passage of the Unpaid Wages Prohibition Act in New York State. This bill creates penalties for nonpayment or payment under the minimum wage. Enforcement remains spotty.[19]

Even when there are laws and redress agencies, enormous problems remain. The Hempstead office of the New York State Department of Labor

> seems designed to discourage immigrants from filing claims of non-payment of
> wages. A Spanish speaking interviewer is only available for three hours once every
> two weeks. Moreover because no one who answers the phone—if it is answered at
> all—speaks Spanish, it is impossible for Spanish-speaking workers to learn the
> hours of the Spanish-speaking interviewer.[20]

Also, many wage claims that are filed are not investigated for long periods of time, sometimes asa long as eighteen months.

The New York State Division of Human Rights, charged with enforcing antidiscrimination laws, takes up to five years to investigate and decide discrimination cases. These practices, combined with requests for documentation concerning taxes, witnesses, and authorization of work "effectively turn a blind eye to the entire underground economy, the arena of the greatest labor abuses."[21]

Another often invisible occupation taken by immigrants is domestic work. In the hierarchy of domestic work, living with an employer is considered the lowest rung of the ladder. Women are isolated without transportation and often are compelled to work hours without defined limits. Hidden in the homes of upper-middle-class suburbs are immigrant women who work up to fifteen-hour shifts six days a week for wages amounting to $2 an hour. The popular Spanish term for this job, *encerrado*, "gets to the heart of the matter—locked up."[22]

Some domestics work by the day cleaning, doing laundry, and taking care of children. These female workers face problems similar to those of their male counterparts: working long hours for less than minimum wage, being subjected to the whims of employers, and having little guarantees of payment or benefits. Dina Aguirre worked for three weeks for a family in Garden City without getting paid. "I worked from seven in the morning until 7 at night and sometimes until 11. I asked the woman to pay me and she said, 'I don't owe you anything, because you ruined my blouse.' She said, 'Give me your address and I will send you a bill for all that you owe me.'" Aguirre was finally paid, but only after suing in small claims court. Even when domestic workers go to court for back wages, often they remain unpaid. Yanira Juarez worked for an employer in Bellport, where she won her claim in court for more than $2,000 in back wages, but she was never actually paid. "I returned and returned again, with a friend who spoke English to tell her that I needed the money. She took my address and said, I will send it, I'm still waiting."[23] Other employers deny even having employed the worker, or falsely accuse them of stealing.[24]

The Workplace Project is organizing domestic workers by circulating an advice book about scornful bosses and their overworked maids, as well as forming Justice Committees of domestic workers who will appear at employers' homes to show their court orders and demand back wages. They plan to follow this up with a cooperative for domestic workers.

These low-paid, tenuous employment practices make decent housing for immigrants hard to find, especially in suburbia, where there is little inexpensive housing and a market that favors single-family homes. Most communities have laws limiting the number of unrelated people sharing a home. Town and village officials do not have nearly enough inspectors to handle even a fraction of the hundreds of thousands of illegal apartments believed to exist on Long Island.[25]

Often then, immigrants are forced to live in substandard, illegal makeshift housing with five or six other families who share a single kitchen and bathroom. The situation is even worse for undocumented immigrants, who have no legal recourse and sometimes are forced into renting beds by the day or night. Often "an extra bed in someone's home is rented in shifts to day and night laborers who pay $300 dollars a month and call them hot beds because they are rarely without a warm body."[26] Landlords frequently let small rooms at inflated rents, from $250 to $500 a month; they can get as much as $5,000 a month leasing a house. In 1988 the Long Island Regional Planning Board estimated that there were at least 90,000 illegal apartments, "which is obviously an underestimation considering the massive new immigration and the difficulty in detection."[27]

Suburban neighborhoods by day present a tidy picture. By nightfall, when residents come home from work, the streets change to reveal telltale cracks in the suburban facade. Cars on lawns, groups of people walking because they can't speak enough English to get a driver's license, loud music, cookouts on the street, and general noise are signs that homes meant to house a family have now become rental tenements. Only catastrophe makes this situation fully apparent: a fire, a raid, or a fight.

In May 1999 in Huntington Station a fire engulfed a single-family house crowded with thirty-three Salvadoran immigrants, killing three people and leaving sixteen injured and thirty homeless.[28] Jose Santos Fuentes died of exposure in 1997, after falling into a creek next to his bed under a Glen Cove overpass.[29] Another fire, in Freeport in 1996, revealed twenty-two people, most of them Central American immigrants, crammed into makeshift cubicles of plywood and cardboard on every floor, from the basement up to the third-floor attic. A raid by police and building inspectors in Hicksville turned up nearly 100 immigrants living in a hodgepodge of one- and two-story buildings. The building's residents all worked, but they were living on the edge. Some, like the Delgado family, had pooled their income to pay $2,700 a month to house fifteen people in an office suite that had been converted into seven tiny bedrooms, two small kitchens, two bathrooms, and a tattered former reception area that served as a living room. The Delgado family still lives in this office suite, but now their bags are always packed in case of a raid.[30]

Even when inspections are made, there is no guarantee that living conditions will improve. Huntington's public safety director, Bruce Richards, said that in 1994,

"inspectors found men living in outdoor sheds on property, and more people living in two apartments carved illegally out of the garage. The sheds were removed and the owner, Estrella Martinez, paid $375 in fines." In 1997 Mr. Richards checked out a report of an overflowing cesspool on the same property and discovered at least 15 people-all of them, apparently undocumented, living on the property: in a camper parked next to the garage; in four rooms in the cellar, two of which he likened to crawl space; and in an upstairs attic.[31]

The house was declared unfit for occupants and Ms. Martinez fined $1,100, but in January 1998 inspectors returned to investigate another complaint and found people again occupying illegal apartments and the cellar. She was given a summons and told to report to court. This situation is not unusual. Landlords calculate the fines in their cost of doing business.

As Marge Rogatz, president of the nonprofit Community Advocates in Nassau County, explained, "We are turning our backs on the low income people working in our communities. We need them to run all kinds of enterprises, but we are perfectly willing to have them come to work from living in a place we don't want to know about."[32]

The black market in housing is a result of the unwillingness to build low-income housing, or to change the zoning regulations that only allow single-family dwellings. The situation persists because of "the extraordinary collusion of landlords, tenants, real estate brokers and contractors tacitly abetted by judges and bureaucrats who are partly unwilling and partly unable to stop it."[33] Without new laws and protections, safety and health conditions cannot be assured.

The integration of this new population into the schools has also been difficult. Since 1990 Long Island has the highest level of students with limited English in New York State. Most of these limited-English districts are on the South Shore of Long Island. Some Long Island districts report that students speak thirty or more languages and dialectics.[34] Non-English-speaking students are expensive to educate; they need bilingual classes. Some school districts have tried to incorporate bilingual education into their curricula, at least for Hispanic students. The financial strain is greatest in poor districts that already are underfunded.

One solution is to place non-English-speaking students into special education classes, intended officially for the learning disabled. A 1994 special education report on teaching English as a second language noted that "the over representation of minorities and the foreign born in special education classes was not restricted to ... Long Island. It reflects the failure of suburban school systems nationwide to adapt as their populations have changed." The report indicated that in many schools there is only "forty-five minutes of English instruction daily for students expected to master high school level mathematics, biology and history."[35]

One science teacher in Westbury, Long Island, taught twenty Haitian Creole-speaking students with no assistance. Eventually he became so frustrated that he slammed the door on a fourteen-year-old boy's finger, severing the tip. He landed in jail. The Haitian community then pressed school officials for Creole-speaking teachers and aides, but the Westbury school did not respond. Creole-speaking teachers were available, but the Haitian parents hadn't enough clout to ensure that their children's needs were met.[36]

Stringent residency requirements make it difficult for immigrant students to attend school. In many Long Island schools and other suburban districts in the country, one needs to prove residency by showing "lease contracts, mortgage statements and notarized letters from absentee landlords." Nine-year-old Daniel Amaya, whose family did not have these precious documents because they lived in a doubled-up dwelling, where such documents are difficult to attain, was barred from a Hempstead public school. Mrs. Amaya stated, "I have no idea who the owner is. I live with my two sisters." A meeting was arranged for immigrant women and children to explain the requirements. Unfortunately the Salvadoran group spoke no English and no official came to translate. Daniel Amaya captured the essence of this frustration when he said, "I don't understand anything they are saying, but they are really angry at all of us."[37]

In spite of these cultural skirmishes, the new immigrants have had an impact on Long Island. Street signs in a town such as Brentwood are in Spanish and English. In a delicatessen in Patchogue, a sign advertises a *cerveza light*. "The nearby mainstreet market sells baccaloo (dried cod fish) as well as t-bone steaks. Across the street at La Vida Christiana children receive religious instruction and adults learn English."[38] You can buy *platanos* (bananas used for cooking), Jamaican meat patties, curries of all varieties, and *Kim Chee* (Korean pickled cabbage). Video stores carry films in Indian dialects, Spanish, and Chinese.

In Hicksville, a little India has developed encompassing a five block area offering food markets, restaurants, an Indian-owned hair salon and a duplex movie theatre

showing only Indian films. The two biggest annual events [in Brentwood] . . . are
the St. Patrick's Day Parade in March and the Adelante Day Parade, which cele-
brates Hispanic struggle, in June.[39]

There is such variety now that ethnic neighbors don't automatically bond.
"Twenty years ago, if you saw a Hispanic person, you held him and said, 'I'm
Spanish,'" Roberto Portal explained. "Now we are so many that if we see a His-
panic, we go across the street."[40]

Suburbs are now becoming—albeit not always willingly— multiclass, multi-
ethnic, and multiracial. This assimilation continues to be knotty and remains in
flux. Can older suburbs accommodate these new ethnic groups, or will outmoded decentralized government structures and prejudice keep them hidden
baja del agua—underwater? Will these new populations revitalize the dream and
energize subrubia to change once again?

Conclusion: Crossroads

In a market-driven society the development of new homes is as important to economic health as the Dow Jones: housing is a major indicator of growth or decline. In reality American free enterprise means that good houses are built for those who have the means to purchase entree into safe neighborhoods with decent schools and beautiful surroundings. Yet housing is also a social indicator that measures the extent to which class and racial integration are possible. Housing is the outward, visible sign of whether access to a better life can be gained by all citizens, as a fulfillment of the democratic promise. Although free-market ideas seem to dictate public policy decisions today, there have been moments in U.S. history in which social concerns weighed equally heavily. The tension between these competing philosophies shapes the contours of the modern suburb.

The very idea that gave birth to the mass-produced suburb—decent housing as a right for all—is seldom heard. Instead America is back in the Gilded Age, where market ideology has free rein. The social disparities of the Gold Coast era once again are palpable. A society based on the common good has been replaced by a get-rich-quick mentality that pervades the culture. The belief that long-standing social problems are not solved by government intervention is with us again.

In 1990 the United States became the first nation to have more suburbanites than city and rural dwellers combined. Home ownership has reached its highest level in history, 66.7 percent of America's households. In spite of recent demographics, there is a conspicuous absence of creative thinking or even interest in building large-scale affordable housing in suburbia. In a social and political climate where escape rather than engagement is paramount, the private housing industry turns a deaf ear to social concerns. New developments that appropriate old language take on new meanings: the planned community has become a metaphor for living in a private enclave. Private builders are more interested in building new communities for the upper middle class than providing suburban housing for the less affluent.

Recent developments confirm this tendency. The fastest growing housing option is the gated community, built for the frightened middle and upper middle classes who seek to close themselves off from the greater community and the problems they entail. Another private option is the fantasy theme park village, which appeals to a yearning for an older, ordered sense of community amid social fragmentation. Against the prevailing tide are the new towns and cohousing movement designed for people who seek a participatory, more democratic and less elite notion of community.

Gated communities—walled-off, tight security developments—originally were designed for retirees in the Southwest and West, but they have spread rapidly to include nonretirement, mostly white middle-class families living in all parts of the country. By one estimate in 1997 there were nearly 20,000 gated communities containing more than 3 million households and nearly 8.5 million residents. Gated communities create bunkered environments surrounded by walls, gates, and security personnel. These suburban developments are organized around rigidly enforced rules and regulations, as opposed to democratic decision-making by residents themselves.[1] Employing a fortress mentality, gated communities reinforce the notion of exclusion and isolation and play on anxieties prevalent in the 1990s of criminals and other dangerous outside forces. Motivated by these apprehensions, residents opt out of civic life and instead choose communities that employ private government, schools, and police.[2]

Security is chiefly the appeal of gated housing.[3] Walled enclaves give home owners a buffer against their free-floating forebodings. As a resident of Green Valley, Nevada, explained, "There were these . . . forces if you know what we mean. There were too many things we could not control."[4] In a world dominated by media stories where rape, child molestation, car jackings, and random shootings are depicted as commonplace occurrences, the walls and gates are supposed to ward off unexpected, frightening daily intrusions as well as random harmless encounters.[5] Walls also eliminate diversity. As Gerald Frug, professor of local government at Harvard Law School, says, "These private communities are totally void of random encounters. So you develop this instinct that everyone is just like me and then you become less likely to support schools, parks or roads for everyone else."[6]

Wealthy suburbanites have a long history of walling themselves off from society's perils. To some extent Long Island's Gold Coast set the stage for this. Today the enclosed habitat has become more general and widespread. The existence of gated communities again raises the issue of whether private commercial solutions provided by developers can substitute for concerned, engaged public citizens in open communities.

Another recent option is the so-called neotraditional community, which tries to capture a sense of living in a world without the stress and strife that are by-products of modern living. Taking their cues from theme parks, these communities are built to capture a fantasy of life in a nineteenth-century American small town. The imaginary village is designed as an escape into the good old days, a time when many Americans believe that life was simple and safe, and townspeople knew and trusted each other. Here set design takes the place of social imagination. Many neotraditional-inspired towns are located throughout the United States in Mashpee, Massachusetts; Kentlands, Maryland; Manchester, New Hampshire; and outside Madison, Wisconsin, to name a few.

Seaside, Florida, begun in 1981, is the architectural model for many neotraditional communities. Seaside was built by the well-known architectural team of Elizabeth Plater-Zyberk and Andres Duaney, founders of the Congress for a New Urbanism, a group of more than 1,600 planners. Seaside explicitly rejected the design of the mass-produced postwar suburb. Its architects and planners believed that the architecture itself would encourage neighborly interaction. Unlike Levittown, no two houses are alike. The houses are wood shingled, with deep front porches and shiny tin roofs, like old houses in rural America.[7]

The simulated nineteenth-century village look recreates a time when kids' lemonade stands were on every corner, and crime was something that happened somewhere else. In contrast to Greenbelt or Levittown, where residents have an acute memory of their town being built and their part in it, Seaside is a packaged collection of nostalgia from a past that never was—except perhaps on television.

Seaside and Seaside lookalikes mimic the settings of 1950s sitcoms. The front porch beckons, the houses are wood, and a small-town sense of harmony prevails. To achieve this sentimental look, Seaside prohibits the distinctive characteristics of older suburbs: picture windows, front lawns, sliding glass doors, and vinyl or aluminum siding.

Whether a sense of place can be architecturally engineered remains to be seen. Critics such as Herbert Muschamps of the *New York Times* and Alex Krieger of the Harvard Urban Design School feel that the New Urbanists who build these towns overemphasize the role architecture plays in creating community and oversell the capacity of its designs to reinvent neighborliness.[8] In the 1920s Mumford and others criticized the use of new mass-production techniques to replicate the houses and artifacts of the past; the same criticism can be made of neotraditionalist architecture. Why, as society rushes toward a high-tech, information-packed millennium, do architects and residents flee to the past to avoid the challenge of the new? Does living in a seemingly TV-like, old-fashioned house in a community premised on nostalgia ward off modern anxieties and new suburban phobias? Or is it part of the escapist impulse, where buying a ready-made community substitutes for participating in the process of decision making and the more messy problems of society at large?

Fittingly, the Disney Corporation, renowned for theme parks, became central to the popularization of planned communities like Seaside. In 1994 the Disney Corporation started building Celebration, a community designed to house 20,000. Located south of Orlando, Florida, Celebration—heralded by its developers as a new "City on a Hill"—contains private hospitals, public and private schools, and shopping arcades mixed with residences.[9] Celebration was built combining principles of the New Urbanist architecture and Disney theme parks: the small-town American look, with open, pedestrian-friendly streets, mom and pop stores, village centers, and a diversity of house design. People flocked to Celebration, believing that the Disney success in theme park design would carry over into the building of communities. About 5,000 people competed in a lottery for the first 350 houses.[10]

At first glance Celebration appears to be a model community, Lego-like, with neat narrow streets. According to Carl Hiaasen, "Celebration invokes nothing so much as a small-town neighborhood of the 1950s, remembered over fondly. The houses, which feature wooden shutters and open porches, could have been lifted off the lot of TV's *Leave It to Beaver*."[11] Disney brochures advertise the development as a "hopscotch-and-tag neighborhood to be viewed from front-porch swings."[12] Unlike the sitcoms its design imitates, Celebration is rigidly controlled. Residents are not allowed to change the color of the house or the drapery, the pattern of the shrubbery, or where to park their cars. Nor will the community ever achieve the comfort that comes with age or acquire a feeling of being lived in, as the streets are washed every night, like in Disney World.

Not only is the environment controlled in Celebration, but every aspect of the community is subject to the approval of the private Disney corporate board. Some parents, for instance, disliked certain aspects of the Disney-run school's curriculum and asked to hold a meeting of concerned parents. After being denied this right by the Disney Corporation, the news hit the papers: there was trouble in Celebration. Instead of calling meetings, the Disney Corporation commenced a public relations campaign by holding pep rallies for the school and calling the concerned parents "negative" and school supporters "positive" in its newsletter. As Roger Burton, a parent involved in the Disney-run school, explains, "I knew Celebration was going to be a very controlled situation, but controlled in a good way. But as soon as you run into a problem, you find there is no mechanism to change things. The only person you can call is a corporate Vice President, but he's not interested in the school, not really, he's interested in selling real estate."[13]

In Celebration everything is private, even the town hall. Like malls, the Disney Corporation even decides what political signs are permissible. Robert Stern encapsulated Celebration's antidemocratic foundations when he explained that "in a free wheeling capitalist society, you need controls—you can't have community without them. It's right there in de Tocqueville: in the absence of an aristocratic hierarchy, you need firm rules to maintain decorum. I'm convinced these controls are actually liberating to people. It makes them feel their investment is safe. Regimentation can release you."[14] Release you from what, we might ask. The right to choose your own way of life?

Celebration has reformulated a new kind of society: a combination of secure capitalist investment and control of everyday life, within a supposedly safe haven. Disney has developed a community for the nineties, shorn of politics and transformed into a commodity—something people buy and consume rather than produce, a lifestyle rather than a participatory achievement.

These Cities on a Hill and gated communities represent a rejection of the idea of community based on democratic participation and conflict as a way to resolve issues and promote change. In one sense Levitt and other master builders were forerunners of the gated community and the New Urbanism. Massproduced suburbs and these newer developments each hold the promise of escape from urban life and city strife. The master builders constructed individually owned homes in communities controlled by the builder. Strict mandates governed race as well as enforcement of middle-class proprieties, such as when laundry may be hung and how tall the grass may grow. Levitt named the town after himself, owned the newspapers, and fined home owners for failing to follow his regulations.

Levittown residents, however, took control of their community in many ways. They changed their houses and took part in establishing baby-sitting co-ops, schools, and libraries. When Celebration residents tried to take an active role in their school they were stopped by a Disney media blitz. In Levittown there was controversy, but it was worked out through discussion and debate, not public relations. The community was not privately owned and operated and therefore was part of the county and state political structure. Even more important, the original idea of Levittown was to give home owners a piece of the American dream: an affordable house in a new suburban setting.

Gated and theme park communities speak to a suburban future where class concerns about security and the protection of an amenity-packed lifestyle outweigh concerns for democratic community participation and diversity. There are, however, more forward-looking suburban housing alternatives taking their cues from the new town movement of the 1920s and 1930s and the visionary planners of the Regional Planning Association of America. New towns and the cohousing movement reject suburban sprawl and the lack of community, but they also incorporate diversity, democracy, and civic participation.

Columbia, Maryland, is the leading example of the contemporary new town. Columbia was built by developer James Rouse, who was quite knowledgeable about the work of the RPAA and applied its principles in planning the community. Columbia commenced in 1967 and continued growing well into the 1970s, housing 83,000 people in 1998. Unlike Levittown, which was homogeneous in population and architecture, Columbia is a diverse community in age, race, and choice of homes and was one of the first suburban communities to offer integrated housing; twenty percent of the population is African American.

The community consists of nine small villages, each with several hundred houses: single-family dwellings, apartments, town houses, rentals, senior and single-person homes. Like Radburn and Greenbelt, there are curvilinear streets, pedestrian walks, foot and bike paths, and open parklands (more than a third of Columbia's land).[15] Located between Washington, D.C., and Baltimore, and connected to these cities by public transportation, Columbia is a safe suburban environment with many urban amenities, including concerts, restaurants, a public library, and a dinner theater. As long-time residents Bonnie and Gordon Pollokoff explain, "My closest friends live there; there is a communal feeling in this racially integrated 'Newtown' as we call it. It provides us with the best of city and suburb."[16]

Learning from Levittown and other suburban-sprawl communities, Rouse included a master plan based on continuing development. The plan foresaw growth as community centered rather than random blocks of individual houses. Community activities such as neighborhood committees, PTA groups, and village decision making were included in the plan. Columbia's master plan determined the mix of houses and their layout, design, and color. Columbia also has its restrictions and rules, and some residents complain that there are too many— their paint must be approved, for example, and grass kept at a certain length, otherwise residents are fined. Generally, though, residents feel they have a voice in decision making and that management is open to their ideas. Columbia has active home owners and neighborhood associations, and people rarely move out. As the Pollokoffs point out, "They wouldn't live anywhere else."[17]

Another democratic, small-scale option is the cohousing movement. The Communities Directory lists more than 500 cohousing communities across the nation—up from 300 in 1990—and the Center for Communal Studies at the University of Southern Indiana estimates that more than 200,000 Americans live in some type of communal arrangement.[18] There are large communities such as Earthhaven in North Carolina and smaller ones such as Ganas in Staten Island, Davis in California, and Ecovillage, near Ithaca. Beginning in Denmark in the 1960s and helped along by an influential book by Kathryn McCamant and Charles Durrett, *Cohousing: A Contemporary Approach to Housing Ourselves*, cohousing took root in the United States in the late 1980s. In these communities, residents get together and act as their own developers, making architectural, environmental, and social decisions. The cohousing movement explicitly seeks diversity of age, type of family, race, and economic class. Couples and single parents live next door to older people who eschew the isolation found in many retirement communities.

Cohousing combines the benefits of owning your own home with a sense of belonging to an extended family with a shared daily life. It is reminiscent of the rural commune movement of the 1960s, in that members share chores and household items. It differs from the 1960s in its emphasis on financial solvency and pragmatic outlook. Central to the philosophy of cohousing is the emphasis on shared commodities, such as snowblowers, cars, sports equipment, and washing machines. As Michael Samboro, who is active in setting up a cohousing community near New York City, explains,

> Look, we've got to move past the way we currently live, where it's me and my TV, me and my car, me and my possessions. We're all languishing under the weight of individual consumption. And we're lonely, many of us. I want to live in a place where I know people will watch my back, watch my kid's backs, and who trust that I'll do the same for them.[19]

Cantine's Island in Saugerties, New York, is one of the newest cohousing initiatives, begun in 1996. Sabrina Greensea, a single mother of two teenage daughters, moved there from California in the late 1990s because she never got to know many people outside her own family. She chose cohousing because "I've always wanted to live in a place where people drop in on one another. I never wanted to live in isolation."[20] This theme is echoed by Pegg Wonder, age thirty-nine, who moved with her husband from Palo Alto, California, to the Ganas community on Staten Island. "Sometimes the separation between me and other people was too much to bear. Here, I've got myself a giant extended family, people who really take care of me."[21]

In cohousing between eight to sixty future residents get together to design and make decisions about their intended community. They are assisted by the Cohousing Company, founded by authors McCamant and Durrett, and an array of nonprofit housing groups. This process often takes years. Cohousers design their own houses according to individual desires and needs. Their houses are generally smaller than usual, because they also design a common building that is community-owned and the center for shared social activities, evening meals, day care, laundry, workshops, meetings, and home office space. This large common area subsumes many of the functions that normally take place in the individual home.

People who choose to live in cohousing communities desire social interaction, interdependence, and cooperation.[22] The ability to compromise and reach decisions by consensus in long, biweekly meetings is essential for cohousing members. Not everyone is prepared for this kind of intense participation. Many try it out and find it is not for them.

Some cohousing communities, wanting to make some of their dwellings permanently affordable to low-income families, have secured government subsidies. Most of the developments are suburban, within commuting distance to urban areas. These communities provide residents with a sense of security without having to install a private security system. There is always a friendly neighbor to assist if needed.[23] Many are built with pedestrian walkways and bike paths; cars are parked on the edge of the community. The cohousing movement implements the ideas of the Regional Planning Association of America. Another source of inspiration is second-wave feminism, based on the principle that men and women share housework, cooking, and child care.

Claudia Weisburd, an early resident who grew up in the Kingsbridge section of the Bronx, said she tried to incorporate some aspects of her old neighborhood into the design. "People were out on the stoops, they knew each other. And everyone spent a lot of time outdoors. It is very important that the community not be isolated. The Ecovillage is a mile and a half from downtown Ithaca. It's not desirable, I think, to be an enclave."[24]

While it is hard to gauge what impact these democratic alternatives will have, their ideas and practices seem hopeful in that residents choose to engage with others, acknowledge the society and its unsolved problems, and hold up the principles of participatory decision making so visibly absent from the social dialogue of escapism and nonengagement ascendant in the suburban housing options of the 1990s.

As the greater society has changed, so too has suburbia. What we see today is a running away from the larger issues. Suburbia has never been a haven from social issues; rather, suburbia has been shaped by them. Private developments attempt to provide a temporary resting place, but they mask important issues—the aging, now congested and unaffordable suburbs, the lack of housing for young middle-income and poor families, single, older people, and new immigrants—bubbling under the surface. Inexpensive suburban integrated housing remains a key issue.

In our view the history of the suburbs is fundamentally a history of America's attempts to provide housing to all of its citizens. It took decades and a major depression and war to place the needs of the ill-housed on the front burner. What will it take to make housing for all a national priority once again? The technology is certainly at hand; ideas and inspirations are available, the need for decent housing is manifest, but the disparity between rich and poor grows each day. Access to a decent place to live is an essential component of genuine democracy. Yet large-scale social solutions are marginalized as market ideology dominates public discourse. In a nation of suburbs there are dynamic examples of integrated communities; yet, they remain the exception. Turning the exception into the rule will require resources and a great leap of imagination. Without such a shift, today's suburbs are in danger of becoming a vast sprawl of exclusion—a marker of social disintegration, rather than the fulfillment of the American dream.

Endnotes

INTRODUCTION

1. Lewis Mumford, "The Wilderness of Suburbia," *The New Republic, 28*, September 1921, 44.

2. Frederick Lewis Allen, "Suburban Nightmare," *The Independent*, 13 June, 1925.

3. Christine Frederick, "Is Suburban Living a Delusion?" *The Outlook*, 22 February, 1928, 290–91.

4. John Seeley, R. Alexander Sim, and E. W. Loosley, *Crestwood Heights: A Study of the Culture of Suburban Life* (Toronto: University of Toronto Press, 1956), 42–43.

5. John Keats, *The Crack in the Picture Window* (New York: Houghton-Mifflin, 1957), 61.

6. Ibid. 47.

7. After the blitz of 1950s and 1960s literature there was a hiatus, followed by a few new histories of suburbia, broader in scope, with a more nuanced vision and less snobbish. Significant were Kenneth Jackson's *Crabgrass Frontier,* Gwendolyn Wrights' *Building the Dream,* Robert Fishman's *Bourgeois Utopia,* and Barbara Kelly's *Expanding the American Dream: Building and Rebuilding Levittown.* Also clarifying the suburban reality are novels, particularly those of Alice Hoffman, Alice McDermott, Jon Katz, and Nelson De Mille; memoirs, such as Betsy Israel, *Grown Up Fast,* Donald Katz, *Home Fires,* D. J. Waldie *Holy Land,* and David Beers, *Blue Sky Dream,* and cultural histories such as Thomas Hine, *Populuxe,* Elaine Tyler May, *Homeward Bound,* Stephanie Coontz, *The Way We Never Were,* and Donna Gaines, *Teenage Wasteland.* Robert Caro's, *The Power Broker, Robert Moses and the Rise and Fall of New York* is particularly useful in illustrating how the suburban infrastructure was created.

8. Kunstler quoted in Richard O' Mara, "Suburban Gloom," *The Capital Times,* (Madison Wisconsin), 3–4 May 1997.

9. Andres Duany and Elizabeth Plater-Zyberk, *Towns and Town Making Principles* (New York: Rizzoli, 1991), 6.

10. William Upski Wimsatt, *Bomb the Suburbs* 2d. ed. (The Subway and Elevated Press Company 1997), 10, 11, 99.

CHAPTER ONE

1. The first inhabitants of Nassau County were indigenous people, Algonquian-speaking extended family groups such as the Secatoques, the Marsepeagues, the Matinecocks, and the Setalcotes. Later, as slavery was introduced, African Americans

were brought to Long Island. Emancipated in 1827, black Americans formed small communities in Nassau and Suffolk counties. The dominant ethnicity was Anglo-Saxon. For a good account of native Americans see John A. Strong, *The Algonquin Peoples of Long Island from Earliest Times to 1700* (Interlocken, New York: Empire Books, 1997), 25–33.

2. Warren S. Thompson and P. K. Wheltpon, "The Population of the Nation," in *Recent Social Trends in the United States* (New York: McGraw Hill, 1939), 9. This was obviously changing; by 1930 the rural population was 44 percent.

3. Ruth Grefe, unpublished diary, donated to authors, April 1992.

4. Robert McKay, "Long Island Country Houses," *Long Island Historical Journal,* 2 (Spring 1994): 187. During this period 43 percent of the new sumptuous retreats were built.

5. *New York Herald* cited in ibid.

6. Cited in Dennis P. Sobin, *The Dynamics of Community Control,* Empire State Historical Publication Series 59 (Port Washington: Ira Friedmanine,1968), 30.

7. Lessard quoted in Rhoda Amon, "The Architect of Desire," *Newsday* at LI History.com. (Series "Long Island: Our Story," n.d.).

8. Prince of Wales cited in McKay, "Long Island Country Houses," 181.

9. Sobin, *Dynamics of Community Control,* 47–48, 119–20.

10. Ibid., 69; Robert A. Caro, *The Power Broker: Robert Moses and the Rise and Fall of New York* (New York: Vintage, 1975), 150.

11. Ibid.

12. Sobin, *Dynamics of Community Control,* 37.

13. Geoffrey L. Rossano, "Long Island Goes to the Auto Races," *Long Island Historical Journal* 3, 2 (Spring 1991): 235.

14. Malcolm M. Wiley and Stuart A. Rice, "The Agencies of Communication," *Recent Social Trends in the United States,* One volume edition. (New York: McGraw Hill, 1933), 194.

15. Cited in Rossano, "Long Island," 235. See also Roger Wines, "Vanderbilt's Motor Parkway: America's First Auto Road," *Journal of Long Island History* (Fall 1962).

16. Sobin, *Dynamics of Community Control,* 100.

17. Ibid.

18. Ibid., 99–104. Sobin citing the pamphlet *The History of Lake Success* (no author, ca. 1949).

19. McKay, "Long Island Country Homes," 181–83.

20. Cited in ibid., 184.

21. Sobin, *Dynamics of Community Control,* 99.

22. Rossano, "Long Island," 234.

23. Ibid., 239. Frank Luther Mott, *American Journalism: A History, 1690–1960* (New York: Macmillan, 1962), 546–92; Stuart Ewen, *PR: A Social History of Spin* (New York: Basic Books, 1996), 39–59.

24. Sobin, *Dynamics of Community Control,* 69–70.

25. Matthew Josephson, *The Robber Barons* (Harcourt Brace Jovanovitch, 1934. Reprint, 1962), 339.

26. Cited in ibid.; Amon, "Architect of Desire."

27. Clara Gillens, interview by authors, January 1992.

CHAPTER TWO

1. Frederick Louis Allen, *The Big Change* (New York: Harper and Row, 1952), 124; and John Faragher et al., *Out of Many: A History of the American People* (Englewood Cliffs, NJ: Prentice Hall, 1994), 729.

2. Robert A. Caro, *The Power Broker: Robert Moses and the Rise and Fall of New York* (New York: Vintage, 1975), 144.

3. Robert S. Lynd and Helen Lynd, *Middletown* (New York: Harcourt Brace, 1929), 225–27.

4. Caro, *Power Broker,* 143.

5. Ibid., 145–46.

6. Benjamin Hampton, *History of the American Industry* (1931. Reprint. New York: Covici, 1970), 222. See also Stuart Ewen and Elizabeth Ewen, *Channels of Desire: Mass Images and the Shaping of American Consciousness* (New York: McGraw-Hill, 1982; rev. ed., Minneapolis: University of Minnesota Press, 1992).

7. Eric Barnouw, *Tube of Plenty* (New York: Oxford University Press, 1975), 45; *Country Life,* February 1922, cited in ibid.

8. David Nye, *Electrifying America* (Cambridge, MA: MIT Press, 1990), 239.

9. See Dolores Hayden, *The Grand Domestic Revolution* (Cambridge, MA: MIT Press, 1982).

10. "The Cape Cod Cottage," *Architectural Forum,* March 1949, 104.

11. James quoted in Nye, *Electrifying America,* 256.

12. "Cape Cod Cottage," 105.

13. Edward Filene, *The Way Out: A Forecast of Coming Change in Business and Industry* (New York: Doubleday, 1925), 203–5.

14. Lewis Mumford, *American Taste* (San Francisco: The Westgate Press, 1929), 16–22, 27–31, 34.

15. Ibid.

16. Ibid.

17. Wright quoted in Jan Cohn, *The American House as Cultural Symbol* (East Lansing, MI: Michigan State University Press,1979), 108.

18. Dorothy Parker, *Day Dreams,* Marion Meade, ed. (London: Heinemann, 1988), 97.

CHAPTER THREE

1. Robert A. Caro, *The Power Broker: Robert Moses and the Rise and Fall of New York* (New York: Vintage, 1975), 144–47. Westchester barred its parks to anyone not a resident of the county, and New Jersey was accessible only by privately operated ferries that took a long time. Long Island was accessible by the Brooklyn Bridge (1883), the Williamsburg Bridge (1903), the Queensborough Bridge (1909), and the Manhattan Bridge (1909).

2. Peggy and Seth Mills, interview by authors, March 1993.

3. Caro, *Power Broker,* 153.

4. Ibid., 151.

5. Dennis P. Sorbin, *The Dynamics of Community Control,* Empire State Historical Publication Series 59 (Port Washington: Ira Friedman Inc., 1968), 113.

6. On Long Island Moses built the Van Wyck, Long Island, Willowbrook, Northern State, and Seaford-Oyster Bay Expressways, the Wantaugh, Bethpage, Grand Central, Southern State, Meadowbrook, and Cross Island Parkways, and the Cross Bay, Queensborough, Bronx Whitestone, and Triborough Bridges, and the Robert Moses Causeway, as well as twenty-one parks. See http://www.boone.calstatela.edu/g476winter98Kirby-Moses.html.

7. Caro, *Power Broker,* 157.

8. Ibid., 157–59.

9. Ibid., 318.

10. Ibid., 318–19.

11. Bernie Bookbinder, *Long Island People and Places Past and Present* (New York: Newsday Books/Harry Abrams, 1983), 202.

12. Caro, *Power Broker,* 238.

13. Bookbinder, *Long Island People,* 139.

14. Louise Simpson, interview by authors, April 1991.

15. Harve Sinklar-Herring, interview by authors, September 1991.

16. Jon C. Teaford, *Post-Suburbia, Government and Politics in the Edge Cities* (Baltimore, MD: Johns Hopkins University Press, 1997), 33.

17. Peggy Mills, interview by authors, March 1993.

18. Kenneth Jackson, *Crabgrass Frontier: The Suburbanization of the United States* (New York: Oxford University Press, 1985), 174–75; *Who Built America: From the Gilded Age to the Present,* vol. 11. American Social History Project, ed. (New York: Pantheon Books, 1992), 274–75.

19. Nathaniel Schneider Keith, *Politics and the Housing Crisis Since 1930* (New York: Universe Books, 1973), 17; Gwendolyn Wright, *Building the Dream: A Social History of Housing in America* (Boston: MIT Press, 1983), 195.

20. *New York Times,* 19 January 1923, 13 February 1923, 19 March 1923, 29 August 1923, 16 August 1924, 15 December 1924, 11 August 1992, *Newsday,* 7 November 1982. See Jane Gombieski, "Klokards, Kleagles, Kludds, and Kluxers: The Ku Klux Klan in Suffolk County, 1915–1928," *Long Island Historical Journal* 6 (Fall 1993): 41–62, for an informative analysis of the growth of the KKK and its activities on Long Island.

21. Sarah Delany and Elizabeth Delany, *Having Our Say: The Delany Sisters' First Hundred Years* (New York: Kodansha International, 1993), 139.

22. Wright, *Building the Dream,* 212.

23. Edward Smits, *Nassau Suburbia USA* (Garden City, NY: Doubleday, 1974; rev. ed., 1990), 184.

24. Marilyn E. Weingold, *American Mediterranean: An Environmental, Economic, and Social History of the Long Island Sound* (Port Washington, NY: Kennikat Press, 1974), 91.

25. *Architectural Forum,* "Sub Divisions and the FHA," May 1935, 487.

26. Ibid., "Nassau Shores," 465.

27. Keith, *Politics and the Housing Crisis,* 17.

28. Ibid., 18.

29. Ibid., 19.

30. Richard O. Davies, *Housing Reform During the Truman Administration* (Columbia: University of Missouri Press, 1966), 11.

CHAPTER FOUR

1. Edward Filene (1860–1937), an important commercial figure and social thinker, has been largely ignored by historians of the twentieth century. To date there is no major biography of Filene, whose thought influenced the evolution of modern consumerism. In the 1920s he became famous for the creation of a new kind of department store where all classes could shop: the fifth floor for the wealthy, the fourth for the upper middle class, the third for the middle class, the second and first for workers, and the basement contained goods at prices affordable for the masses. He also helped found the consumer union movement, the U.S. Credit Union movement, as well as funding cooperative stores and starting the 20th Century Foundation.

2. Robert Kanigel, *The One Best Way: Frederick Winslow Taylor and the Enigma of Efficiency* (New York: Viking, 1997).

3. Edward A. Filene, *The Way Out: A Forecast of Coming Change in Business and Industry* (New York: Doubleday, 1925), 176, 184.

4. Ibid., 201.

5. Ibid., 203–5.

6. RPAA membership over ten years may have reached twenty-five.

7. RPAA members were disproportionately influential in the New Deal's policies and projects, particularly the Tennessee Valley Authority, the Civilian Conservation Corps, the Rural Electrification Administration, and the Greenbelt Communities.

8. Members of the RPAA drew inspiration from a range of sources. They were influenced by Ebenezer Howard, the father of the English Garden City Movement. Howard believed that the reformation of the physical environment could contribute to the transformation of the social environment. The group looked to American ideas as well, drawing from Henry David Thoreau's emphasis on nature, Thorstein Veblen's critique of conspicuous consumption, and John Dewey's ideas of participatory democratic culture.

9. Mumford quoted in Carl Sussman, ed., *Planning the Fourth Migration: The Neglected Vision of the Regional Planning Association of America* (Cambridge, MA: MIT Press, 1976), 13. For an excellent history of the RPAA see Roy Lubove, *Community Planning in the 1920s: The Contribution of the Regional Planning Association of America* (Pittsburgh: University of Pittsburgh Press, 1963).

10. Henry Wright, "The Road to Good Houses," *Survey Graphic* 7 (May 1925): 165–68.

11. Mumford quoted in Daniel Schaffer, *Garden Cities for America: The Radburn Experience* (Philadelphia: Temple University Press, 1982), 61.

12. Lewis Mumford, "A Region to Live in," *Survey Graphic* 7 (1925): 151–52.

13. Ibid.

14. Sussman, *Planning the Fourth Migration*, 45.

15. Mumford quoted in ibid., 44.

16. Clarence Stein, "New Towns for New Purposes," in Lewis Mumford, ed., *Roots of Contemporary American Architecture* (New York: Reinhold, 1952), 336.

17. Mumford quoted in Sussman, *Planning the Fourth Migration*, 13.

18. Chase quoted in ibid., 23.

19. Schaffer, *Garden Cities for America*, 114.

20. Lubove, *Community Planning in the 1920s*, 67–82.

21. Stein in Mumford, ed., *Roots of Contemporary American Architecture*, 339; Gwendolyn Wright, *Building the Dream: A Social History of Housing in America* (Boston: MIT Press, 1983), 205–7.

22. "Limited Dividend Roll Call," *Architectural Forum*, January 1935, 98–103. Most businessmen who invested were involved in major department store and retail trade like their contemporary, Edward Filene.

23. Lubove, *Community Planning in the 1920s*, 79.

24. Christopher Gray, "Amalgamated Housing Still Works," *New York Times*, 3 July 1994.

25. Schaffer, *Garden Cities for America*, 106.

26. Ibid., 123.

27. Ibid. This pioneering large-scale building method in housing was a forerunner to Levittown, where speed was essential: 1,200 units were erected in four years.

28. Ibid., 124.

29. A Sunnyside house cost between $4,800 and $17,000 depending on size; with a 10 percent down payment, the average house or cooperative apartment cost a minimum of $42 a month, or $504 a year, to maintain, "necessitating an annual family income of $2500, an amount earned by only 40% of all urban families." Ibid., 127.

30. Ibid.

31. *New York Times*, 26 June 1994. According to a 1994 *Times* article, Sunnyside in the 1990s is still considered one of the most successful planned communities in the United States.

32. Mumford quoted in Schaffer, *Garden Cities for America*, 127.

33. Stein quoted in Mumford, ed., *Roots of Contemporary American Architecture*, 345.

34. Ibid., 205–6.

35. Clarence Stein, *Towards New Towns for America*, (Liverpool: University of Liverpool Press, 1951), 46. For a useful bibliography on the new town movement see Susan L. Klaus, *Links in the Chains: Greenbelt, Maryland, and the New Town Movement in America: An Annotated Bibliography on the Occasion of the Fiftieth Anniversary of Greenbelt, Maryland*, vol. 13 (Washington, DC: Center for Washington Studies, 1987).

36. Geddes Smith quoted in Stein, *Towards New Towns for America*, 44.

37. Lewis Mumford, "America Can't Have Housing," *The New Republic*, 1934, 15–19.

38. Catherine Bauer, *Modern Housing* (New York: Houghton Mifflin Co. 1934), 242. Catherine Bauer was the daughter of Jacob Bauer, the New Jersey highway commissioner who initiated the modern superhighway that bypassed major towns. See *Notable Ameri-*

can Women. Modern Period, A Biographical Dictionary (Cambridge, MA: Harvard University Press, 1980).

39. Mumford quoted in Stein, *New Towns*, 15.

CHAPTER FIVE

1. Catherine Bauer, "We Face a Housing Shortage," in M. B. Schnapper, ed., *Public Housing in America* (New York: H. W. Wilson, 1939), 30.

2. Thomas S. Holden, "Construction and Finance," *Atlantic Monthly,* March 1938.

3. Ibid. *The New Republic* quoted in Frederick Ackerman, "Debt as a Foundation for Houses," in *Architectural Forum* April 1934, 255–56; "Some Statistics on the Housing Shortage," *Architectural Forum,* April 1934, 301–2.

4. Ackerman, "Debt as a Foundation," 256–57.

5. Clarence Arthur Perry, *Housing for the Machine Age* (New York: Russell Sage Foundation, 1939), 25.

6. Chase qouted in Schnapper, ed., *Public Housing in America,* 266.

7. Richard O. Davies, *Housing Reform During the Truman Administration* (Columbia: University of Missouri Press, 1966), 16.

8. Holden quoted in *Atlantic Monthly,* 321.

9. Kenneth Jackson, *Crabgrass Frontier: The Suburbanization of the United States* (New York: Oxford University Press, 1985), 203–4, quoting a Federal Emergency Relief administrator testifying before the House Banking and Currency Committee, 18 May 1934.

10. Editorial, *Architectural Forum,* July 1934.

11. FDR quoted in Ronald Tobey, Charles Wetherell, and John Brigham, "Moving out and Settling in: Residential Mobility, Home Owning, and the Public Enframing of Citizenship, 1921–1950," *American Historical Review* 95 (December 1990): 1418.

12. Russell Buhite and David Levy, *FDR's Fireside Chats* (New York: Penguin, 1993), 82, 110, 50.

13. Allen Brinkley, "The New Deal and the Idea of the State," in Steve Fraser and Gary Gerstle, eds., *The Rise and Fall of the New Deal Order, 1930–80* (Princeton, NJ: Princeton University Press, 1989), 97.

14. Hanson and FDR quoted in ibid., 96.

15. Ibid., xiv.

16. Schlesinger quoted in Nathaniel Schneider Keith, *Politics and the Housing Crisis Since 1930* (New York: Universe Press, 1973), 21–25; Jackson, *Crabgrass Frontier,* 195–96; "The Federal Home Loan Bank System," *Architectural Forum,* April 1935, 116–21.

17. "The Brewing of FHA's Title 11," *Architectural Forum,* November 1934, 380–81.

18. "Subdivisions and the Federal Housing Administration," *Architectural Forum,* May 1935, 157–60.

19. Jackson, *Crabgrass Frontier,* 195–203; Gwendolyn Wright, *Building the Dream: A Social History of Housing in America* (Boston: MIT Press, 1983), 240–47.

20. Robert Bremner, *From the Depths: The Discovery of Poverty in the United States,* (New York: NYU Press 1956), 21.

21. Wagner and La Guardia quoted in Davies, *Housing Reform*, 13–14.

22. Wright, *Building the Dream*, 224–25.

23. Ibid., 227.

24. "The New Deal's First Year," *Architectural Forum*, April 1934, 253.

25. Keith, *Politics and the Housing Crisis*, 29.

26. Herbert U. Nelson, executive vice president of the National Association of Real Estate Boards, proclaimed "In our country, we prefer that governmental activity shall take the form of assisting and aiding private business rather than undertaking great public projects of a governmental character." Davies, *Housing Reform*, 17.

27. *Architectural Forum*, December 1935.

28. Broadus Mitchell, *Depression Decade: From New Era Through New Deal, 1929–1941* (New York: Harper and Row, 1947), 333.

29. The Straus family migrated from Bavaria to the United States in 1854. They moved to New York City after the Civil War, where they became associated with the development of Macy's, and in 1896 Nathan Straus, Sr., acquired ownership. Nathan Sr. was a prominent philanthropist, giving coal to people without heat in the depression of 1894 and advocating programs for child health. Nathan Jr. (1889–1961), after completing college, started as a reporter for the *New York Globe*. In 1914 he founded the weekly humor magazine *Puck*, and in 1917 he enlisted in the navy. After his return he ran for the New York Senate, was elected, and served for six years. After a stint as director of USHA, he wrote two books on the housing issue and bought the New York City radio station WMCA in 1943. Believing that owning a radio station was "the best way of reaching the largest number of people in disseminating the truth," Straus did not accept advertising and ran programs on social issues. See *Contemporary Authors*, vol. 89 (Detroit: Gale Research, 1961); *New York Times*, Obituary, 14 September 1961.

30. Jackson, *Crabgrass Frontier*, 223–25; Wright, *Building the Dream*, 229–30.

31. "TVA Homes Examined," *Architectural Forum*, March 1938, 60.

32. "Houses in Half the Time," *Architectural Forum*, March 1939, 230.

33. Rachel L. Swarns, "Sixty Years Later and Still a Success," *New York Times*, 18 December 1995.

34. Eleanor Roosevelt was so interested in housing that in 1934 she championed Arthurdale, an experiment in housing for 165 unemployed mining families in West Virginia. She raised money for the school and health clinic and insisted that the new houses have indoor plumbing, root cellars, gardens, and livestock. Some of the houses had combination barns, poultry houses, and pigpens. Employment opportunities were offered by two private industries, and the cooperative agriculture and community enterprises were created by the Arthurdale Association. See Blanche Cooke, "One First Lady to Another," *New York Times*, 17 January 1996, op. ed., and "Houses," *Architectural Forum*, June 1937, 498.

35. "$6.05 Per Room in Manhattan," *Architectural Forum*, January 1936, 67–68. First Houses was declared a New York City landmark in 1974.

36. Keith, *Politics and the Housing Crisis*, 39.

37. Charles Lewis, "Let Private Capital Build Houses," in Schnapper, ed., *Public Housing in America*, 307.

38. "Why Not Subsidies for Business," in Schnapper, ed., 325.

39. Ibid.

40. Robert Wagner, "Low Cost Homes for Low Incomes," in ibid., 232–33.

41. Ibid., 227.

42. Davies, *Housing Reform*, 19–20.

CHAPTER SIX

1. Mary Lou Williamson, ed., *Greenbelt: History of a New Town, 1937–1987* (Norfolk, VA: Donning, 1987), 12.

2. Ibid., 29.

3. Tugwell cited in ibid., 32.

4. Ibid.

5. Clarence Stein, *Towards New Towns for America* (Liverpool: University of Liverpool Press, 1951), 127.

6. Ibid.

7. Draper quoted in Leta Mach, "Constructing the Town of Greenbelt," in Williamson, ed., *Greenbelt*, 33.

8. Stein, *New Towns*, 134.

9. Draper quoted in Mach, "Constructing the Town," 33.

10. Ibid., 34–35. No churches could be built because of the legal separation of church and state.

11. "Model City, Greenbelt Maryland," *Grand Street* 50 (Fall 1994), 103.

12. Barbara Likowski and Jay McCarl, "Social Construction," in Williamson, ed., *Greenbelt*, 72.

13. Stein, *New Towns*, 130.

14. Likowski and McCarl, "Social Construction," 72.

15. "Model City," 106.

16. Likowski and McCarl, "Social Construction," 72.

17. Stein, *New Towns*, 130.

18. Likowski and McCarl, "Social Construction," 73.

19. Ibid., 75.

20. "Model City," 106.

21. Likowski and McCarl, "Social Construction," 79.

22. "Houses," *Architectural Forum*, June 1937, 473.

23. "They Dressed Them Up," *Architectural Forum*, November 1934, 382.

24. Tom Bernard, "New Homes for Sixty Dollars a Month," *American Magazine*, April 1948, 104.

25. Townsend quoted in Charlie Zehren, "The Dream Builder," *Newsday*, 28 September 1997, 51.

26. "They Dressed Them Up," 382.

27. Ibid., 383–84.

28. Ibid, 383.

29. Ibid, 384.

30. "Harmon Builds Again," *Architectural Forum,* May 1937, 64. Harmon, who was also from a successful building family, built developments in New Jersey, Long Island, and Westchester.

CHAPTER SEVEN

1. "The Industry Capitalism Forgot," *Fortune,* August 1947, 61.

2. Joseph Mason, *History of Housing in the U.S.: 1930–1980* (Houston, TX: Gulf Press, 1982), 31.

3. *The Role of the Housebuilding Industry: Building America* (Washington, DC: National Resources Planning Board, July 1942), 13.

4. Mason, *History of Housing,* 32.

5. Ibid., 33–34.

6. "Channel Heights Housing Project," *Architectural Forum,* March 1944, 65–74.

7. Blandford quoted in Nathaniel Schneider Keith, *Politics and the Housing Crisis since 1930* (New York: Universe Press, 1973), 49–50.

8. The Seabees, the navy's Fighting Construction Battalions, served a critical apprenticeship in mass production. Builders, architects, engineers, electricians, plumbers, welders, steelworkers, and bricklayers made up the ranks of the Seabees. They built housing, barracks, airstrips, docks, hangars, and advanced bases, often under fire in a thousand remote and fearful spots from the South Pacific to the Antarctic. The Seabees' motto was "CAN DO." After the war, many came back to play important roles in the housing industry. William Levitt did two years of duty with the Seabees, and with characteristic arrogance claimed, "That little branch of the navy that had the pleasure of my company learned much more about building from me than I did from them."

9. Arnold Silverman, "Defense and Deconcentration: Defense Industrialization During World War II and the Development of the Contemporary American Suburb." Paper delivered at Hofstra University, June 1988, 2 (brought to our attention by Robert Keeler).

10. *Newsday,* 16 February 1944.

11. Advertisements for *Better Homes and Gardens* in *Printer's Ink,* 24 July 1942, 21 August 1942, 11 October 1942 (brought to our attention by Andrew Mattson).

12. Ads from *Stars and Stripes* in Keith Winsell, "Utopia in Transition" in Mary Lou Williamson, ed., *Greenbelt: History of a New Town, 1937–1987* (Norfolk, VA: Donning, 1987), 149.

CHAPTER EIGHT

1. Gwendolyn Wright, *Building the Dream: A Social History of Housing in America* (Boston: MIT Press, 1983), 253.

2. Thomas Reeves, *The Life and Times of Joe McCarthy* (New York: Stein and Day, 1982), 133; Wright, *Building the Dream,* 242.

3. William Levitt, "The Builder and Banker, a Partnership in Democracy," *United States Investor* (20 November 1948): 40.

4. Nathaniel Schneider Keith, *Politics and the Housing Crisis Since 1930* (New York: Universe Press, 1973), 56, 57.

5. Reeves, *Joe McCarthy*, 133.

6. Richard O. Davies, *Housing Reform During the Truman Administration* (Columbia: University of Missouri Press, 1966), 69.

7. Jack Anderson and Ronald May, *McCarthy: the Man, the Senator, the Ism* (New York: Beacon, 1952), 143.

8. Davies, *Housing Reform*, 69.

9. Anderson and May, *McCarthy*, 145; Reeves, *Joe McCarthy*, 134.

10. Wright, *Building the Dream*, 46. President Truman chimed in with this argument when he said, "Children and dogs are as necessary to the welfare of this country as is Wall Street and the railroads."

11. Levitt, "The Builder and the Banker," 43.

12. U.S. Senate, Joint Committee Study and Investigation of Housing, Hearings, 80th Cong., 1st sess., 1947–48, 10 (hereafter cited as Housing Hearings).

13. Housing Hearings, 11.

14. Ibid., 20.

15. Nathan Straus, *Two-Thirds of a Nation: A Housing Program* (New York: Knopf, 1952), 277.

16. Lee F. Johnson, "The Housing Act of 1949 in Your Community," in ibid., 207.

17. Housing Hearings, 149.

18. Ibid., 174–77.

19. "Let's Have Ourselves a Housing Industry," *Fortune*, September 1947, 4.

20. Ibid., 1–4.

21. Housing Hearings, 57.

22. Ibid., 5108. See, e.g., Hartwell Dickson, "Low Down on the Slow Down," *Collier's*, November 1947; Joseph M. Guilfoyle and John S. Cooper, "No New House for You," *Saturday Evening Post*, March 1948; and Thurmond Arnold, "Why We Have a Housing Mess," *Look*, 1 April 1947, 21–23.

23. House Hearings, 5112.

24. Ibid., 5112–13.

25. Ibid., 5110.

26. Ibid., 5111.

27. Ibid., 113.

28. Ibid., 149.

29. Ibid., 117.

30. Edward Angly, "Let's Rebuild Our Building Codes," *Collier's*, 15 November 1947, 5.

31. Arnold, "Why We Have a Housing Mess," 21–23.

32. Housing Hearings, 5157.

33. Boyden Sparkes, "They'll Build Neighborhoods, Not Houses," *Saturday Evening Post*, 28 October 1946, 46.

34. Housing Hearings, 5158.

35. Ibid.

36. Reeves, *Joe McCarthy*, 139; Anderson and May, *McCarthy*, 148.

37. Reeves, *Joe McCarthy*, 139–40; Housing Hearings, 5154.

38. Housing Hearings, 5057–58.

39. William Levitt, "The Builder and Banker, a Partnership in Democracy," *United States Investor* 46 (1947): 1948.

CHAPTER NINE

1. "The Fortune Survey," *Architectural Forum*, April 1946, 180–81, 184, 186, 188.

2. Cited in Nathan Straus, *Two-Thirds of a Nation: A Housing Program* (New York: Knopf, 1952), 96.

3. Stuart Ewen, *PR!: A Social History of Spin* (New York: Basic Books, 1996), 302–16.

4. W. W. Jennings, "The Value of Home Owning as Exemplified in American History," *Social Science* (January 1938), cited in John Dean, *Home Ownership: Is It Sound?* (New York: Harper and Row, 1945), 4.

5. Fritz Burns, "To Own—Certainly," cited in Dean, *Home Ownership*, 5.

6. Dean, *Home Ownership*, 3–4.

7. Cited in Straus, *Two-Thirds of a Nation*, 75.

8. Nathan Straus, *The Seven Myths of Housing* (New York: Knopf, 1946), frontispiece; Robert Lynd, foreword, in Dean, *Home Ownership*, vii, ix, x.

9. Straus, *Seven Myths of Housing*, 74.

10. Charles Lewis, "The American Family and Its Shelter," *Architectural Forum*, April 1939, 9.

11. Dean, *Home Ownership*, 16.

12. "The Urge to Own," *Architectural Forum*, November 1937, 378.

13. Advertisement, *Newsday*, 7 July 1947.

14. Straus, *Two-Thirds of a Nation*, 74, 76–81.

15. Dean, *Home Ownership*, 66.

16. Cited in John Liell, "Levittown: A Study in Community Development" (Ph.D. diss., Yale University, 1952), 72.

17. Dean, *Home Ownership*, 51; Charles Abrams, "Good Houses for Everybody," in Bruce Bliven and A. G. Mezerik, eds., *What the Informed Citizen Needs to Know* (New York: Duell, Sloan & Pearce, 1946), 172.

18. Dean , *Home Ownership* 47.

19. Straus , *Two-Thirds of a Nation*, 86.

20. Four hundred fifty square feet for one person living alone, 750 square feet for a couple, 1,000 square feet for a family of three, and 1,150 square feet for a family of four. Ibid., 87.

21. Ibid.

22. *New York Times,* 1 June 1950, cited in ibid.

23. Ibid., 64–65.

24. Italics in text, Straus, *Seven Myths,* 111–13.

25. Straus, *Seven Myths;* The National Association of Real Estate Boards, *The Confidential Weekly Letter,* November 1939, 139.

26. Lynd, foreword, in Dean, *Home Ownership,* viii.

27. Liell, "Levittown," 137. As Lewis Mumford pointed out, "To plan adequately for the dwelling house however, one must plan at the same time for all the communal institutions and functions which enable people to do in larger groups what they cannot perform as families: these communal functions cannot be conceived as afterthoughts." Ibid., 194.

28. Bryn J. Hovde, "Prerequisites of Planned Developments," *Architectural Forum,* April 1944, 88.

CHAPTER TEN

1. The most conservative reports from the National Housing Agency estimated that at least 5 million housing units were needed immediately and a total of 12.5 million over the next decade. Cited in Richard O. Davies, *Housing Reform During the Truman Administration* (Columbia: University of Missouri Press, 1966), 25.

2. "Large Scale Housing," *Architectural Forum,* February 1938, 111–12.

3. "The Industry Capitalism Forgot," *Fortune,* August 1947, 169.

4. Ibid.

5. "Large Scale Housing," *Architectural Forum,* 110.

6. "The Builder's House, 1949," *Architectural Forum,* April 1949, 81.

7. "It Takes More than 30,000 Parts to Build a Typical House" (editorial), *Architectural Forum,* April 1937.

8. "Domestic Interiors," *Architectural Forum,* October 1937, 239–46.

9. "The Low Cost House," *Architectural Forum,* November 1938, 312.

10. "Planning the Postwar House," *Architectural Forum,* January 1944, 76.

11. Ibid., 75.

12. "A *Life* Roundtable on Housing," Russell Davenport, moderator, *Life,* February 1948, 77.

13. "Building with Pre Fabs, *Architectural Forum,* April 1949, 133–34.

14. U.S. Senate, Joint Committee Study and Investigation of Housing, Hearings, 80th Cong., 1st sess., 1947-1948, 5158, and repeated by William Levitt in *Life* roundtable in 1948.

15. "The Industrialized House: The Greatest House Building Show on Earth," *Architectural Forum,* March 1947, 105. Another merchant builder, the Byrne Organization, comprised of Texans, who had also built war housing, used similar construction methods by erecting factories in Quonset huts near the site. They built thousands of houses—between ten and fifteen a day—outside Baltimore in Glen Burnie and in Harundale, Maryland, for $6,950.

16. "Fabrication," *Architectural Forum*, July 1946, 141.

17. Park Forest was planned by Nathan Manilow, one of the biggest builders in Chicago; Jerrold Lobel, architect; and Philip Klutznick, commissioner of the Federal Public Housing Authority and well-known advocate of public housing.

18. "A *Life* Roundtable," 78; "American Community Builders," *Architectural Forum*, August 1948, 70–75.

19. "Construction Financing," *Architectural Forum*, February 1948, 12–13.

20. Eric Larabee, "The Six Thousand Houses That Levitt Built," *Harper's*, September 1948, 87.

21. "The Look House," *Look*, 3 August 1948, 43–45.

22. Albert Wood, letter to Alicia Patterson, 21 September 1944, in Robert Keeler's private archives.

23. "The Long Island Builders' House," *Architectural Forum*, July 1950, 102.

24. Tom Bernard, "New Homes for Sixty Dollars a Month," *American Magazine*, April 1948, 104.

25. Ibid.

26. According to Kenneth Jackson, "The Levitts were among the nation's largest home builders even before the construction of the first Levittown." Kenneth Jackson, *Crabgrass Frontier: The Suburbanization of the United States* (New York: Oxford University Press, 1985), 234.

27. Bernard, "New Homes," 105.

28. Housing Hearings, 5156–57.

29. Larabee, "Six Thousand Houses," 88.

30. Bernard, "New Homes," 104.

31. Ibid., 107.

32. "The Builders' House," 91.

33. Ibid., 88–90.

34. Ibid. Sunnyside also was built this way (see chapter 4). Perhaps Levitt took a cue from FDR, who in 1938 proposed a guaranteed annual wage for building workers who were "lucky to average 125 work days a year, and must therefore get a high daily rate to make up for the days he is idle. . . . In theory the guaranteed annual wage is simplicity itself. John Carpenter now manages to find a hundred and twenty days of work a year at 10 dollars a day, earns $12,000 a year. In consideration of a *guarantee* of twice as much work a year—200 days—let him agree to accept *an annual* wage of $16,000. This would mean a reduction in his daily wage of one third to $6.67, but increase in his annual income by $400 dollars. Thus the labor costs on a house would be cut by a third, houses would be cheaper, more people would buy them, more would be built, everyone would stand to win." FDR cited in "The Guaranteed Wage," *Architectural Forum*, March 1938, 207–8.

35. "The Builders' House," 90–91.

36. Larabee, "Six Thousand Houses," 83.

37. Frank Lloyd Wright, *Architectural Forum*, January 1938 (issue written and edited by Frank Lloyd Wright), 79.

38. Cited in Robert F. Keeler, "Alicia Patterson and the Shaping of Long Island," in Natalie A. Naylor and Maurren O. Murphy, eds., *Long Island Women: Activists and Innovators* (Interlaken, NY: Empire State Books, 1998), 271–72.

39. Robert Keeler, 272.

40. Housing Hearings, 5159–60.

41. Joseph M. Guilfoyle and J. Howard Rutledge, "Levitt Licks the Housing Shortage," *Coronet*, September 1948, 113. Levitt ends and means cited in Larabee, 85.

42. John Liell, "Levittown: A Study in Community Development," (Ph.D. diss., Yale University, 1952), 114–15. Some people estimate $2,000 or more.

43. William J. Levitt, "A House Is Not Enough," in Sidney Furst and Milton Sherman, eds., *Business Decisions That Changed Our Lives* (New York: Random House, 1964), 64–65.

44. Ibid., 70.

45. "Planning the Postwar House," *Architectural Forum*, January 1944, 77.

46. "The Industry Capitalism Forgot," *Fortune*, August 1947, 66.

47. Quoted in "Levitt's 1950 House," *Architectural Forum*, March 1950, 136.

48. "The Builders' House," 85–86. Alfred Levitt figured out that housewall shingles, paper, insulation, plasterboard, etc., cost 25 cents a foot—exactly the same amount as double glazing.

49. "The Most Popular Builders' House," *Architectural Forum*, April 1950, 134.

50. Michele Ingrassia, "The House That Levitt Built," *Newsday*, 28 September 1997.

51. Ibid.

52. Frank Lloyd Wright, *Architectural Forum*, January 1938, 78.

53. Joseph Barry, "Frank Lloyd Wright: The Man Who Liberated Architecture," *House Beautiful*, November 1955, 240, 241, 244 .

54. Ingrassia, "The House that Levitt Built."

55. *Architectural Forum*, July 1948, 15.

56. John Dean, *Home Ownership: Is It Sound?* (New York: Harper and Row, 1945), 25.

57. *Business Week*, September 1944, quoted in ibid., xi.

58. Liell, "Levittown," 113. "Levitt's 1950s House," *Architectural Forum*, April 1950, 136.

59. The most conservative reports from the National Housing Agency estimated that at least 5 million housing units were needed immediately and a total of 12.5 million over the next decade. Cited in Richard O. Davies, *Housing Reform During the Truman Administration* (Columbia: University of Missouri Press, 1966), 25.

60. Ibid., 167.

61. "The Urge to Own," *Architectural Forum*, November 1937, 377.

62. "The Builders' House," 86. Opening the house in this manner "made the kitchen a control station from which the housewife can easily reach any part of the house. Previously, kitchens were designed without women in mind, domestic chores were done by wives and servants, kept hidden from family life. The idea that the kitchen should central, not isolated was taken from the feminist scientific housing movement.

63. Larabee, "Six Thousand Houses," 82; "Industry Capitalism Forgot," 167.
64. Liell, "Levittown," 111.
65. *Architectural Forum*, September 1948, 243; idem, December 1949, 157.
66. Liell, "Levittown," 111.
67. "Up from the Potato Fields," *Time*, 30 July 1950.
68. *Architectural Forum*, May 1949, 24, 28, 32.

CHAPTER ELEVEN

1. John Liell, "Levittown: A Study in Community Development" (Ph.D. diss., Yale University, 1952), 216, 231, 226.
2. Abraham Levitt, William J. Levitt, and Alfred S. Levitt, *Levittown* (New York: Levitt and Sons, July 1948).
3. Liell, "Levittown," 171.
4. Barbara M. Kelly, *Expanding the American Dream: Building and Rebuilding Levittown* (Albany, NY: SUNY Press, 1993), 50–51; Pat and Bob Smith, interview by Julius Marta, 22 April 1988.
5. Liell, "Levittown," 184.
6. Quoted from *Coronet*, September 1948, in Geoffrey Mohan, "Suburban Pioneers," *Newsday*, 28 September 1997, 25.
7. Liell, "Levittown," 185.
8. Harry Henderson, "The Mass Produced Suburbs," *Harper's*, November 1953, 25.
9. Ibid., 39.
10. Michele Ingrassia, "The House That Levitt Built," *Newsday*, 28 September 1997, 28.
11. Henderson, "Mass Produced Suburbs," 27. Henderson reports in interviewing women that home-decorating ideas "primarily came from pictures of rooms in national magazines. Nobody copies an entire room but they take different items from different pictures." Early-American and modern furniture advertised in magazines and shown on TV became standard in Levittown houses. Rarely seen in Levittown were family heirlooms.
12. Ibid., 28.
13. Dan Gossard, interview by Anthony Mariano, April 1999.
14. Liell, "Levittown," 176.
15. Ibid., 177–80.
16. Agnes Geraghty, interview by daughter Cara, May 1992.
17. "Markets in the Meadows," *Architectural Forum*, March 1949, 114. As a writer in *Architectural Forum* observed in 1949, "If the first half of the 20th century has witnessed the gradual centralization of business—with the foci of sales shifting from the previously self sufficient small towns to the city, and from the neighborhood to the downtown shopping district—the second half promises to complete the reversal of this trend. . . . The consumer, thanks to the automobile, has become mobile enough to transcend the fixed

concentrations of retail stores, where congestion and lack of parking space makes shopping an ordeal" (p. tk).

18. *Time*, 16 July 1956, 80–81.

19. In that same year, 1956, twenty-two additional shopping centers were built in Nassau County: the Mid Island, Hicksville, Greenacres, and Valley Stream malls, to name a few. See Jon C. Teaford, *Post Suburbia: Government and Politics in the Edge Cities* (Baltimore, MD: Johns Hopkins University Press, 1997), 56.

20. Robert Sweeney, interview by authors, 5 November 1992.

21. Norman Appelton, interview by authors, 11 February 1991.

22. It is hard to estimate how many nontraditional families were in Levittown at this time, but there were at least 10 percent to 20 percent.

23. Betty Scott, interview by authors, May 1989.

24. Clifford Clark, *The American Family Home* (Chapel Hill: University of North Carolina Press, 1986), 210.

25. Geraghty, interview by Cara.

26. Liell, "Levittown," 110.

27. "Same Rooms, Varied Decor," *Life*, January 14, 1952, 90–93.

28. Elizabeth Sweeney Herbert, "This Is How I Keep House," *McCall's*, April 1949, 41–42, is representative of popular magazine articles of the period that also fit the needs of the consumer industries in their search for Mrs. Consumer.

29. See Clark, p. 234; Susan Strasser, *Never Done*, (New York: Pantheon, 1982), Chapter 14; Ruth Schwartz Cowan, *More Work for Mother* (New York: Basic Books, 1983) Chapter 7. These studies indicate that housework was not less time-consuming, but rather housework was modernized. Consumption became a part of everyday life and had to be included in the housework equation.

30. Henderson, "Mass Produced Suburbs," 29; idem, "Rugged American Collectivism," *Harper's*, December 1953, 80–81. Actually, this sentiment probably was true only for the first child: after a community of mothers was established part of its function was to aid women during pregnancy.

31. Henderson, "Rugged American Collectivism," 84.

32. Ibid.

33. Ibid.

34. Thomas Hines, Populuxe (City: Publisher, date), 18.

35. Henderson, "Rugged American Collectivism," p. 83

36. Addams quoted in William O'Neill, *Everyone Was Brave* (Chicago, Illinois: Quadrangle, 1969), 34.

37. Elizabeth Ewen, *Immigrant Women in the Land of Dollars* (New York: Monthly Review Press, 1985).

38. The authors interviewed over 200 people: some in groups, some individually. Most interviews were conducted in homes in Levittown, Roosevelt and Freeport. A few interviews were conducted at people's work sites and at McDonald's. The interviews concerned the suburban experience over a forty-year period. Ages ranged from twenty-three

to ninety. Those interviewed seem to remember their pioneer days vividly; in fact they remember the period from 1947 to 1957 better than any period of their lives. This early period became an important signpost as described by Ernest Schactel, *Metamorphosis* (New York: Basic Books, 1959).

39. Doris Kalisman, interview by authors, March 1989.

40. Mathilda Albert, interview by authors, March 1989.

41. Clare Worthing, interview by authors, March 1989.

42. Virginia Crowther, interview by authors, April, 1989.

43. Henderson, "The Mass Produced Suburbs," 31.

44. Martha Mordin, interview by authors, 14 March 1987.

45. Helga Baum, interview by authors, March 1989.

46. Doris Kalisman, interview by authors, March 1989.

47. Roberta Stim, interview by authors, March 1989.

48. Joseph Maloney, "The Lonesome Train in Levittown," *Inter-University Case Program* (University, AL: University of Alabama Press, 1958), 1–4.

49. Henderson, "Mass Produced Suburbs," 26.

50. Henderson, "Rugged American Collectivism," 83.

51. Interview with Barbara Croswell , April, 1990.

52. Maloney, "Lonesome Train," 1.

53. Albert, interview by authors.

54. Baum, interview by authors.

55. Mohan, "Suburban Pioneers," 11.

CHAPTER TWELVE

1. Donald Katz, *Home Fires* (New York: HarperCollins, 1992), 121.

2. Phyllis McGintley, "Suburbia: Of Thee I Sing," *Harper's,* December 1949, 79.

3. John Keats, *The Crack in the Picture Window* (New York: Houghton Mifflin, 1957), 139.

4. Ibid., 139.

5. Katz, 122.

6. Betty Friedan, *The Feminine Mystique* (New York: Dell, 1963), esp. chap. 1 and 2; Marilyn French, *The Woman's Room* (New York: Harcourt Brace, 1977), 108.

7. Friedan, *Feminine Mystique* ,14.

8. Sheila Rowbotham, *A Century of Women: The History of Women in Britain and the United States* (London: Viking, 1997), 367. By the early 1960s the job market for educated women had improved. Clerical, elementary education, nursing, and sales were still the primary available arenas, but there was growth in higher education, heath, administration, and female unionization. Although equal pay legislation provided an important breakthrough, women still received only 60 percent of the rate for men in the 1960s. Even though the door to work opened slightly, the stereotyped suburban housewife remained the dominant image, good or bad, of the American way of life. *The Feminine Mystique*

took on all the old prejudices against working mothers, but for Friedan it was the stay at home, so called good mother, who turned to insanity, drink, and tranquilizers.

9. Letter no. 685, 1 November 1963, Betty Friedan papers, ser. 3, Schlesinger Library, Cambridge, MA. (Letters are numbered according to date received.)

10. Letter no. 688, 23 October 1963.

11. Ibid.

12. Grace Grillo, interview by Maureen Tarulli, May 1994.

13. Gertrude Shedlick, interview by William Shedlick, April 1993.

14. Virginia Gaurnari Brown, interview by daughter Linda Brown, May 1994.

15. Lewis Mumford, *The City in History,* (New York: Harcourt, Brace and World, 1961), 486.

16. William Levitt, "What! Live in Levittown?" *Good Housekeeping,* July 1958, 176.

17. Ibid., 47, 175.

18. Mae Brandon, interview by authors, January 17, 1991; Barbara Kelly, *Expanding the American Dream: Building and Rebuilding Levittown* (Albany, NY: SUNY Press, 1983), 56.

19. D.J. Waldie; *Holy Land, A Suburban Memoir* (New York: Norton, 1996) 27, Kelly, 30, John Liell, "Levittown: A Study in Community Development" (Ph.d. diss., Yale University; 1952), 173.

20. David Beers, *Blue Sky Dream: A Memoir of America's Fall From Grace* (New York: Doubleday, 1996), 51.

21. Ron Rosenbaum, "The House That Levitt Built," *Esquire,* December 1988, 388.

22. Ralph G. Martin, "How Individuality Got a Second Chance," *House Beautiful,* February 1956, 96.

23. Ralph G. Martin, "Life in the New Suburbia," *New York Times,* 12 January 1950; Kelly, *Expanding the American Dream,* 52; Waldie, *Holy Land,* 12.

24. Ibid., 1, 2.

25. Beers, *Blue Sky Dream,* 39–40.

26. Waldie quoted in Joan Didion, "Trouble in Lakewood," *The New Yorker,* 23 July 1993, 47. Waldie was then the City of Lakewood's Public Information Officer.

27. "Zippy's Roots in . . . ? Levittown," *Boston Globe,* 5 October 1997. We would like to thank James Campen for calling this article to our attention.

CHAPTER THIRTEEN

1. "The House We Live In," *Newsday,* 19 August 1948.

2. Charles and Meta Meredy, interview by authors, February 1991.

3. Madeline Ryttenberg, "Freeport Slums, A Monument to Voters No," *Newsday,* 28 August 1951.

4. Ibid.

5. "The House We Live In."

6. John Rice, "A History, Village of Roosevelt—Good Place to Live—A Splendid Challenge," *News Bulletin,* 1, no. 2 (Roosevelt Chamber of Commerce, May 1991).

7. Madeline Ryttenberg, "States' Worst Slum Shames Freeport," *Newsday*, 25 March 1949.

8. Since Long Island politicians were Republicans and most property owners still believed in segregation, the only group that represented the people in Bennington Park were the Protestant, Catholic, and Jewish local clergy.

9. Ryttenberg, "States' Worst Slum."

10. "AVC Demands End to Slums in Freeport," *Newsday*, 13 January 1950.

11. Bernie Bookbinder, "Freeport Slum Clearance Plan Gets Big Boost," *Newsday*, 21 August 1951.

12. Ibid.

13. Ibid.

14. As late as 1945 the high school in Freeport had a KKK emblem over its main entrance. Residents report that such forms of racism dated from the period when whites expected all blacks to act like servants.

15. John Dean, "None Other than Caucasians," *Journal of Land and Public Utility Economics*, 3, no. 4 (November 1947).

16. Gwendolyn Wright, *Building the Dream: A Social History of Housing in America* (Boston: MIT Press, 1983), 247–48.

17. Thurgood Marshall, letter to Harry Truman, 1 February 1949, NAACP file, box 751, quoted in Andrew Wiese, "Driving a Thin Wedge of Suburban Opportunity: Black Suburbanization in the Northern Metropolis, 1940–1960" (master's thesis, Columbia University, 1988), 80.

18. Ron Rosenbaum, "The House That Levitt Built," *Esquire*, December 1988, 382.

19. *Newsday*, 12 March 1949.

20. Ibid. Robert Keeler's book *Newsday* argues that the newspaper had a stake in Levittown and suburban development and was tied into to the Levitt publicity machine.

21. John Liell, "Levittown", 144. In Levittown, Pennsylvania, in 1957 a black family, William and Daisy Myers and their three small children moved in. "What they got initially was harassment, threats and protests from residents who opposed their presence. For over two months the Myers family endured stone throwing mobs, hate mail, threatening phone calls and other forms of harassment. Local police guarded the Myers residence around the clock. They were joined by state police under the direction of Gov. George Leader. Finally a court decree that threatened to jail protesters brought the violence and intimidation to an end." Brent Glass, letter to the *Philadelphia Inquirer*, 28 February 1993, protesting Thomas Hine article on the fortieth anniversary of Levittown.

22. William Levitt quoted in Michael Danielson, The *Politics of Exclusion* (New York: Columbia University Press, 1976), 132.

23. Nancy Arroyo, interview by authors, March 1990.

24. Ibid.

25. "Builder Gets Award: Thomas Romano Is Honored for Non-Discriminatory Homes," *New York Times*, 2 April 1950.

26. Sidney Schaer, "Ronek Park, Equal Opportunity Suburb," *Newsday*, 28 September 1997, 19. Andrew Weise, "Racial Cleansing in the Suburbs: Suburban Government, Urban Renewal and Segregation on Long Island, New York, 1945–1960," in Marc Silver and Martin Melkonian, *Contested Terrain: Power, Politics and Participation in Suburbia* (New York: Greenwood Press, 1993), 6. For an interesting argument of the effect of the second wave of people leaving urban areas in the 1960s see Ray Suarez, *The Old Neighborhood: What We Lost in the Great Suburban Migration* (New York: Free Press, 1999).

27. "Federal Policies Relative to Equal Housing Opportunity Statement by the President," *Weekly Compilation of Presidential Documents*, 7 (14 January 1971): 892.

28. The proportion of blacks living outside the South rose from 23 percent to almost 50 percent between 1940 and the mid-1960s. Richard Cloward and Frances Fox Piven *Poor Peoples Movements: Why They Succeed and How They Fail* (New York: Pantheon, 1977), 192.

29. See Michael Brown and Steven Erie, "Blacks and the Legacy of the Great Society: The Economic and Political Impact of Federal Social Policy," *Public Policy, 29*, 3 (Summer 1981); Nicholas Lehman, *The Great Black Migration and How It Changed America* (New York: Alfred Knopf, 1991), 201–2; Thomas Edsall and Mary Edsall, *Chain Reaction: The Impact of Race, Rights and Taxes on American Politics* (New York: W. W. Norton, 1991), write, "Fully half of all blacks holding professional and managerial jobs are employed by local, state or federal government agencies as compared to just over a quarter of whites" (p. 18).

30. Hazel Dukes, interview by authors, February 1991.

31. Jean Wyatt, interview by authors, February 1989.

32. Helena White, interview by authors, October 1990.

33. Turner Bond, interview by son, Steven Bond, May 1999.

34. "L.I. Community Striving to Keep Racial Balance," *New York Times*, 27 June 1967.

35. John Rice, interview by authors, April 1991.

36. John Scott, interview by his daughter Raquel Scott, May 1999.

37. "L.I. Community," *New York Times*.

38. Marquita James, "Blacks in Roosevelt, Long Island," Salvotore La Gumina, ed., *Ethnicity in Suburbia, The Long Island Experience* (New York: Nassau Community College, 1980), 97. Rice, interview by authors; Ruth Grefe, Reginald Brown, and Ilda Northern, interview by authors, March 1992.

39. "Confessions of a Blockbuster" (1967), quoted in Hillel Levine and Lawrence Harmon, *The Death of an American Jewish Community: A Tragedy of Good Intentions* (New York: Free Press, 1992), 195–96.

40. "State Extends Order to Curb New Outbreak of Alleged Blockbusting," *New York Times*, 6 June 1967.

41. Interview with Yvonne Simmons, March 1991.

42. *New York Times*, 6 July 1967.

43. Simmons, interview by authors.

44. James, "Blacks in Roosevelt, Long Island," 95.

45. Alvin and Shelly Dorfman, interview by authors, November 1990.

46. Ivan and Cynthia Ashby, interview by daughter, Natalie Ashby, March 1997.

47. Louise Simpson, interview by authors April 1991.

48. Ramona Crooks interview by authors, November 1990.

49. Simmons, interview by authors; *New York Times,* 27 June 1967; Douglas Massey and Nancy Denton, "Trends in the Residential Segregation of Blacks, Hispanics and Asians: 1970–1980," *American Sociological Review,* 52 (1987): 802–25.

50. Grefe, Brown, and Northern, interview by authors, February 1991.

51. "A Message of Vital Importance from the Clergymen of Your Community," February 1963 leaflet (loaned by Ruth Grefe).

52. Ibid.

53. "L.I. Community," *New York Times.*

54. Ibid.

55. Ruth Grefe, interviewed by authors, March 1992. Roosevelt still has one of the highest tax rates in the county, but this money goes to Hempstead, the town to which Roosevelt belongs. To use a common Roosevelt expression, Roosevelt is a town where there is "taxation without representation."

56. Saul Alinsky, quoted in Levine and Harmon, 7.

CHAPTER FOURTEEN

1. Ramona Crooks and Michael Kirwin, interview by authors, March 1992.

2. Robert Ryan, "Blockbusting: What Happened in Freeport?" *New York Herald Tribune,* 20 December 1964; "Blockbusting Realtors to Be Censored by State," *Freeport Leader,* 4 February 1965; Ken Byerly, "Seek Freeport Blockbusting Probe," *Newsday,* 17 November 1964; Gregory Wynne, "Freeport Seeks to Stem Influx of Welfare Families," *Long Island Press,* 13 October 1964.

3. Linda Charlton, "L.I. Community Thriving," *Newsday,* 13 April 1968.

4. Louise Simpson, interview by authors, April 1991.

5. Marquita James, quoted in Ronald Smothers and Marlene Cimons, "Negroes in Freeport List School Demands," *Newsday,* 20 December 1968.

6. Ibid.; *Newsday,* 23 December 1968.

7. Marquita James, interview by authors, December 1992.

8. Jim O'Neill, Charles Coleman, and Lewis Grossberger, "Melee Disrupts Freeport High," *Newsday,* 25 April 1969.

9. "200 Youth in Racial Rampage," *Long Island Press,* 26 April 1969; Bill Van Haintz and Jim O'Neill, "4 Hurt as Negro Youths Roam Roosevelt Streets," *Newsday,* 26 April 1969.

10. Marlene Cimons and Lewis Grossberger, "Freeport Whites Demand Law and Order," *Newsday,* 29 April 1969.

11. Mandel quoted in Marlene Cimons, "Fixing the Blame in Freeport," *Newsday,* 30 April 1969.

12. Isa Abdul Kareem, interview by authors, April 1991.

13. Louise Simpson, interview by authors April 1991.

14. Chris Sprowal, interview by authors, February 1993.

15. Michael Patterson, "Freeport Race Row Cooled by Empathy," *Newsday*, 16 November 1970.

16. Julius Pearse, interview by authors, November 1992.

17. Idan Simowitz, "Tears . . . Anger . . . Demands," *Long Island Press*, 29 April 1969.

18. Jomer Rand, interview by authors, January 1993.

19. Michael Alonge, "Freeport Whites Set to Boycott," *New York Daily News*, 29 April 1969.

20. Marlene Cimons and Lewis Grossberger, "In Freeport, Anger," *Newsday*, 29 April 1969.

21. Ibid.; Simowitz, "Tears."

22. *Long Island Press*, 16 May 1969.

23. Ibid.

24. Victoria Mares, "Two Races Find Common Ground," *Newsday*, 7 July 1970.

25. Pearse, interview by authors.

26. "Freeport—A Village Where the Races Go Their Separate Ways," *Newsday* 21 July 1970; "Ramsey Issues Press Release," *Long Island Kernel*, 23 July 1970.

27. Letter from Kathleen Glass, *Newsday*, 25 July 1971, Freeport Library Ethnic Groups files.

28. Louisa Monteiro, interview by authors, February 1990.

29. Robert Sweeney, interview by authors, October 1992.

30. Dan Mandel, interview by authors, April 1991.

31. Alvin Dorfman, interview by authors, November 1990.

32. Dan Hertzberg, "Freeport Is Fighting Block-Busting," *Newsday*, 1 June 1971.

33. Paul Schreiber, "Blockbusting in Freeport," *Newsday*, 4 June 1971.

34. Michele Ingrassia, "Freeport Defends For Sale Ban," *Newsday*, 24 June 1977; "Block Busting Realtors to Be Censored by State," *The Leader*, 24 June 1974; "Village Bans For Sale Signs," *Long Island Graphic*, 24 June 1974.

35. Kathleen Kerr, "Role of House Listers Disputed," *Newsday*, 11 January 1985.

36. Marjorie Kaplan, "Freeport Tackles White Flight," *Newsday*, 6 May 1979.

37. Barbara Patton, interview by authors, April 1991.

38. Ramona Crooks and Michael Kirwin, interview by authors.

39. Marjorie Kaplan, "Finding Their Dream House," *Newsday*, 6 May 1974.

40. Ibid. The commission was created by the Poverty Program.

41. Harriet Popkin et al., interview by authors, April 1988.

42. "Mayor Lauds Lawsuit Targeting Racial Steering in Local Housing," *Newsday*, 19 December 1985.

43. Organizations like Homefinders exist in Shaker Heights, Cleveland. Others are in Oak Park, Illinois, and Teaneck, New Jersey, but in these towns did not engage in direct real estate sales (*Newsday*, 11 January 1985). For an interesting analysis of these attempts at inte-

grated housing see Andrew Weise, "Neighborhood Diversity: Social Change, Ambiguity and Fair Housing Since 1968," *Journal of Urban Affairs* 17, 2 (Summer 1995): 107–29.

44. "Freeport Race Row Cooled by Empathy," *New York Daily News,* 21 November 1971.

45. Rand, interview by authors.

46. Ibid.

47. Dan Hertzberg, "Black, Blue-Collar Coalition Sought," *Long Island Kernel,* 24 May 1973.

48. Rand, interview by authors.

49. Pearse, interview by authors.

50. Ibid.

CHAPTER FIFTEEN

1. Geoffrey Mohan, "Levittown Today," *Newsday,* 28 September 1997, 45.

2. Jon C. Teaford, *Post-Suburbia: Government and Politics in the Edge Cities* (Baltimore, MD: Johns Hopkins University Press, 1997), 166.

3. Roberta Coward and Karen Roberts, interview by authors, May 1990.

4. Lee E. Koppleman and Pearl M. Kramer, "Anatomy of the Long Island Economy: Retrospective and Prospective," *Long Island Historical Journal* 6, 2 (Spring 1994): 148.

5. Quoted in Jane Fritsch, "The Parking Lot Lottery," *New York Times,* 8 October 1997.

6. Herbert Muschamps, "Becoming Unstuck on the Suburbs," *New York Times,* 28 October 1997.

7. Nancy Arroyo, interview by authors, March 1989.

8. Barbara Ware, interview by authors, March 1990.

9. Roberta Stim, interview by authors, March 1989.

10. Koppleman and Kramer. "Anatomy of the Long Island Economy," 148–49.

11. Clara Gillens, interview by authors, March 1990.

12. Ware, interview by authors, March 1990.

13. Coward, interview by authors, May 1990.

14. Gillens, interview by authors.

15. Ware, interview by authors.

16. Pat Sullivan, interview by authors, March 1990.

17. Ibid.

18. Ware, interview by authors.

19. Ibid.

20. Gillens, interview by authors.

21. Helga Baum, interview by authors, March 1989.

22. Divorce happened more frequently to their children. As one pioneer put it, "In our generation, we just coped" (Baum, interview by authors).

23. Rose Cimino, interview by authors, April 1989.

24. Dorothy Bass, interview by authors, April 1989.

25. Donna Gagliano, interview by authors, April 1989.

26. Ibid.

27. Karen Roberts, interview by authors, March 1990.

28. Interview with Roberta Coward.

29. Roberts, interview by authors.

30. John Juliano, interview by authors, April 1991. Although we cannot estimate numbers, everyone interviewed was well aware of this new situation.

31. See Diane Jean Schemo, "Facing Big City Problems, Long Island Suburbs Try to Adapt to the Future," *New York Times*, 16 March 1994.

32. Bass, interview by authors.

33. Cimino, interview by authors.

34. Bruce Weber, "Alone Together, the Unromantic Generation," *New York Times*, 5 April 1987.

35. David M. Halbfinger, "New Buyers Renew Levittown, Now Fifty," *New York Times*, 28 September 1997.

36. Diana Schemo, "Killing Casts a Rare Light on Gay Life in Suburbia," *New York Times*, 28 January 1992.

37. Ibid.; Marilyn Goldstein, "Being Gay in the Suburbs," *Newsday*, 6 March 1986. For more information see, Michael Norman, "Suburbs are a Magnet to Many Homosexuals" *New York Times*, 11 February 1986, Jane Gross, "A Milestone in Fight for Gay Rights: A Quiet Suburban Life," *New York Times*, 30 June 1991; David Dunlap, "Gay Parents Ease into Suburbia," *New York Times*, 16 May 1996, states that 32 percent of gays live in the suburbs nationwide.

38. Lenore David and Sally Rosen, interview by authors, February 1993.

39. Ibid

CHAPTER SIXTEEN

1. Robert Fishman, *Bourgeois Utopias: The Rise and Fall of Suburbia* (New York: Basic Books, 1987),17, 184.

2. Andrew C. Revkin, "A Bucolic Nightmare: Gridlock in Suburbia," *New York Times*, 16 October 1997. In New Jersey, largely an amalgamation of suburbs linked by highways, there are more registered cars than licensed drivers–6.4 million vehicles to 5.7 million drivers— and the gap has been steadily widening. People drive 60 billion miles a year. See N. R. Kleinfield, "Born to Drive," *New York Times*, 25 September 1997.

3. William Kowinski, *The Malling of America: An Inside Look at the Great Consumer Paradise* (New York: William Morrow, 1981), 34–35. See also Jennifer Steinhaver, "On Long Island: The Mall as History Book," *New York Times*, 21 December 1997.

4. Frank Rich, "The Mall Pall," *New York Times*, 4 December 1996.

5. Sarah Boxer, "I Shop Ergo I Am: The Mall as Society's Mirror," *New York Times*, 28 March 1998.

6. Joseph P. Fried, "In the Louima Police Brutality, a Legal Dream Team and Questions of Overkill," *New York Times*, 9 November 1997. Johnny Cochran was a lawyer for the Buffalo case. In many ways this resembles Robert Moses' idea of building the bridges on the Northern State Parkway so low that city buses couldn't access Jones Beach.

7. "On Long Island, the Mall as History Book".

8. "A Teenage Pall at the Mall," *New York Times*, 23 January 1993.

9. William Glaberson, "The Mall as Cocoon," *New York Times*, 21 April 1992.

10. Betsy Israel, *Grown-Up Fast: A True Story of Teen Age Life in Suburban America* (New York: Poseidon Press, 1988), 65.

11. *Pump Up the Volume*, written and directed by Allan Whyle, New Line Cinema, 1995.

12. Lilia Paige, interview by authors, May 1990.

13. Diana Jean Schemo, "Facing Big City Problems, Long Island Suburbs Try to Adapt," *New York Times*, 16 March 1994.

14. Ibid.; Josh Barbanel, "From Long Island Teller Machines to Gas Stations, Suburban Robberies Are on the Rise," *New York Times*, 18 February 1992.

15. Jonathan Rabinowitz, "Malls Stress Visible Security to Counter Fears," *New York Times*, 27 November 1992.

16. Robert Reza, the respected doctor who grieved for the disappearance of his bride until he confessed to killing her and disposing her body in garbage bags after a Christmas eve quarrel, and Joel Rifkin, who placidly planted corpses in his garden in East Meadow, are other examples of this phenonmenon. See Ron Rosenbaum, "The Devil in Long Island," *New York Times*, 22 August 1993 and Lorraine Delia Kenny, "Amy Fisher, My Story, Learning to Love the Unlovable," *Socialist Review* 24, 3 (1994).

17. Tom cited in Thomas Lueck, "Island of Lost Souls," *New York Times*, 23 January 1993.

18. Agnes Geraghty, interview by Cara Geraghty, 1992.

19. Virginia Guarnari and William Brown, interview by Linda Brown, May 1991.

20. Schemo, "Facing Big City Problems"; Bruce Lambert, "Suburban Nassau, at 50, Attempts to Create a Central Hub," *New York Times*, 18 January 1997.

21. Schemo, "Facing Big City Problems"; David Halbfinger, "Wealthy Nassau Makes Itself a Financial Mess," *New York Times*, 6 October 1999.

22. Beers, *Blue Sky Dream*, 211.

23. Ibid.

24. Schemo, "Facing Big City Problems." This analogy is suggested by Katherine S. Newman, an anthropologist at Columbia University.

25. Herbert Muschamps, "Becoming Unstuck On the Suburbs," *New York Times*, October 28, 1997.

26. Rita Arditta with Tatiana Schreiber, "Breast Cancer: The Environmental Connection," *Resist* (newsletter), no. 246, May–June 1992, 6–7.

27. For more information see Diane Jean Schemo, "Long Island Presses for Answers on Breast Cancer," *New York Times*, 5 October 1992; Peter Marks, "U.S. to Finance Project Study Breast Cancer on Long Island," *New York Times*, 25 November 1993; idem, "On Long Island, Fear from Eclectic Fields," *New York Times*, 6 January 1994; Diane Jean Schemo, "L.I. Breast Cancer Is Possibly Linked to Chemical Sites," *New York Times*, 13 April 1994.

28. Jane Gross, "In Levittown, Cancer Steals Peace of Mind," *New York Times*, 26 June 1998.

29. Grace Grill, interviewed by Maureen Turicci, May 1990.

30. Rosenbaum, "The Devil in Long Island."

CHAPTER SEVENTEEN

1. Charlie LeDuff and David Halbfinger, "Wages and Squalor for Immigrant Workers," *New York Times*, 5 May 1999.

2. *New York Times*, 24 July 1997.

3. Sara Mahler, "First Stop Suburbia," *NACLA* [North American Committee on Latin America] *Report on the Americas* 26, 1 (July 1992): 19.

4. LeDuff and Halbfinger, "Wages and Squalor."

5. Ibid.

6. Norman Appelton, interview by authors, January 1991.

7. Doreen Carvajal, "New York Suburbs Take on a Latin Accent," *New York Times*, 29 July 1993.

8. Jennifer Gordon, "We Make the Road by Walking: Immigrant Workers, the Workplace Project and the Struggle for Social Change," *Harvard Civil Rights Civil Liberties Law Review* (Summer 1995): 411.

9. Mahler, "First Stop Suburbia," 20–48.

10. Doreen Carvajal, "Making Ends Meet in a Nether World," *New York Times*, 13 December 1994.

11. Mahler, "First Stop Suburbia," 20–24.

12. Gordon, "We Make the Road by Walking," 412–13.

13. Ibid., 408, 418, 419.

14. Doreen Carvajal, "Out of Sight, Out of Mind, But Not Out of Work," *New York Times*, 8 July 1995.

15. Ibid.

16. Gordon, "We Make the Road by Walking," 408–9.

17. Ibid., 432.

18. Evelyn Nieves, "Day Laborer Stakes Out His Own Patch," *New York Times*, 10 May 1998.

19. *New York Times*, 24 July 1997; *New York Times* editorial, 31 August 1997; *New York Times*, 19 September 1997.

20. Gordon, "We Make the Road by Walking," 420–21.

21. Ibid., 418–21. See also Kenneth C. Crowe, "The Big Payback," *Newsday*, 7 January 1996.

22. Doreen Carvajal, "For Immigrant Maids, Not a Job But Servitude," *New York Times*, 25 February 1996.

23. Ibid.

24. *New York Times*, 24 July 1997.

25. LeDuff and Halbfinger, "Wages and Squalor."

26. Doreen Carvajal, "Making Ends Meet"; idem, "A Mayor Asks Help on Illegal Tenancies," *New York Times,* 11 October 1996.

27. Ibid., "A Mayor Asks Help"; LeDuff and Halbfinger, "Wages and Squalor."

28. Robert McFadden, "Fire in a Crowded Home of Immigrants Kills 3 and Injures 16 on L.I.," *New York Times,* 2 May 1999,

29. LeDuff and Halbfinger, "Wages and Squalor."

30. McFadden, "Fire in a Crowded Home."

31. Ibid.

32. Bruce Lambert, "Raid on Illegal Housing, Shows the Plight of Suburbs Working Poor," *New York Times,* 7 December 1996.

33. Frank Bruni, with Debra Sontag, "Behind a Suburban Facade in Queens, A Teeming Angry Urban Arithmetic," *New York Times,* 8 October 1996.

34. John Rather, "New Immigrants Transforming the Population," *New York Times,* 17 March 1996, Long Island edition.

35. Diana Jean Schemo, "Education as a Second Language," *New York Times,* 25 July 1994.

36. Doreen Carvajal, "Cultures Clash in Suburbs, Schools Struggle to Cope With Influx of Immigrant Students," *New York Times,* 8 January 1995.

37. Doreen Carvajal, "Immigrants Fight Residency Rules, Blocking Students in Long Island Schools," *New York Times,* 7 June 1995.

38. Sylvia Moreno, "Long Island Census Shows 3.9% Hispanic," *Newsday,* 27 April 1981.

39. Patrick Boyle, "Brentwood's a Melting Pot of Promise," *Newsday,* 1 December 1996; Lyn Dobrin, "The Spice Root in Hicksville." *Newsday,* 16 October 1995.

40. Ibid. New York Suburbs Take on a Latin Accent.

CONCLUSION

1. For further information see Evan McKenzie, *Privatopia: Homeowner Associations and the Rise of Residential Private Government* (New Haven: Yale University Press, 1994), and Edward J. Blakely and Mary Gail Snyder, *Fortress America: Gated Communities in the United States* (Washington, D.C.: Brookings Institution, 1997).

2. Timothy Egan, "Many Seek Security in the Private Communities," *New York Times,* 3 September 1995.

3. Ibid.

4. David Guterson, "No Place Like Home, on the Manicured Streets of a Master Planned Community," *Harper's,* November 1992, 59.

5. Robert Lang and Karen Danielsen, "Gated Communities in America: Walling Out the World," *Housing Policy Debate,* 8, 4 (1997): 872.

6. Egan, "Many Seek Security."

7. Philip Langdon, "A Good Place to Live," *Atlantic Monthly,* March 1988, 39–56. In contrast to Levittown, streets are built narrowly and on straight angles so that one can see neighbors. Many streets culminate in community gathering places such as pools, bath houses and gazebos. The streets are accessible by foot or bike and lead to public spaces

where residents can get a meal or mail a package. Small businesses, rather than malls, mark the landscape.

8. Herbert Muschamps, "Can New Urbanism Find Room for the Old?," *New York Times*, 2 June 1996; Sarah Boxer, "A Remedy for the Rootlessness of Modern Suburban Life," *New York Times*, 1 August 1998; Michael Pollan, "Breaking Ground; The Parting of the Green Sea, Seed, Re Seed, Secede," *New York Times*, 4 June 1998.

9. Michael Pollan, "Town Building Is No Mickey Mouse Operation," *New York Times*, 14 December 1997.

10. Carl Hiaasen, *Team Rodent: How Disney Devours the World* (New York: Ballantine, 1998): 51–52.

11. Ibid., 52.

12. The amusement park and television touch can be seen in the sales rooms for Celebration. One enters the sales office through an actual porch built onto the front of a giant billboard depicting a life-size, full-scale model house. These models seem so real that people have been known to put signs on their houses such as "This Is a Real Home, Not a Model Home, Do Not Enter." "Spaghetti Dinners and Fireflies in a Jar" (no author), from the World Wide Web, http://www.bitmark.com/christyfischer/celerat.htm, Celebration (1997); Christina Fischer, "Celebration," World Wide Web, Celebration (1997).

13. Pollan, "Town Building."

14. Ibid.

15. Recreational amenities in Columbia include three man-made lakes, tennis courts, swimming pools, and modern health facilities. The schools are among the best in the state, and there are educational facilities ranging from day care (twenty-nine centers) to a community college. Major department stores, industry, and businesses make it possible for residents to work, shop, and live there.

16. Bonnie and Gordon Pollokoff, interview by authors, August 1997.

17. Ibid. See also Paul Goldberger, "James Rouse, Developer, Dies at 81" *New York Times*, 10 April 1996; "A Brief History of Columbia," reprinted from *Creating a New City; Columbia, Maryland*, ed. Robert Tennenbaum (MD: Perry Publishing Co., 1997); World Wide Web Columbia, http://cityguide.lycos.com/midatlantic/columbiaMD.html, InfoConnection, "James W. Rouse, A Life Well Lived," Enterprise Foundation Inc., 1996.

18. Andrew Jacobs, "Yes It's a Commune. Yes It's on Staten Island," *New York Times*, 29 November 1998

19. Eleanor J. Bader, "Cohousing," typescript in *Dollars and Sense* (forthcoming).

20. Ibid.

21. Jacobs, "Yes It's a Commune."

22. Donna Spreitzer, "N Street" (Master's thesis, University of California), http://www.cohousing.org/library/spreitzer/thebibliography.

23. Naomi Davis, "Co Housing and Other Cooperative Housing," *Baltimore Resource Journal*, World Wide Web, http//sec/abcsucdavis.edu.stanfor/cohousing.html.

24. Mary McAleer Vazard, "Putting Up Housing with a Built-in Sense of Community," *New York Times*, 7 September 1997.

Index

CPSIA information can be obtained
at www.ICGtesting.com
Printed in the USA
BVHW072033140822
644578BV00014B/162